Java™
Programming
for Windows®:

*Using Microsoft AFC,
WFC, AND XML*

Java™ Programming for Windows®:

Using Microsoft AFC, WFC, AND XML

Mark Watson

Morgan Kaufmann Publishers, Inc.
San Francisco, California

Senior Editor	Diane D. Cerra
Director of Production and Manufacturing	Yonie Overton
Senior Production Editor	Elisabeth Beller
Cover and CD Label Design	Ross Carron Design
Cover Photo	© The Field Museum, Cat# A105143-36136, Chicago; Photo by James Balodimas and Julie Pitzen
Text Design	Sybil Ihrig, Helios Productions
Copyeditor	Ken DellaPenta
Proofreader	Jennifer McClain
Indexer	Anne Leach
Printer	Courier Corporation

Designations used by companies to distinguish their products are often claimed as trademarks or registered trademarks. In all instances where Morgan Kaufmann Publishers, Inc. is aware of a claim, the product names appear in initial capital or all capital letters. Readers, however, should contact the appropriate companies for more complete information regarding trademarks and registration.

Morgan Kaufmann Publishers, Inc.
Editorial and Sales Office
340 Pine Street, Sixth Floor
San Francisco, CA 94104-3205
USA

Telephone 415 / 392-2665
Facsimile 415 / 982-2665
Email mkp@mkp.com
WWW http://www.mkp.com

Order toll free 800 / 745-7323

© 1999 by Mark Watson

03 02 01 00 99   5 4 3 2 1

Library of Congress Cataloging-in-Publication Data

Watson, Mark, date.
    Java programming for Windows : using Microsoft AFC, WFC, and XML / Mark Watson.
        p.   cm.
    Includes bibliographical references and index.
    ISBN 1-55860-516-9
      1. Java (Computer program language) 2. Microsoft Windows (Computer file)
    3. Microsoft AFC. 4. Windows foundation class library. 5. XML (Computer program language)
    QA76.73.J38W383   1999
    005.2'768—dc21
                                               98-34742
                                                CIP

For Carol, Julie, David, and Calvin

Contents

Preface xiii

Acknowledgments xv

Introduction xvii

**Chapter 1 Using the Microsoft Java
SDK Version 3.0** *1*

1.1 Testing the installation 3

1.2 Setting up the Java
development environment 4

1.3 Installing the book examples from
the CD-ROM 5

1.4 A simple Java programming example 10

1.5 Using J++ version 1.1 with the
examples in this book 12

1.6 Using J++ version 6.0 with the
examples in this book 15

Chapter 2 The AFC and WFC Class Libraries *17*

2.1 Introduction to AFC 19

2.2 AFC components 24

2.3 AFC event handling 26

2.4   The AFC tree component 35

    2.4.1   Design of the EventTree class 35

    2.4.2   Implementing the EventTree class 38

    2.4.3   Testing the EventTree class 46

2.5   AFC text components 49

2.6   AFC split viewer components 53

2.7   AFC tabbed components 57

2.8   Introduction to WFC 62

2.9   WFC architecture 63

2.10 WFC Java packages 64

2.11 WFC event model 66

2.12 Integration of WFC and Web pages 67

2.13 Using WFC for graphics 68

2.14 Example WFC application 71

Chapter 3   *Implementation of an Internet*
News Browser Using AFC *87*

3.1   Requirements for portable Java classes
for using the NNTP protocol 88

3.2   Design of portable Java classes for using
the NNTP protocol 89

3.3   Implementation of portable Java classes
for using the NNTP protocol 91

3.4   Design of a Panel class for the news reader
user interface 100

3.5   Implementation of a Panel class for the
newsreader user interface 104

3.6   Design of a stand-alone Java application
for reading Internet news 125

3.7   Implementation of a stand-alone Java
application for reading Internet news 126

Chapter 4   *Introduction to JavaBeans* *129*

4.1   Designing a JavaBean component for
listing current news stories from Web
news services 131

4.2   Implementing a JavaBean component
for listing current news stories from
Web news services 132

4.3   Using the JavaBean component for
listing current news stories from Web
news services 137

Chapter 5   *Using ActiveX Components in*
Java Programs *141*

5.1   How to access ActiveX controls in
Java programs 143

5.2   Wrapping the Internet Explorer 4.0
ActiveX control as a JavaBean 145

5.3   Example of writing an ActiveX
control in Java 153

5.4   Using WFC with the Internet Explorer
4.0 ActiveX control 159

Chapter 6   *Using Applets with CAB and*
JAR Archives *165*

6.1   A simple example Java applet 166

6.2   Packaging an applet in a CAB archive file 169

6.3   Using a CAB archive file on a Web page 170

6.4   Packaging an applet in a JAR archive file 171

6.5   Using a JAR archive file on a Web page 172

Chapter 7   *Extensible Markup Language*
(XML) and the Channel
Definition Format (CDF) **173**

7.1   Overview of XML 176

   7.1.1   The Microsoft XML parser is
written in Java 179

7.2   Design of a Java browser for
XML documents 186

7.3   Implementation of a Java browser
for XML documents .188

7.4   Overview of CDF 192

7.5   Example CDF document 193

7.6   Implementing a customized CDF
Web server in Java 196

Chapter 8   *Custom Desktop/WebTop in Java* **207**

8.1   Taking over the desktop 208

8.2   Adding Java applets to the
Microsoft Active Desktop 215

Chapter 9   *Three-Tier Application Example* **219**

9.1   Design of the three-tier system 220

9.2   Implementation of the three-tier system 223

Chapter 10   *Game Library Using Direct3D* **237**

10.1   Requirements of a game library 238

10.2   Implementation of a game library
using Direct3D 241

10.3   Design of a 3D game for simulating
           flight around orbiting planets 254

10.4   Implementation of a 3D game for
           simulating flight around orbiting planets 255

Chapter 11   ***JScript and DHTML*** ***267***

11.1   Introduction to JScript 268

11.2   JScript interaction with Dynamic HTML
           document objects 270

11.3   JScript interaction with Java applets 275

Chapter 12   ***J/Direct*** ***281***

12.1   Introduction 282

12.2   Using native dialog boxes 283

12.3   Interaction with the Windows 95/98
           and NT desktop environment 285

12.4   Adding a Java newsreader program to
           the Windows task bar 299

12.5   Wrap-up 303

Appendix   ***JavaDoc Documentation for***
               Example Programs ***305***

A.1   Class Hierarchy 305

A.2   Index of all fields and methods 309

Bibliography ***323***

Index ***325***

Preface

The Java programming language is the best general-purpose programming language. I base this opinion on professional use of other programming languages like C, C++, Pascal, LISP, Prolog, Smalltalk, Algol, and Fortran. There are two prevalent uses for the Java language: writing portable "write once, run anywhere" applications to the standard Java APIs, and using Java for specific platforms, like Microsoft Windows, set top boxes, and other specific platforms that may require the use of nonstandard Java APIs.

This book focuses exclusively on exploiting the power and elegance of the Java language for creating Windows applications. We will discuss partitioning applications into separate "portable Java" and "platform-specific Java" parts. We will use the Microsoft Application Foundation Classes (AFC) and Windows Foundation Classes (WFC) libraries to write high-performance Windows applications that have the standard Windows look-and-feel.

This book also introduces you to the important Extensible Markup Language (XML) technology by developing tools for XML and Microsoft's Channel Definition Format (CDF). We develop a Java Web server that supports XML. I finish this treatment by developing a three-tier application that uses the XML-enabled Web server to pull data from a relational database, encapsulate it in XML, and feed it to a thin client Java applet.

I also provide a short tutorial for using Microsoft's Java API for real-time 3D animation: DirectX and Direct3D. I provide a Java class library that allows you to experiment with Direct3D without getting too caught up in the technical difficulties of the Component Object Model (COM) interface.

There are many practical uses on the Windows platform of the combination of JScript (Microsoft's implementation of the standard JavaScript language, with extensions) and Java. I provide several short examples of communication between JScript and Java. A short introduction to Dynamic HTML (DHTML) is also provided with several short examples.

Mark Watson
Sedona, Arizona

Acknowledgments

I would like to thank my wife Carol for her constant encouragement for this book project; Microsoft for making publicly available the Java SDK 3.0, the XML parser, and the many fine example Java sample programs with the Java SDK; and the anonymous programmers at Microsoft who wrote the example programs with the Java SDK that both complement the SDK documentation and provide important information not always found in the documentation.

I would like to thank Object International Software, Ltd. (*www.oi.com*) for providing the TogetherJ object modeling tool, MicroGold Software, Inc. (*www.microgold.com*) for providing the WithClass object design tool, and Popkin Software (*www.popkin.com*) for providing their System Architect modeling tool. I used these three tools both for developing the examples in this book and for generating UML class diagrams used in this book. I would like to thank JavaSoft for their support with several of my Java programming projects. I would also like to thank Microsoft for making the J++ 6.0 (preview) release available for creating the WFC examples in this book.

Introduction

The Java programming language was developed by Sun Microsystems to support small information appliance devices and network applications. The language initially gained popularity as a means of adding simple animations to Web pages. Today, the Java language provides a portable programming language for a wide range of applications. For example:

- Thin client front ends to remote information servers. (For example, an applet is downloaded to your Web browser and provides stock market information from a database located on the same computer as the Web server.)
- Network applications (e.g., distributed database applications).
- Artificial intelligence (AI) based software. (Java's flexible memory allocation with garbage collection and a large set of built-in data classes makes the Java language a strong candidate for AI programming projects.)
- Electronic commerce using smart cards. (For example, a credit-card-type device contains a small Java processor, memory, and software to allow you to keep electronic funds and your personal financial information in your wallet.)

- Windows 95/98 and NT-specific applications and network programming (the topic of this book).

Even though one of the advantages of the Java language and runtime environment is portability between computing platforms, we should note that the last two types of applications listed above are definitely not portable. There will certainly be competing and probably incompatible smart financial cards, and Windows 95/98 and NT applications using the Microsoft-specific APIs discussed in this book will probably not run on other computing platforms (except for the Apple Macintosh). However, while I was writing this book, Microsoft released the Internet Explorer 4.0 (IE 4.0) Web browser for several Unix environments, so even some of the Windows-specific examples should at least run on a variety of platforms if you run IE 4.0.

Portability

Many of the Java programming examples developed in this book will be nonportable because we will be using Microsoft APIs to take maximum advantage of the Windows computing platform. This does not mean that we should completely ignore portability issues. We will use the Java package system to organize the software developed in this book into four broad categories:

- Portable utilities that should run on any Java platform (package **com.markwatson.util**)
- Microsoft-specific utilities and applications (package **com.markwatson.ms**)
- Microsoft-specific short demonstration programs (package **com.markwatson.demo**)

Using JavaPureCheck

I frequently use the utility **JavaPureCheck** to verify my programs for compatibility with the old JDK 1.02 API (useful for Web page applets), the JDK 1.1.x API (useful for my general-purpose Java programming), and to indicate where I am using nonstandard API calls. **JavaPureCheck** is available at the Web site *www.suntest.com*, or if you cannot find it there, use a Web search engine to search for Web pages containing "JavaPureCheck".

■ Microsoft-specific large demonstration programs (package **com.markwatson.apps**)

Most of the Microsoft-specific libraries are compatible with both the older JDK 1.02 and the latest JDK 1.1.x. All of the utility classes and examples developed in this book support JDK 1.1.x and rely on the new delegation event model (so they will not be compatible with JDK 1.02).

One of the great things about object-oriented programming languages is the relative ease of building applications from reusable tools. When I am designing and writing software, I usually initially write code "quick and dirty"—spending more time on new algorithms, figuring out how to use new APIs, and so on, rather than thinking about class design for reuse. After my code is working, I then like to redesign and implement it for reuse and maintainability. The examples in this book were originally built as small snippets of code whose purpose was to figure out how the Microsoft APIs work, and so on. However, I redesigned and implemented everything before including the examples in this book; you will hopefully find the example code both easy to read and easy to reuse in your own projects.

The material in this book is presented in a specific order for the following reasons:

- We start with a solid introduction to using the Application Foundation Classes (AFC) (portable Java). AFC applications provide a Windows look-and-feel, but Java AFC applications will run on other platforms like OS/2 and Unix (including Linux).

- We then introduce Microsoft's Windows Foundation Classes (WFC) that tightly couple Java applications to the Windows 32 API. We will see that WFC makes it relatively easy to write native Windows applications in Java.

- We then create a Java class library for automatic retrieval of information from Internet news servers (using NNTP protocol) (portable Java).

- AFC is used to implement a versatile component for reading network news (portable Java).

- Then the network news component is packaged as a JavaBean (portable Java).

- Then the network newsreader JavaBean is converted to an ActiveX control (nonportable Java).

- The Extensible Markup Language (XML) and Channel Definition Format (CDF) are introduced with code examples for encoding and decoding XML and CDF (portable Java).

- The Abstract Window Toolkit (AWT) is used to create classes for a custom Java desktop/WebTop (portable Java).

- We then build a sample custom ActiveX Desktop using HTML and Java (nonportable Java).
- The Microsoft Direct3D Java API is introduced and wrapped in a set of Java classes that make it easier to write online games (nonportable Java).
- The game class library is used to write a simple space game (nonportable Java).
- The JScript scripting language is introduced (nonportable Java).
- JScript is used to couple a JavaBean and an ActiveX component (nonportable Java).

Portability of Java applications that use the AFC

The original AFC libraries that shipped with the prerelease version of the Microsoft Java SDK were indeed portable. I used them under Windows, OS/2, and Linux. The next release, version 2.0, of the Microsoft Java SDK contains an AFC library that is not portable, but I have directions on my Web site for easily making the AFC portable by removing two Windows-specific class files if you are using version 2.0 of the SDK. Please check *www.markwatson.com* (click on the "Books" link, then click on the "Errata" link). The latest release of the SDK, version 3.0 (which was in prerelease form as I finished this book), provides AFC libraries that are portable to all Java platforms.

- The J/Direct API is introduced with examples showing how to directly interact with the Windows 95/NT desktop and other WIN32 examples (nonportable Java).

Standards

Microsoft has been occasionally criticized for creating their own standards because they are such a powerful force in the computer and information technology industries. I prefer not to get caught up in such discussions. Instead, I try to concentrate on what technologies help me to work more effectively for both my own research projects and for the work that I do for my consulting customers.

The combination of a standard Web Document Object Model, standard HTML, the widespread use of a newly standardized Extensible Markup Language (XML), and standard scripting languages like Netscape's JavaScript and Microsoft's JScript will make distributed, collaborative applications for exchanging and sharing information easier to write and to maintain. I live in the United States (in beautiful Sedona, Arizona), but a day hardly ever goes by that I don't communicate with someone in a foreign country through email and the World Wide Web. The effect of the standardization of Web technologies on all of our lives in the near and distant future is hard to predict accurately, but the effect will certainly be profound.

The Java programming language has quickly become a standard language for writing distributed applications. It is possible to write both great portable Java client-side applications and great Windows-platform-specific Java client-side applications that couple and cooperate tightly with the Windows 95 and Windows NT operating systems. This book will provide a good foundation for developing portable Java applications, for developing platform-specific Java applications when it makes sense to exploit specific features of the Windows platform, and for working with evolving standards for information exchange like HTML, JavaScript/JScript, and XML.

Using the Microsoft Java SDK Version 3.0

The Microsoft Java SDK version 3.0 is available free of charge from the Web site *www.microsoft.com/java*. The SDK is installed by downloading the setup file and then running it. Since the setup file is a large download, it is better to save it as a local file rather than opening it directly from Microsoft's Web site. The SDK setup file will prompt you for a destination directory (**c:\SDK-Java.30** is the default location). The setup program creates eight subdirectories:

- **AFC102**—a version of the AFC classes libraries that are compatible with the older JDK 1.02 API standard. These libraries are not used for the examples in this book.

- **Bin**—contains the Java compiler (**jvc.exe**), Java Virtual Machine (**jview.exe**), and other development tools.

- **Include**—contains header files required if you are interfacing C/C++ code with Java.

- **Lib**—contains library files for using Java with C/C++ applications.

- **RelNotes**—HTML document files covering installation, AFC, Java Virtual Machine, and so on.

- **Src**—Java source files for classes that provide low-level and low-overhead access to Windows WIN32 API.

- **Docs**—the HTML documents for the entire Microsoft Java SDK. The **index.html** file in this directory should be bookmarked in your Web browser for fast access to the excellent online documentation that is provided with the Java SDK.

- **Samples**—contains many great examples of writing Java programs to exploit the Windows 95 and NT environments. This book contains examples of techniques that I find most useful in my own work, but you are advised to spend time at least

The Microsoft SDK may change when it is updated

Recently, Microsoft has been very aggressive in bringing out new updates and improvements in their Java development tools. It is likely that future versions may differ in setup and configuration. You can check my Web site at *www.markwatson.com* (click on the "Books" link, then click on "Errata") to get updates and bug fixes for any material in this book.

running the samples to see additional techniques that you may find useful for writing your own programs.

During the setup process, you will be asked if you want to install the Java Virtual Machine (JVM) included with the SDK. You can choose not to install it during setup (e.g., you may be running the latest Microsoft Web browser that already contains the JVM). The executable **msvmjava.exe** (contained in the **Bin** directory) can be run at a later time to install the JVM. You will probably need to reboot your computer after installing either the Java SDK or the JVM.

Hopefully, you have installed the Microsoft Java Virtual Machine and classes on your system. If you have not already done so, please change directory (i.e., use the **cd** command) to **\SDK-Java.30\Bin** and type

```
clspack -auto
```

If you do not do this, you will not be able to compile all of the example programs in this book.

1.1 Testing the installation

To test the installation of the Microsoft Java SDK, open the folder SDK-Java.30\Samples\AFC and double-click on the HTML file **afcsamp.htm**. (I am assuming that you have the Microsoft Internet Explorer 4.0 or higher release installed.)

IE 4.0 should open with an HTML page with links to several sample applets that show off most of the user interface classes in the AFC library. You can also use the AFC and most of the examples in this book with the older Internet Explorer 3.0 if you install the JVM from the Java SDK.

If the demo applets do not run, manually install the JVM if you have not already done so.

1.2 Setting up the Java development environment

In order to use the Java SDK 3.0 (or later release), you must make sure that the Microsoft Java class libraries and the directory **c:\mjava\classes** are in your **CLASSPATH** and that the directory **c:\SDK-Java.30\Bin** is in your **PATH**. The Java SDK setup program should set up the **PATH** and **CLASSPATH** environment variables correctly, but you will have to manually add **c:\mjava\ classes** to your **CLASSPATH**.

For example, if you are running Windows NT and if you have NT and the Java SDK installed on the **c:** disk drive, then make sure that your **CLASSPATH** environment variable includes

```
c:\WinNT\Java\classes\classes.zip
c:\mjava\classes
```

and your **PATH** environment variable includes

```
c:\WinNT\Bin
c:\SDK-Java.30\Bin
c:\SDK-Java.30\Bin\PackSign
```

If the Java SDK installation program did not correctly set up these two environment variables, then you must open the Windows NT "control panel," open the **System** control, and edit your environment settings.

If you are running Windows 95 (and both Windows and the Java SDK are installed on the **c:** drive), then make sure that your **CLASSPATH** environment variable includes

```
c:\windows\java\classes\classes.zip
c:\mjava\classes
```

and that your **PATH** environment variable includes

```
c:\windows
c:\SDK-Java.30\Bin
c:\SDK-Java.30\Bin\PackSign
```

If the Java SDK installation program did not correctly set up these environment variables, then you will have to manually edit the **c:\autoexec.bat** file.

You can test to see if your **PATH** environment variable is set correctly by opening an MS-DOS–style window and typing the following two commands:

```
jcv
jview
```

If either of these commands is not recognized, then either the SDK for Java is not installed correctly or your **PATH** environment variable is not set up correctly. You may have to reboot Windows 95 for changes to your **c:\autoexec.bat** file to take effect.

1.3 Installing the book examples from the CD-ROM

Installing the CD-ROM book examples is simple. Open an MS-DOS–style command prompt window, and type the following two commands:

```
c:
xcopy d:\mjava c:\mjava /s
```

You will be asked if **c:\mjava** should be a file or directory; specify that **c:\mjava** should be a directory. Here, I assume that **d:** is your CD-ROM drive. Substitute your CD-ROM drive letter if it is different on your system.

I recommend that you use **xcopy** instead of dragging the **mjava** folder to your **c:** drive because this will avoid any problems with read-only files in the **mjava** directory and subdirectories. It is very important that the subdirectory names in the directory **c:\mjava\classes** are properly named. Sometimes, especially under Windows 95, the first letters of directory names get automatically capitalized. If you get any error messages when compiling like

```
Undefined package: com.markwatson.util.*
Undefined package: com.markwatson.news.*
```

then make sure that the directory names in

```
c:\mjava\classes\com\markwatson
```

are all lowercase letters.

The **c:\mjava** directory should contain the following directories (shown in italics) and files (some files with the extensions **.html** and **.class** are not shown):

```
3tier
   C.BAT
   DBInterface.java
   DBXMLServer.java
   ViewXML.java
   test.html
ACTIVEX
   BOOKS.HTM
   BrowserBean.java
   C.BAT
   R.BAT
   R2.BAT
   REGISTER.BAT
   TestBean.java
   TestBean.tlb
```

```
          unregister.bat
APPLETS
   C.BAT
   TestApplet.java
   test.html
   APPS C.BAT
   Images
      DOC.GIF
      FOLDER.GIF
   NewsFrame.java
   R.BAT
   R2.BAT
   config.news
C_ALL.BAT  (compiles all source files to c:\mjava\classes)
DEMO
   C.BAT
   EventDemo.java
   EventDemo2.java
   Images
      DOC.GIF
      FOLDER.GIF
   R.BAT
   SampleTree.java
   SplitViewerDemo.java
   TabViewerDemo.java
   TextDemo.java
   TreeDemo.java
   test.java
DESKTOP
   C.BAT
   DesktopFrame.java
   R.BAT
   config.news
HTML  (directory contains JavaDoc files)
JAVABEAN
   C.BAT
   MAKEFILE
   NEWSBEAN.JAR
   NewsBean.java
   NewsBeanInfo.java
   NewsIcon16.gif
   NewsIcon32.gif
   R.BAT
```

```
    README.TXT
    config.news
JDIRECT
    C.BAT
    JDMessageBox.java
    R.BAT
    TaskBarHandler.java
    TaskBarNews.java
    TestTaskBarHandler.java
    config.news
    r_desk_news.bat
    r_desk_test.bat
JSCRIPT
    C.BAT
    DOWN.GIF
    FontTest.html
    JavaInterfaceTest.html
    NETSCAPE
    RIGHT.GIF
    TestApplet.java
    ToggleTest.html
    WriteTest.html
MAKE_CAB.BAT  (makes a CAB file)
MAKE_JAR.BAT  (makes a JAR file)
MS  (contains the Microsoft Java XML parser source files)
Make_javadoc.bat  (creates JavaDoc files of all examples)
NEWS
    C.BAT
    NewsArticleHeader.java
    NewsGroup.java
    NewsPanel.java
    NewsServer.java
    R.BAT
    README.TXT
README.TXT  (information on example programs)
TEST.CAB  (a sample CAB file)
TEST.JAR  (a sample JAR file)
UTIL
    AppTestFrame.java
    C.BAT
```

```
       ConfigFile.java
       EventTree.java
       Images.java
XML
   C.BAT
   R.BAT
   SampleReader.java
   XMLBrowser.java
   XMLServer.java
   XMLServerConnection.java
   chan1.htm
   chan2.htm
   cust.xml
   prescription.xml
   test.html
   test.xml
```
classes (contains compiled class files for examples)
d3d
```
   C.BAT
   Game.java
   GameData.java
   GameEngine.java
   GameObject.java
   PlanetGameObject.java
   R.BAT
   README.TXT
   TestGame.java
   blue2.bmp
   green2.bmp
   planet1.x
   planet2.x
   target.x
```
j++ (contains a sample J++ project)
`test_cab.html` (HTML file to show loading of a CAB file)
`test_jar.html` (HTML file to show loading of a JAR file)

1.4 A simple Java programming example

The directory **c:\mjava** contains several subdirectories. In order to test the proper installation of the Java SDK, please type the following commands to build the first demo program (contained in the file **c:\mjava\demo\test.java**):

```
cd c:\mjava\demo
c.bat
jview com.markwatson.demo.test
```

The command file **c.bat** compiles all Java source code in the current directory and creates compiled class files in the **c:\mjava\classes** directory. The command **jview** is used to run stand-alone Java applications using the Microsoft Java Virtual Machine. You should see a Java stand-alone application appear, as in Figure 1.1.

Listing 1.1 shows the command file **c.bat** that is used to compile all Java source files in any of the subdirectories of **c:\mjava** and place the compiled Java class files in **c:\mjava\classes**. If you get compiler errors when running **c.bat**, then you probably do not have your **CLASSPATH** environment set up correctly.

Listing 1.1

```
jvc /g /cp %CLASSPATH% -d ..\classes *.java
```

In Listing 1.1, the **–d** compiler option specifies that the compiled Java class files are written to the directory **..\classes** (which is **c:\mjava\classes**).

Listing 1.2 shows the simple 41-line program in the file **c:\mjava\demo\test.java**.

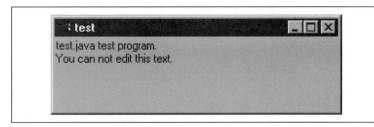

Figure 1.1   *The application window for the file c:\ mjava\ demo\ test.java*

Listing 1.2

```
// test.java
//
// This is a simple Java application to check for the
// proper installation of the Microsoft Java SDK
//

package com.markwatson.demo;

import java.awt.*;
import com.ms.ui.*;
import com.ms.ui.event.*;
import com.ms.fx.*;

public class test extends UIFrame {
  public static void main(String args[]) {
    test demo = new test();
    demo.setBackground(FxColor.lightGray);
    demo.setSize(300,100);
    demo.setVisible(true);
  }

  public test() {
    super("test");
    // enable window events so that we can handle window closing:
    enableEvents(AWTEvent.WINDOW_EVENT_MASK);
    // create the text viewing area:
    UIDrawText text =
```

(continued)

Listing 1.2 *(continued)*

```
    new UIDrawText("test.java test program.\n" +
        "You cannot edit this text.\n");
  add(text);
}

public void processEvent(UIEvent evt) { // JDK 1.1 event model
  switch (evt.getID())  {
  case Event.WINDOW_DESTROY:
    System.exit(0);
  default:
    super.processEvent(evt);
  }
}
}
```

This test program is placed in the package **com.markwatson.demo**, and the compiler (see Listing 1.1) puts compiled Java class files in the directory **c:\mjava\classes**, so compiling the Java source file in Listing 1.2 creates the file

```
c:\mjava\classes\com\markwatson\demo\test.class
```

You should check that the compiled class file **test.class** is in the correct directory and make sure that you understand the concept of Java packages. Java packages are discussed in the online documentation at Microsoft's site *www.microsoft.com/java* and at Sun/JavaSoft's site *java.sun.com*.

1.5 Using J++ version 1.1 with the examples in this book

When I wrote this chapter (January 1998), J++ version 1.1 did not support the JDK 1.1 inner classes and other language features. In this section, I will give advice on how to patch J++ to use the new Java compiler **jvc.exe** that ships with the Java SDK 3.0 (or later). Please note that the examples in this book were developed using just the Java SDK 3.0 and that the instructions in this section may become inaccurate as new versions of J++ and the free Java SDK are released.

When you install J++, a directory **DevStudio** is created. You must copy the following files from the **SDK-Java.30\Bin** directory to the **DevStudio\SharedIDE\Bin** directory:

```
jvc.exe
msjvc.dll
jps.dll
```

After you have installed J++, rebuild the **classes.zip** in your Windows directory by changing the directory to **\SDK-Java.30\Bin** and type

```
clspack -auto
```

Installing J++ will overwrite the **classes.zip** file that is added to your system during the installation of the Java SDK, so it is very important for you to reinstall the newer libraries from the Java SDK.

The directory **c:\mjava\j++\test** contains a project that I built to build and run the **test.java** program seen in Listing 1.1. After creating an empty Java project with J++, I did the following:

- Added the source file **c:\mjava\demo\test.java**

- In the project settings, made the changes indicated in Figures 1.2, 1.3, and 1.4

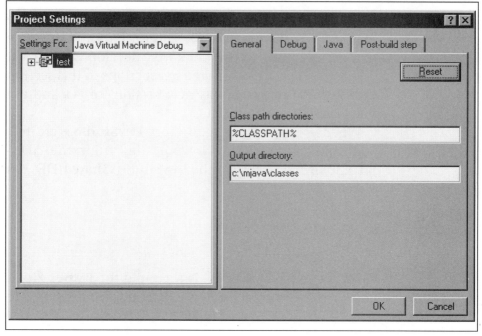

Figure 1.2   *Set up the J++ project to use the **CLASSPATH** environment variable and to place compiled Java class file(s) in the directory c:\ mjava\ classes*

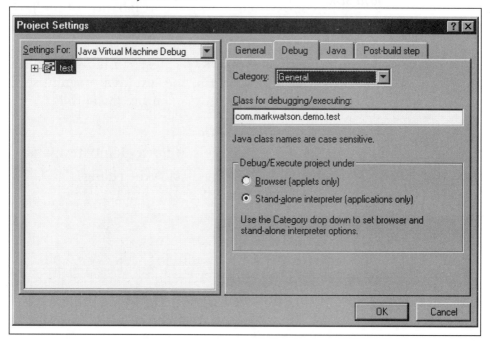

Figure 1.3   *Specify the full package name of the Java class to execute*

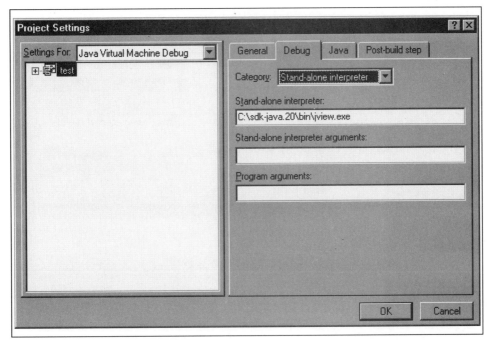

Figure 1.4   *Specify the path to the **jview.exe** that is included with the Java SDK. This path might change with new releases of the Microsoft Java SDK.*

1.6 Using J++ version 6.0 with the examples in this book

I added this section in March 1998 when Microsoft released the preview version of J++ version 6.0. This preview edition also marked the first public release of the Windows Foundation Classes (WFC). Figure 1.5 shows the use of the J++ version 6.0 Java Integrated Development Environment (IDE).

I was able to build projects using J++ version 6.0 (preview release) without modifying J++. The directory **c:\mjava\j++_6.0** contains a sample project for a simple Java application. In Chapter 2 we will discuss both the

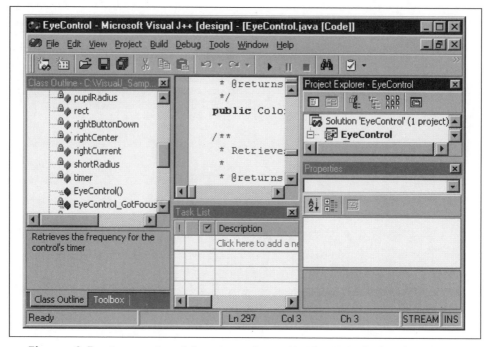

Figure 1.5   *J++ version 6 (preview release 1). The IDE window has been reduced from full-screen mode.*

Microsoft AFC (for building portable Java applications that have the look-and-feel of a Windows 98 program) and the Microsoft WFC (for building native Java applications for Windows) class libraries. At the end of Chapter 2, we will develop a simple application using J++ version 6.0 that uses the WFC and creates a standard Windows **.exe** application.

The AFC and WFC Class Libraries

The Application Foundation Classes (AFC) library was designed and implemented by Microsoft to make Java applications appear more like standard Windows 95 and NT applications. It is interesting that this is accomplished with a pure Java library; you can run Java AFC applications under Linux and OS/2 and they look like typical Windows 95 applications.

Many of the AFC Java classes are similar to the standard Java Abstract Window Toolkit (AWT) classes with similar names. In many cases, AFC and AWT classes can be used together. I have used a combination of pure AFC, a mixture of AFC and AWT, and pure AWT examples in this book. The AFC library is divided into several packages:

- **com.ms.fx**—provides classes that encapsulate colors, glyphs, fonts, curves, text, and textures

Portability of the AFC class library

When I wrote this chapter in October 1997, the prerelease version of the AFC class library was very portable (I used it under OS/2 and Linux with no major problems). However, the next version of the Java SDK, release 2.0, contained a version of the AFC class library that might not run on all Java platforms. I have directions at my Web site *www.markwatson.com* for patching newer versions of the AFC to work under OS/2 and Linux. I recommend using Linux for testing for portability of your Java applications because Linux is free and is fairly simple to install on most PCs if you have an extra disk partition. IBM's Java support in OS/2 is also very good. As I was finishing this book in January 1998, Microsoft released version 3.0 (prerelease) of the Java SDK that contains a portable version of AFC.

- **com.ms.ui**—provides components for menus, dialogs, list boxes, scroll bars, push buttons, check boxes, edit boxes, and tree controls
- **com.ms.ui.event**—provides support for the Java 1.1 event model
- **com.ms.ui.resource**—provides support for using WIN32 resource files with Java applications
- **com.ms.util.cab**—provides access to cabinet (CAB) file creation and extraction services

This chapter (and the examples in this book) will use the first three packages (**com.ms.fx**, **com.ms.ui**, and **com.ms.ui.event**). In addition to the **com.ms.ui.event** package, I also use Java (JDK 1.1 and later) inner classes and the standard Java 1.1 event classes. The **com.ms.ui.-resource** and **com.ms.util.cab** packages are not used in the examples in this book.

As we will see in this chapter, the Java classes in the **com.ms.fx** and **com.ms.ui** packages provide a great-looking and high-level toolkit for building visually attractive, functional, and efficient Java applications and applets.

The Microsoft Java SDK version 2.0 (or later) contains useful online documentation that augments the material in this chapter. Microsoft's documentation refers to user interface (UI) items as *controls* while I prefer (and will use) the term *component*.

Microsoft introduced the Windows Foundation Classes (WFC) as I was finishing this book in January 1998. I added several sections to the end of this chapter to cover WFC. Java applications that use WFC have the following properties:

- Tightly coupled to the Windows native APIs
- Efficient user interface code
- Abstract handling of Windows API data and methods, making it easier to write native Windows applications in Java

2.1 Introduction to AFC

Both the standard Java AWT and AFC use the concept of containers that group UI components (or controls). There are AFC classes that wrap most of the standard

Table 2.1 *Comparison of AWT and AFC classes*

AWT Class	AFC Class	AFC Interface Implemented
Canvas	UICanvas	IUIComponent
Panel	UIPanel	IUIContainer
Applet	UIApplet	IUIContainer
Dialog	UIDialog	IUIContainer
Frame	UIFrame	IUIContainer
Window	UIWindow	IUIContainer
LayoutManager	UILayoutManager	IUILayoutManager

AWT classes as seen in Table 2.1. The **UICanvas** class is typically used for drawing graphics, and the **UIPanel** class is used as a container for other components. The **UIApplet** class is used for Java programs that need to run in an environment managed by a Web browser. The **UIDialog** class is used as a container for components that appear in a pop-up window. The **UIFrame** class provides support for a new window. The **UIWindow** class is the base class of **UIFrame** (and you usually will not use it directly). The **UILayoutManager** class is the superclass for a set of utility classes that manage the placement of components in a container (usually an instance of class **UIPanel** or of a subclass of **UIPanel**).

Table 2.2 shows additional classes for components that are not available in AWT.

We will start with a discussion of components and containers in the standard AWT. The Universal Modeling Language (UML) (Harmon and Watson 1997) class diagram in Figure 2.1 shows the relationship between the AWT **Component** and **Container** classes. The class diagram shows several commonly used methods that we will discuss in this section. In UML class diagrams, a rec-

Table 2.2 *Additional AFC classes*

AFC Class	Superclass	Interface Implemented
UIStatic	UICanvas	IUICanvas
UIButton	UIPanel	IUIContainer
UIStatus	UIPanel	IUIContainer
UIDrawText	UIPanel	IUIContainer
UIThumb	UIPanel	IUIContainer
UIScroll	UIPanel	IUIContainer
UIViewer	UIPanel	IUIContainer
UISelector	UIPanel	IUIContainer
UIPopup	UIWindow	IUIContainer

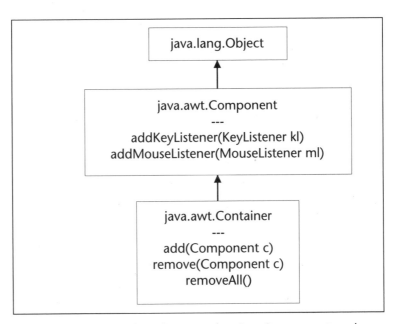

Figure 2.1 *UML class diagram showing **Component** and **Container** classes*

Using Java packages

The Java language provides a mechanism for separating class names into different **package** names. Most of the AFC classes that we will use in this book are located in the package **com.ms.ui**. We can, for example, refer to the AFC class **UIComponent** using the fully qualified package name **com.ms.ui.UIComponent**. Most of the examples that I wrote for this book are placed in the package **com.markwatson**.

tangle represents an individual class. A rectangle, at a minimum, contains the name of the class that the rectangle represents. A rectangle can also show methods (usually just public methods) and class data.

We see in Figure 2.1 that the class **Component** is derived from class **Object** and that class **Container** is derived from class **Component**. A solid arrow in UML class diagrams indicates class inheritance; the arrowhead points to the super- (or base) class.

Figure 2.2 shows the UML class diagram for the AFC classes **com.ms.ui.UIComponent** and **com.ms.ui.UIContainer**. The AFC versions of the AWT classes **Component** and **Container** implement interfaces that are defined in the AFC library. The **UIContainer** class implements the **IUIContainer** interface. The container interface extends the component interface, providing public method signatures for adding, deleting, and positioning contained components. The **UIComponent** class implements the following interfaces:

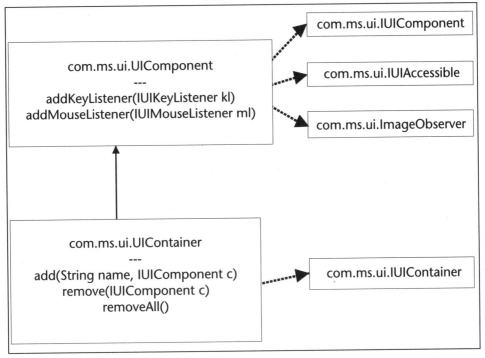

Figure 2.2   *UML class diagram for **UIComponent** and **UIContainer** classes*

- **IUIComponent**—provides the method signatures for handling many events (e.g., adding listeners for mouse and keyboard events) and for getting/setting component properties (e.g., size, visibility, location in parent container, position on screen, etc.)

- **IUIAccessible**—provides public methods for retrieving visual information (e.g., bounds, keyboard shortcut, etc.)

- **ImageObserver**—defines methods for waiting for image graphics to load and be displayed

2.2 AFC components

The **UIComponent** class is abstract; it is used as the base class for all other component and container classes in the AFC library. Components that are created by sub-classing **UIComponent** can either be stateless or maintain their own state. Stateless components do not have to manage their own events.

The **UIComponent** class provides public methods for the following:

- Handling events (e.g., adding keyboard and mouse listeners for the delegation event model, as seen in Listing 2.1)

- Checking the bounds of the component

- Creating images that can appear in the component

- Making the component visible

- Changing the font used by the component

- Getting the location (relative to parent container or the screen)

- Getting the parent container

- Getting the state code for codes defined by the **IUIStateComponent** interface (i.e., **STATE_SYSTEM_CHECKED**, **STATE_SYSTEM_FOCUSED**, **STATE_SYSTEM_HOTTRACKED**, **STATE_SYSTEM_MIXED**, **STATE_SYSTEM_PRESSED**, **STATE_SYSTEM_SELECTED**, **STATE_SYSTEM_FOCUSABLE**, **STATE_SYSTEM_SELECTABLE**, and **STATE_SYSTEM_INVISIBLE**)

- Getting/setting the value of any text associated with the component

Using the online documentation that is provided with the Microsoft Java SDK

The top-level documentation for the Java SDK is available by opening the following file using Internet Explorer 4.0, which you should have installed for some of the examples later in this book:

```
c:\SDK-Java.30\Docs\default.htm
```

The AFC user interface classes (in package **com.ms.ui**) documentation is available by opening the following file using Internet Explorer 4.0:

```
c:\SDK-Java.30\Docs\SDKJDOC\def_ui.htm
```

It is a good idea to bookmark the **def_ui.htm** page in IE 4.0 in order to access it quickly; you will find yourself frequently referring to the online class documentation when you are programming using the AFC library.

- Getting the action state of the component (e.g., is redrawing, is visible, etc.)
- Getting/setting the foreground and background colors
- Getting/setting the size

AFC components that have state (e.g., buttons and check boxes) are derived from the class **UIStateCompo-**

nent. (See the online Java SDK documentation for a list of states that are managed.)

2.3 AFC event handling

The AFC class library supports both old JDK 1.02–style event handling (by defining **handleEvent** methods for each component and UI object) and the new JDK 1.1 delegation-style event handling. Delegation event handling involves explicitly specifying event classes that will be called for events affecting a given component or UI object. Typically, the delegation event model is much more efficient. The older event model allowed events to trigger event handlers in a UI object's container; that container could trigger event handlers in its container, and so on. We will use the new delegation event model in this book (as seen in Listing 2.1).

The AFC class library defines a hierarchy of 12 classes for event handling. We will use only a few of these classes in the examples in this book. The remaining classes are either used internally by AFC or are not required for our examples. We will use

- **UIBaseEvent**
  - **UIEvent**
  - **UIInputEvent**
    - **UIKeyEvent**
    - **UIMouseEvent**
  - **UIItemEvent**
  - **UITextEvent**

It is important for you to understand the new delegation model for handling events. The examples that are developed later in the book are complex; we will use a very simple example here to demonstrate how to capture mouse and keyboard events in a simple program. Figure 2.3 shows a screen shot of the program seen in Listing 2.1.

The class **EventDemo** is defined in Listing 2.1. The class **EventDemo** is derived from the AFC class **UIFrame** and contains a **public static void main** method so that the class can be run as a stand-alone Java application. Figure 2.4 shows the UML class diagram for **EventDemo**.

In order to build and run the example in Listing 2.1, do the following in a DOS-style window:

```
cd c:\mjava\demo
c.bat
jview com.markwatson.demo.EventDemo
```

The class **EventDemo** is located in package **com.-markwatson.demo**, so we specify the full package name in addition to the class name that contains a **public static void main** method. A new window (actually a **UIFrame** object) will appear. Try moving the mouse cursor in and out of the window and clicking in the win-

Figure 2.3 *A simple program uses the delegation event model to process mouse events on a button and key down events in the outer component (or container) that holds the button.*

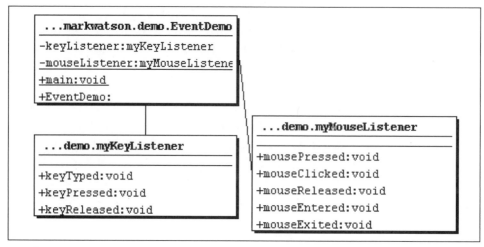

Figure 2.4   *UML class diagram for EventDemo. Public methods are prefaced with a + sign. The data elements keyListener and mouseListener are private so they are prefaced with a − sign.*

dow. The event demo example program prints out the mouse events in the DOS-style window. You can hit the letter *q* or *Q* on the keyboard to terminate the event demo program.

The **EventDemo** class constructor does the following:

- Executes the superclass (**UIFrame**) constructor
- Prints a message to the DOS-style window where you ran the demo program using **jview**
- Creates a new instance of the **UIPushButton** class
- Adds a keyboard listener as an instance of the class **myKeyListener** (which is an inner class defined in Listing 2.1)
- Adds a mouse listener as an instance of the class **myMouseListener** (which is an inner class defined in Listing 2.1)
- Adds the instance of class **UIPushButton** to the **UIFrame** (remember that an instance of class **EventDemo** is also a **UIFrame** object)

Stand-alone Java applications, applets, and JavaBeans

Java programs can execute as stand-alone applications, as applets executing inside a Web browser (like IE 4.0), and can be packaged as reusable components (or JavaBeans) that can be added to other Java applications using a visual building tool like Borland's JBuilder or Symantec's Café. It is possible to package one or more classes so that they can act as applications, applets, and JavaBeans. Almost all of the examples in this book can function as stand-alone applications.

Most source files in the **c:\mjava** subdirectories can be compiled (with their class files installed in the directory c:\mjava\classes) by running the **c.bat** command file that is located in all of the source code subdirectories (e.g., the program in Listing 2.1 is located in the directory **c:\mjava\demo**).

The example program in Listing 2.1 uses the new delegation event model by defining two inner classes (**myKeyListener** and **myMouseListener**). The inner class **myKeyListener** implements the **IUIKeyListener** interface, which means that it must define public methods for

- **void keyTyped(UIKeyEvent ke)**
- **void keyPressed(UIKeyEvent ke)**
- **void keyReleased(UIKeyEvent ke)**

Using the delegation event model will make your programs more efficient than if you used the old event model. Using inner classes makes it simple to implement the new delegation event model.

The inner class **myMouseListener** implements the **IUIMouseListener** interface, which means that it must define public methods for

- **void mousePressed(UIMouseEvent me)**
- **void mouseClicked(UIMouseEvent me)**
- **void mouseReleased(UIMouseEvent me)**
- **void mouseEntered(UIMouseEvent me)**
- **void mouseExited(UIMouseEvent me)**

Listing 2.1

```
// EventDemo.java
//
// Use inner classes that implement listener
// interfaces to handle events

package com.markwatson.demo;

import com.ms.ui.*;
import com.ms.ui.event.*;
import com.ms.fx.*;

public class EventDemo extends UIFrame {
  public static void main(String args[])
  {
    try {
      EventDemo demo = new EventDemo();
      demo.setBackground(FxColor.lightGray);
```

```
      demo.setSize(300,200);
      demo.setVisible(true);
    }
    catch (Exception e) { e.printStackTrace(); }
  }

  public EventDemo() {
    super("Event test demo");
    System.out.println("\nHit the q (or Q) key to quit\n");
    UIPushButton button = new UIPushButton("Push button");
    button.addKeyListener(new myKeyListener());
    button.addMouseListener(new myMouseListener());
    add(button);
  }

  class myKeyListener implements IUIKeyListener {
    public void keyTyped(UIKeyEvent ke) {
      System.out.println("key typed: " + ke.getKeyChar());
      if (ke.getKeyChar() == 'q')  System.exit(0);
      if (ke.getKeyChar() == 'Q')  System.exit(0);
    }
    public void keyPressed(UIKeyEvent ke) {
      System.out.println("key pressed: " + ke.getKeyChar());
    }
    public void keyReleased(UIKeyEvent ke) {
      System.out.println("key released: " + ke.getKeyChar());
    }
  }

  class myMouseListener implements IUIMouseListener {
    public void mousePressed(UIMouseEvent me) {
      System.out.println("mouse pressed");
    }
    public void mouseClicked(UIMouseEvent me) {
      System.out.println("mouse clicked");
    }
    public void mouseReleased(UIMouseEvent me) {
      System.out.println("mouse released");
    }
    public void mouseEntered(UIMouseEvent me) {
      System.out.println("mouse entered");
```

(continued)

Listing 2.1 *(continued)*

```
    }
    public void mouseExited(UIMouseEvent me) {
      System.out.println("mouse exited");
    }
  }
}
```

The example program in Listing 2.1 uses the new delegation event model. There is really no reason for you to use the older event model now that most Web browsers support (at least most of) the JDK 1.1 Java language standard.

One drawback to implementing a listener interface is that you must define all methods in the interface. Event *adapters* are abstract utility classes that implement event listener interfaces and that define stub methods. If you use adapters, then you only have to define the event handling methods that you actually need. If you are using the standard Java AWT classes, then the following adapter classes are available:

- **MouseAdapter**—implements the interface **MouseListener** and defines dummy (or stub) methods for all methods defined in the **Mouse-Listener** interface

- **KeyAdapter**—implements the interface **Key-Listener** and defines dummy (or stub) methods for all methods defined in the **KeyListener** interface

If you use adapter classes, you still use the **addMouse-Listener** and **addKeyListener** methods.

If you are using the AFC classes, then the following adapter classes are available:

- **UIMouseAdapter**—implements the interface **IUIMouseListener** and defines dummy (or stub) methods for all methods defined in the **IUIMouseListener** interface

- **UIKeyAdapter**—implements the interface **IUIKeyListener** and defines dummy (or stub) methods for all methods defined in the **IUIKeyListener** interface

Listing 2.2 shows the file **EventDemo2.java**, which is identical to Listing 2.1, except that adapter classes are used instead of listener classes. Figure 2.5 shows the UML class diagram for **EventDemo2**.

As we see in Listing 2.2, using adapter classes instead of listener interfaces makes our program shorter because

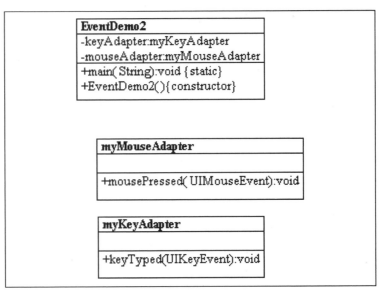

Figure 2.5 *UML class diagram for **EventDemo2**. Public methods are prefaced with a + sign.*

we do not have to define event handling methods that are not required for our specific application.

Listing 2.2

```
// EventDemo2.java
//
// This program is identical to the EventDemo.java
// example, except that we use Event Adapters rather
// than Event Listeners
//

package com.markwatson.demo;

import com.ms.ui.*;
import com.ms.ui.event.*;
import com.ms.fx.*;

public class EventDemo2 extends UIFrame {
  public static void main(String args[])
  {
    try {
      EventDemo2 demo = new EventDemo2();
      demo.setBackground(FxColor.lightGray);
      demo.setSize(300,200);
      demo.setVisible(true);
    }
    catch (Exception e) { e.printStackTrace(); }
  }

  public EventDemo2() {
    super("Event test demo");
    System.out.println("\nHit the q (or Q) key to quit\n");
    UIPushButton button = new UIPushButton("Push button");
    button.addKeyListener(new myKeyAdapter());
    button.addMouseListener(new myMouseAdapter());
    add(button);
  }

  class myKeyAdapter extends UIKeyAdapter {
    public void keyTyped(UIKeyEvent ke) {
```

```
      System.out.println("key typed: " + ke.getKeyChar());
      if (ke.getKeyChar() == 'q')  System.exit(0);
      if (ke.getKeyChar() == 'Q')  System.exit(0);
    }
  }

  class myMouseAdapter extends UIMouseAdapter {
    public void mousePressed(UIMouseEvent me) {
      System.out.println("mouse pressed");
    }
  }
}
```

We see in Listing 2.2 that programs are shorter if we use adapter classes rather than implementing listener interfaces for event handling.

2.4   The AFC tree component

The class **com.ms.ui.UITree** provides a good looking tree control that is simple to use. In this section, we will look at the class API and then derive a subclass **EventTree** that provides the default event handling behavior that we will need for examples developed later in this book. One of the motivations for developing the **Event-Tree** class is to reduce the size of other example programs in this book, thus making them easier to understand. Hopefully, the design of the **EventTree** class is flexible enough to meet your requirements for tree controls in your Java programs.

2.4.1   *Design of the EventTree class*

The design of the **EventTree** class provides a great example for encapsulating third-party libraries in your own programs. There are several reasons why it is a good idea to customize, through inheritance, classes from third-party libraries that you use:

- Increase the portability of your code. In this case, you might want to convert a large application to use Sun/JavaSoft's Java Foundation Classes (JFC) instead of the AFC. If you encapsulate the AFC **UITree** class in your own class, then porting the application will only involve rewriting your class using the underlying JFC tree class instead of **UITree**.

- Add behavior that will be used repeatedly in your applications (e.g., in this case, we add mouse and keyboard event handling). This will make your programs shorter and easier to maintain.

We want to provide the following services in the **EventTree** class:

- The functionality of the base class **UITree**

- Allowance for an instance of **EventTree** to work in single or multiple tree node selection modes

- Easy "built-in" support for two types of tree nodes: folders for nodes that contain other nodes and documents for leaf nodes

- Abstract methods (that must be defined in classes derived from **EventTree**) for returning a list of selected **Strings** for left and right mouse clicks and for returning a character when a key press event occurs in an instance of class **EventTree**

- A utility method that returns an array of **Strings** for all tree nodes that are currently selected

Note on portability and the use of class libraries

As long as the subject of portability has come up, I will share with you my thoughts on what is a politically hot topic in the Java community. I do not believe that there is, at this time, one set of Java class libraries that meet all programming requirements. Java programmers who program mostly (or exclusively) for the Windows platform will sometimes want to take advantage of the nonportable Microsoft class libraries that we cover in this book. Programmers developing distributed client/server and mobile agent software are well advised to use the standard libraries that ship with the Sun/JavaSoft JDK. Programmers writing Java applications for consumer-oriented devices like smart telephones, smart credit cards, and TV set top boxes will likely use proprietary code specific to the device. Programmers writing entertainment software (that does not require real-time 3D graphics) will probably want to use the "slimmed down" Personal Java API from Sun/JavaSoft so that their programs can run on all PCs and TV set top boxes. In the past, programmers have usually had to consider portability of their programs; now the Java language makes portability issues much more manageable.

2.4.2 **Implementing the EventTree class**

We learned how to handle events using the new delegation event model in Section 2.3. Here we will use what
we learned to develop the **EventTree** utility class. The
EventTree class will be derived from the **UITree** class.

Because the **EventTree** class is derived from the
UITree class, we will review the API for **UITree**. The
UITree class is derived from the **UISelector** class. **UISe-
lector** represents collections of selectable objects.

The **UISelector** class is derived from the **UIPanel** class
and implements the **IUISelector** and **TimerListener**
(enables the reception of timer event notifications) interfaces. There are several important public method signatures that are defined in the **IUISelector** interface that
are useful for objects in both the **UITree** and our **Event-
Tree** classes (see the documentation with the Microsoft
Java SDK for the complete API for this interface):

- **public int getSelectedIndex( );**
- **public int[] getSelectedIndices( );**
- **public IUIComponent getSelectedItem( );**
- **public IUIComponent[] getSelectedItems( );**
- **public int getSelectionMode( );**
- **public void setSelectionMode(int mode);**

Additionally, we use from the **UIStateContainer** class
(note that **UITree** is derived from **UIPanel**, which is
derived from **UIStateContainer**) the following API:

- **public synchronized void
  addKeyListener(IUIKeyListener l);**
- **public synchronized void
  addMouseListener(IUIMouseListener l);**

The **UITree** class adds the following important methods to the **UISelector** class (see the documentation with the Microsoft Java SDK for the complete API for this interface) for adding nodes to an instance of **UITree**:

- public IUIComponent add(String s);
- public IUIComponent add(String s, int pos);
- public IUIComponent add(Image i, String s);
- public IUIComponent add(Image i, String s, int pos);
- public IUIComponent add(IUIComponent comp);
- public IUIComponent add(IUIComponent comp, int pos);

The last two add methods are especially important in the applications that you will write that use both **UITree** and our customized version **EventTree**. Instances of classes **UITree** and **EventTree** implement the **IUIComponent** interface; **UITree** is derived from the following classes:

- UITree
  - UISelector
    - UIPanel
      - UIStateContainer
        - UIContainer
          - UIComponent

Indeed, when adding nodes to a tree (either **UITree** of **EventTree**), the most common type of node added will probably be an instance of **UITree**.

For example, the following code is in Listing 2.6 (the class **SampleTree** is defined in Listing 2.5 and is derived from the abstract **EventTree** class):

```
SampleTree et = new SampleTree();
// Create a subtree.  Use an instance of UITree base class,
// and not EventTree or TestTree:
UITree sub_tree = new UITree("item 1: a subtree");

sub_tree.add("subtree item #1");
sub_tree.add("subtree item #2");
et.add(sub_tree);
et.addDocument("item 2);
```

Here, we add a node to the tree **et** that is an instance of class **SampleTree**, which is derived from class **EventTree**, so **et** is also a **UITree** object. Figure 2.6 shows this tree.

Listing 2.3 shows the implementation of the abstract class **EventTree**. The class **EventTree** uses the **Image** class, which is defined in Listing 2.4, to load image files for the tree folder and document icons.

Most of the code for implementing the **EventTree** class is required for implementing the **KeyListener** and **MouseListener** interfaces. Most of the tree component behavior for the **EventTree** class is derived directly through inheritance from the **UITree** base class. There are two class constructors. The default constructor, which has no arguments, defines a new event tree object with a root node labeled **root**. The second class constructor requires a string argument that is the name of the root node of the tree. The public method **setMultiSelect** is used to toggle the multiple selection modes after an event tree object is created. The two methods **addFolder** and **addDocument** are each used to add a new leaf to an event tree object; both methods require a string argument that names the new leaf. Since the **EventTree** class is derived from the **UITree** class, you can also use the **UITree.add** methods to add any object of a class derived from **UIComponent** as a new leaf. The **EventTree** class is abstract; classes derived from **EventTree** must define methods with the following method signatures:

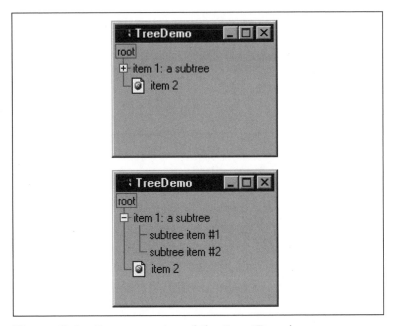

Figure 2.6   *Demonstration of the **EventTree** class*

- **public void leftMouseClicked(String [] targets);**
- **public void rightMouseClicked(String [] targets);**
- **public void keyHit(char c);**

Defining these three methods provides a simple means for adding custom event handling for applications that use the **EventTree** class by deriving new classes from **EventTree**. The method **getSelected** returns an array of strings with the labels of all tree nodes (of leaves) that are currently selected using the mouse. If the event tree is in single selection mode (as opposed to multiple selection modes), then the array will contain a single string element if a tree node is currently selected or return **null** if no node is selected. Internally, event handling in the **EventTree** class is handled by the two inner classes **myMouseListener** and **myKeyListener**.

Listing 2.3

```java
// com.markwatson.util.EventTree.java
//
// This class is derived from the AFC UITree class
// and adds the functionality of handling events for
// returning a list of strings of selected nodes,
// and has abstract methods for leftMouseClick(),
// rightMouseClick(), and keyHit().
//
// Copyright 1997 Mark Watson. This software may be
// used in compiled form without restriction.
//

package com.markwatson.util;

import java.awt.*;
import java.net.URL;
import com.ms.ui.*;
import com.ms.ui.event.*;
import com.ms.fx.*;

public abstract class EventTree extends UITree {

  // use image files from Microsoft Java SDK:
  private static final String imageNames[] = {"folder.gif", "doc.gif"};
  private Image doc;
  private Image folder;

  public EventTree() { this("root"); }

  public EventTree(String root) {
    super(root);
    setExpanded(true);
    setSelectionMode(MULTISELECT);
    Frame tempFrame = new Frame();
    Images images = new Images(imageNames, 2);
    tempFrame = null;
    doc = images.getImage(1);
    folder = images.getImage(0);
    addMouseListener(new myMouseListener());
    addKeyListener(new myKeyListener());
```

```
}

public void setMultiSelect(boolean b) {
  if (b) setSelectionMode(MULTISELECT);
  else   setSelectionMode(SINGLESELECT);
}

public void addFolder(String name) {
  add(folder, name);
}

public void addDocument(String name) {
  add(doc, name);
}

abstract public void leftMouseClicked(String [] targets);
abstract public void rightMouseClicked(String [] targets);
abstract public void keyHit(char c);

String [] getSelected() {
  IUIComponent [] items = getSelectedItems();
  if (items==null) return null;
  int num = items.length;
  String [] names = new String[num];
  for (int i=0; i<num; i++) {
    names[i] = items[i].getName();
    if (names[i]==null) names[i]="";
  }
  return names;
}

class myMouseListener implements IUIMouseListener {

  public void mousePressed(UIMouseEvent me) {
  }
  public void mouseClicked(UIMouseEvent me) {
  }
  public void mouseReleased(UIMouseEvent me) {
    IUIComponent [] c = getSelectedItems();
    if (c!=null) {
     int mod = me.getModifiers();
```

(continued)

Listing 2.3 *(continued)*

```
    int len = c.length;
    if (len<1) return;
    String [] names = new String[len];
    for (int i=0; i<len; i++) {
      names[i] = c[i].getName();
      System.out.println("...." + names[i]);
    }
    System.out.println(".....mod=" + mod);
        if (mod == 16) {
      System.out.println(".....left mouse");
      leftMouseClicked(names);
    }
    if ((mod & 4) != 0)  {
      System.out.println(".....right mouse");
      rightMouseClicked(names);
    }
        }
      }
    public void mouseEntered(UIMouseEvent me) {
    }
    public void mouseExited(UIMouseEvent me) {
    }
  }

class myKeyListener implements IUIKeyListener {
  public void keyTyped(UIKeyEvent ke) {
  }
  public void keyPressed(UIKeyEvent ke) {
    char c = ke.getKeyChar();
    keyHit(c);
  }
  public void keyReleased(UIKeyEvent ke) {
  }
 }
}
```

The **EventTree** class has built-in support for two types of iconic tree nodes: folders and documents. The utility class **com.markwatson.util.Image** (seen in Listing 2.4) is used to read image files.

Listing 2.4

```java
// com.markwatson.util.Images.java
//
// A small utility for loading image files
//

package com.markwatson.util;

import java.applet.*;
import java.awt.*;
import java.awt.image.*;
import java.net.URL;

// This class (like the Microsoft examples) assumes
// that there is a subdirectory 'Images' in the
// current directory.

public class Images
{
  public Images(String image_names[], int num) {
    URL url;
    Toolkit tk = java.awt.Toolkit.getDefaultToolkit();
    images = new Image[num];
    numImages = num;

    for (int i = 0; i < numImages; i++) {
      images[i] = tk.getImage("Images" +
              System.getProperty("file.separator") +
              image_names[i]);
      // (we could use a media tracker to wait for loading)
    }
  }
  public Image getImage(int index) {
    if (index<0 || index >= numImages)  {
      System.out.println("Images.getImage(" + index + "): bad index");
      return null;
    }
    return images[index];
  }
```

(continued)

Listing 2.4 *(continued)*

```
private int numImages = 0;
private Image images[] = null;
}
```

The constructor for the class **Image** does not wait for an image to be loaded from a disk file; it immediately returns to the calling program. This makes the code simple to understand and implement but occasionally results in images appearing on a GUI after an application is initialized and visible.

2.4.3 *Testing the EventTree class*

The **EventTree** class is abstract. In order to use it, we must derive subclasses that define three callback methods:

- **leftMouseClicked(String [] targets)**
- **rightMouseClicked(String [] targets)**
- **keyHit(char c)**

String targets is an array of all node names that are selected (if the **EventTree** is in multiselection mode) or an array containing a single **String** (if the **EventTree** is in single-selection mode).

Listing 2.5 shows a sample class **SampleTree** that is derived from the abstract **EventTree** class. It is important to remember that **EventTree** is an abstract class; we always need to derive a subclass of **EventTree** for our applications.

Listing 2.5

```
// com.markwatson.demo.SampleTree.java
//
// A simple class that is derived from the
```

```java
// com.markwatson.util.EventTree class.
//


package com.markwatson.demo;

import java.awt.*;
import java.net.URL;
import com.ms.ui.*;
import com.ms.ui.event.*;
import com.ms.fx.*;

import com.markwatson.util.*;

public class SampleTree extends com.markwatson.util.EventTree {

  public SampleTree() {
    super();
  }
  public SampleTree(String root) {
    super(root);
  }

  // define methods that are abstract in parent class:
  public void leftMouseClicked(String [] targets) {
    System.out.print("SampleTree.leftMouseClick: ");
    for (int i=0; i<targets.length; i++) {
      System.out.print(targets[i] + "  ");
    }
    System.out.println("");
  }
  public void rightMouseClicked(String [] targets) {
    System.out.print("SampleTree.rightMouseClick: ");
    for (int i=0; i<targets.length; i++) {
      System.out.print(targets[i] + "  ");
    }
    System.out.println("");
  }
  public void keyHit(char c) {
    System.out.println("SampleTree.keyHit(" + c + ")");
  }
}
```

Listing 2.6 shows a simple demo program that implements the class **TreeDemo** for testing the new **SampleTree** class. The **TreeDemo** class is derived from the **UIFrame** base class and it contains a **public static void main** method so that it can run as a stand-alone Java application.

Listing 2.6

```java
// com.markwatson.demo.TreeDemo.java

package com.markwatson.demo;

import java.awt.*;
import java.net.URL;
import com.ms.ui.*;
import com.ms.ui.event.*;
import com.ms.fx.*;

import com.markwatson.util.*;

public class TreeDemo extends UIFrame {
  public static void main(String args[]) {
    TreeDemo demo = new TreeDemo();
    demo.setBackground(FxColor.lightGray);
    demo.setSize(190,160);
    demo.setVisible(true);
  }

  public TreeDemo() {
    super("TreeDemo");
    // enable window events so that we can handle window closing:
    enableEvents(AWTEvent.WINDOW_EVENT_MASK);

    SampleTree et = new SampleTree();
    // create a subtree.  Use an instance of UITree base class,
    // and not EventTree or TestTree:
    UITree sub_tree = new UITree("item 1: a subtree");
    sub_tree.add("subtree item #1");
    sub_tree.add("subtree item #2");
```

```
  et.add(sub_tree);
  et.addDocument("item 2");
  add(et);
}
public void processEvent(UIEvent evt) { // JDK 1.1
  switch (evt.getID())  {
  case Event.WINDOW_DESTROY:
    System.exit(0);
  default:
    super.processEvent(evt);
  }
}
}
```

Figure 2.6 shows the **TreeDemo.java** test program that creates an instance of the class **SampleTree** (which is derived from the class **EventTree**).

2.5 AFC text components

The AFC class library has excellent support for both editable and static text. In Section 2.4 we derived our own application-level class **EventTree** from the AFC class **UITree**. We created our own class to handle our own event handling behavior to the **UITree** AFC class. The event handling for AFC text components is simpler, so in this section we will just give some examples for creating instances of the following AFC classes:

- **UIDrawText**—used to create noneditable text inside other components
- **UIEdit**—used to create editable text inside other components

The class **UIEdit** is derived from **UIDrawText**.

The most commonly used methods in class **UIDraw-Text** are

- **public String getValueText( );**
- **public void setValueText(String value);**

The most commonly used methods in class **UIEdit** are

- **public synchronized void addTextListener(IUI-TextListener l);**
- **public int append(String s);**
- **public void clear( );**

The **IUITextListener** interface adds the following method signature to the **IUIBaseEventListener** interface:

- **public void textValueChanged(UITextEvent e);**

The implementation of class **TextDemo** in Listing 2.7 creates both a read-only and an editable text field. The editable text field has a text listener that is implemented by the inner class **myTextListener**. Whenever any change is made to the editable text, the new value of the text is printed out. When the application is exited, the final version of the editable text is also printed out.

Listing 2.7

```
// com.markwatson.demo.TextDemo

package com.markwatson.demo;

import java.awt.*;
import java.net.URL;
import com.ms.ui.*;
import com.ms.ui.event.*;
import com.ms.fx.*;


import com.markwatson.util.*;

public class TextDemo extends UIFrame {
```

```
public static void main(String args[]) {
  TextDemo demo = new TextDemo();
  demo.setBackground(FxColor.lightGray);
  demo.setSize(190,140);
  demo.setVisible(true);
}

public TextDemo() {
  super("TextDemo");
  // enable window events so that we can handle window closing:
  enableEvents(AWTEvent.WINDOW_EVENT_MASK);

  UIPanel panel = new UIPanel();

  // create the text viewing area:
  UIDrawText text =
    new UIDrawText("You cannot edit this\ntext.\n\n");
  panel.add(text);

  // create an edit text area:
  edit = new UIEdit("you can edit this\ntext\n\n");
  edit.setBackground(FxColor.white);
  // Add a text event listener to the edit text field:
  edit.addTextListener(new myTextListener());
  panel.add(edit);

  add(panel);
}

private class myTextListener implements IUITextListener {
  public void textValueChanged(UITextEvent e) {
    String txt = edit.getValueText();
    System.out.println("text changed: " + txt);
  }
}

private UIEdit edit = null;

public void processEvent(UIEvent evt) { // JDK 1.1
  switch (evt.getID())  {
  case Event.WINDOW_DESTROY:
```

(continued)

Listing 2.7 *(continued)*

```
    // The user closed the window.  Before we terminate
    // the application, we will fetch the text from the
    // UIEdit component and print it:
    String txt = edit.getValueText();
    System.out.println("Final editable text=" + txt);
    System.exit(0);
  default:
    super.processEvent(evt);
  }
 }
}
```

Figure 2.7 shows a sample window frame created by the example program in Listing 2.7 that contains a panel holding two text areas: one static and one editable.

Specifying x-,y-coordinates for components inside a container

In the examples in this book, we usually use a default layout manager that places components inside a container. It is also very simple to specify the exact size and location of components inside any container. The file **c:\mjava\3tier\ViewXML.java** (seen in Listing 9.1) shows how to use a null layout manager, add components to a container, and then call the method **setBounds** on each component after they are added to the container using the **add** method.

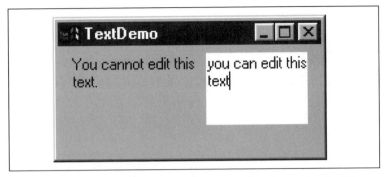

Figure 2.7 *Demonstration of AFC read-only and editable text components*

2.6 AFC split viewer components

The **UISplitViewer** class implements a two-part frame with a dividing bar that can be grabbed with the mouse and moved, changing the relative size of the two parts of the **UISplitViewer**. Figure 2.8 shows an application frame that contains two split viewers: the first is arranged horizontally and contains a tree display and some sample text, and the second split viewer is arranged vertically and contains the first split viewer and a **UIPanel** (on the bottom) that contains editable text and a push button.

The **UISplitViewer** class is derived from the **UIPanel** class. There are five different constructors for the class **UISplitViewer**. In the example program in Listing 2.8, we only use the most versatile constructor (i.e., the constructor with the most arguments for customizing the appearance and behavior):

- public UISplitViewer(IUIComponent nw, IUIComponent se, int style, int size, boolean addScroll);

The third parameter, **style**, can have the value of 0 for a vertically split viewer or the value of **com.ms.ui.UISplit-**

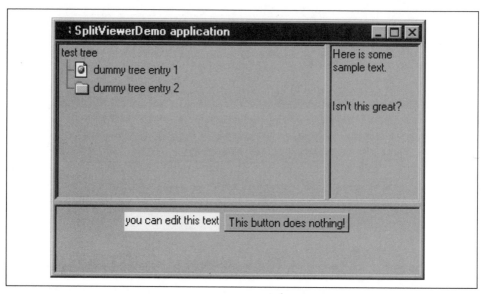

Figure 2.8 *Two nested **UISplitViewers**. This example program is shown in Listing 2.8.*

Viewer.HORIZONTAL for a horizontally split viewer. The first two arguments specify the components that are added to the split viewer component. The fourth argument, **size**, determines the size of the first component that is added to the split viewer. If **size** is negative, then its value specifies the percentage of the height (for vertically split viewers) or width (for horizontally split viewers). If **size** if a positive integer, then it is in units of absolute pixels. I find it most convenient to specify **size** as a negative integer to specify the relative size of the components as a percentage. The fifth argument, **addScroll**, of this constructor is a **Boolean** flag that indicates whether the split viewer is allowed to create and use scroll bars. If this fifth parameter, **addScroll**, is false, then the split viewer will never use scroll bars.

Figure 2.9 shows the UML class diagram for class **SplitViewerDemo**.

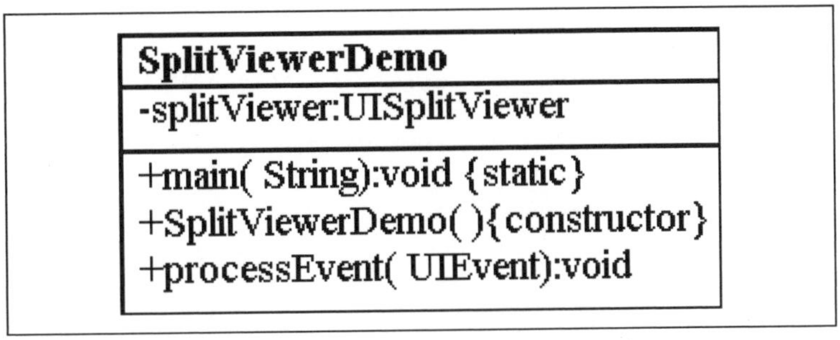

SplitViewerDemo

-splitViewer:UISplitViewer

+main(String):void {static}
+SplitViewerDemo( ){constructor}
+processEvent(UIEvent):void

Figure 2.9   *UML class diagram for **SplitViewerDemo**. Public methods are prefaced with a + sign. The class data item **splitViewer** (of class **UISplitViewer**) is private data.*

Notice in Listing 2.8 that we create two instances of the class **UISplitViewer**; one of the instances contains the other.

Listing 2.8

```
// com.markwatson.demo.SplitViewerDemo

package com.markwatson.demo;

import java.awt.*;
import java.net.URL;
import com.ms.ui.*;
import com.ms.ui.event.*;
import com.ms.fx.*;

import com.markwatson.util.*;

public class SplitViewerDemo extends UIFrame {
  public static void main(String args[]) {
    SplitViewerDemo demo = new SplitViewerDemo();
    demo.setBackground(FxColor.lightGray);
    demo.setSize(500,400);
    demo.setVisible(true);
  }
```

(continued)

Listing 2.8 *(continued)*

```
  private UISplitViewer splitViewer;

public SplitViewerDemo() {
  super("SplitViewerDemo application");
  // enable window events so that we can handle window closing:
  enableEvents(AWTEvent.WINDOW_EVENT_MASK);

  // create tree for the top split viewer (left side):
  SampleTree tree = new com.markwatson.demo.SampleTree("test tree");
  tree.setExpanded(true);
  // dummy tree entries for testing:
  tree.addDocument("dummy tree entry 1");
  tree.addFolder("dummy tree entry 2");

  // create some help text
  UIDrawText text = new UIDrawText("Here is some\n" +
              "sample text.\n\n\n" +
              "Isn't this great?\n");

  // create the top split viewer:
  UISplitViewer top = new UISplitViewer(tree, text,
            0, -75, true);

  // create edit control and button for adding newsgroups:
  UIPanel p = new UIPanel();
  UIEdit edit = new UIEdit("you can edit this text");
  edit.setBackground(FxColor.white);

  UIButton button = new UIPushButton("This button does nothing!");
  p.add(edit);
  p.add(button);

  // create the split viewer that covers the entire panel:
  UISplitViewer entire = new UISplitViewer(top, p,
    UISplitViewer.HORIZONTAL, -70,
    true);

  add(entire);
}
public void processEvent(UIEvent evt) { // JDK 1.1
```

```
switch (evt.getID())  {
case Event.WINDOW_DESTROY:
  System.exit(0);
default:
  super.processEvent(evt);
  }
 }
}
```

We see in Listing 2.8 that it is fairly easy to add split viewer components using the AFC class library. The use of split viewer components is a good alternative to using separate windows (or frames) for different parts of a program's user interface.

2.7 AFC tabbed components

Most users do not like multiple windows for an application's user interface. Using the class **UITabViewer** allows us to have multiple application panels in a single window frame; clicking on a tab brings the panel associated with the tab to the front. Figures 2.10 and 2.11 show a simple tabbed viewer component demo.

The class **UITabViewer** is derived from the class **UIPanel**. Using the tab viewer component is very simple. Figure 2.12 shows the UML class diagram for the **TabViewerDemo** class.

The example in Listing 2.9 that implements the class **TabViewerDemo** only requires two **UITabViewer** class method calls:

- **public UITabViewer( );**
- **public IUIComponent add(String name, IUIComponent comp);**

An application creates a new tab viewer object and then calls the method **add** for each new required tab

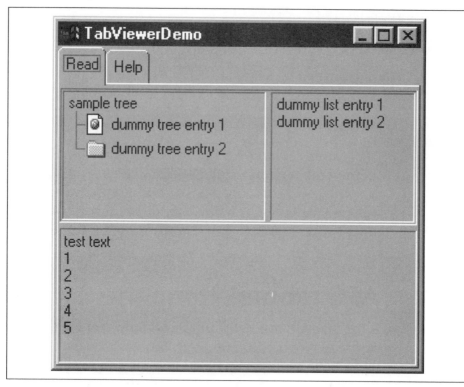

Figure 2.10 *A simple tabbed viewer example with two tabs and two corresponding panels that are shown when a tab is clicked. Here, the first tab is clicked, showing the first panel added to the tabbed viewer component.*

viewer component. The example in Listing 2.9 uses two helper methods:

- **initFirstPanel( )**
- **initSecondPanel( )**

Each helper method creates a single **UIPanel** instance and adds it to the tab viewer. These methods add a variety of AFC components to two separate panels that are added to the tab viewer component.

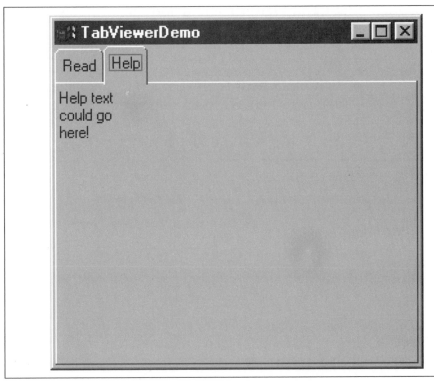

Figure 2.11   *A simple tabbed viewer example with two tabs and two corresponding panels that are shown when a tab is clicked. Here, the second tab is clicked, showing the second panel added to the tabbed viewer component.*

TabViewerDemo
-tabViewer:UITabViewer
+main(String):void {static} +TabViewerDemo( ){constructor} -initFirstPanel( ):void -initSecondPanel( ):void +processEvent(UIEvent):void

Figure 2.12   *UML class diagram for **TabViewerDemo**. Public methods are prefaced with a + sign, while protected and private methods are prefaced with a – sign.*

The **UITabViewer** method **add** takes two arguments:

- **String** name—the name that will appear on the tab
- **IUIComponent** comp—any AFC component that appears whenever its corresponding tab is clicked

Listing 2.9

```
// com.markwatson.demo.TabViewerDemo

package com.markwatson.demo;

import java.awt.*;
import java.net.URL;
import com.ms.ui.*;
import com.ms.ui.event.*;
import com.ms.fx.*;

import com.markwatson.util.*;

public class TabViewerDemo extends UIFrame {
  public static void main(String args[]) {
    TabViewerDemo demo = new TabViewerDemo();
    demo.setBackground(FxColor.lightGray);
    demo.setSize(500,400);
    demo.setVisible(true);
  }

  private UITabViewer tabViewer;

  public TabViewerDemo() {
    super("TabViewerDemo");
    // enable window events so that we can handle window closing:
    enableEvents(AWTEvent.WINDOW_EVENT_MASK);

    tabViewer = new UITabViewer();

    // build two test panels and insert into the tab viewer:
    initFirstPanel();
```

```
      initSecondPanel();

      add(tabViewer);
    }

  private void initFirstPanel() {

      // create tree for the top split viewer (left side):
      SampleTree tree = new SampleTree("sample tree");
      // dummy tree entries for testing:
      tree.addDocument("dummy tree entry 1");
      tree.addFolder("dummy tree entry 2");

      // create a sample list
      UIList list = new UIList();
      // dummy list entries for testing:
      list.add("dummy list entry 1");
      list.add("dummy list entry 2");

      // create the top split viewer:
      UISplitViewer top =
        new UISplitViewer(tree, list, 0, -45, true);

      // create the text viewing area:
      UIDrawText text =
        new UIDrawText("test text\n1\n2\n3\n4\n5");

      // create the split viewer that covers the entire panel:
      UISplitViewer entire =
        new UISplitViewer(top, text,
          UISplitViewer.HORIZONTAL, -50, true);

      tabViewer.add("Read", entire);
    }

  private void initSecondPanel() {

      // create the text viewing area:
      UIDrawText helpText =
        new UIDrawText("Help text\ncould go\nhere!\n");
```

(continued)

Listing 2.9 *(continued)*

```
    tabViewer.add("Help", helpText);
  }

  public void processEvent(UIEvent evt) { // JDK 1.1
    switch (evt.getID())  {
    case Event.WINDOW_DESTROY:
      System.exit(0);
    default:
      super.processEvent(evt);
    }
  }
}
```

The tab panel control is a very good alternative to splitting applications into separate windows (or frames) using a multiple document window design. Most users do not like the use of multiple windows for a single application. We will use tabbed panels in several examples later in this book.

2.8 Introduction to WFC

The WFC classes are used by themselves to build Windows 95 and Windows NT applications. Typically, you will not use the Java AWT user interface classes at all when you use WFC.

The WFC classes provide a very efficient interface to the Windows operating system services. The advantages of using WFC are the tighter integration with the Windows platform and more efficient applications. Java applications using WFC seem to be indistinguishable from native Windows applications. The WFC classes provide Windows programmers with access to (almost) all features of the Windows APIs. Anders Hejlsberg, the Microsoft architect who designed WFC, combined Windows and HTML user interface programming metaphors in the WFC class library; WFC provides a component model that encapsulates both the Windows programming model, including the Graphics Device Interface (GDI), and Dynamic HTML (DHTML). The big disadvantage of using WFC is losing portability to non-Windows platforms.

For client-side application programming, WFC offers an almost identical programming model to using either WIN32 or DHTML for rendering the user interface. Table 2.3 shows code snippets (modified from an example at Microsoft's Visual J++ Web site) that implement a simple user interface on top of both WIN32 and DHTML.

In Table 2.3, notice how the only differences between the DHTML implementation and the WIN32 implementation are the following:

- Import the package **wfc.html** rather than **wfc.ui**
- Use the class **wfc.html.DhPanel** instead of class **wfc.ui.Form**
- Use the class **wfc.html.DhButton** instead of class **wfc.ui.Button**

At the risk of confusing people reading WFC applications, it is too bad that the designers of WFC did not name the classes in the package **wfc.html** with the exact same method names as the corresponding methods in the package **wfc.ui**. In this case, a programmer could have simply changed one import statement to switch between using DHTML and WIN32 for rendering a user interface.

2.9 WFC architecture

The WFC classes are layered on top of both the J/Direct API and the COM interface. Database access is provided through the Active Data Objects (ADO) API. The WFC

Table 2.3 *WFC examples using WIN32 and DHTML*

`import wfc.ui.*;`	`import wfc.html.*;`
```{ // WIN32 implementation Form form1 = new Form(); Button button1 = new Button(); button1.setText("WIN32"); button1.setPosition(25, 25); button1.addOnClick(new EventHandler(this.onClick)); form1.add(button1); }```	```{ // DHTML implementation DhPanel form1 = new DhPanel(); DhButton button1 =new DhButton(); button1.setText("DHTML"); button1.setPosition(25, 25); button1.addOnClick(new DhEventHandler(this.onClick)); form1.add(button1); }```

classes also seamlessly support using DHTML. (See Chapter 11 for a discussion of DHTML.) Figure 2.13 shows the overall architecture of the WFC.

2.10 WFC Java packages

The WFC is defined in the following packages:

- **wfc.core**—provides the core classes
- **wfc.app**—provides application model support
- **wfc.ui**—provides the user interface components
- **wfc.html**—provides DHTML support
- **wfc.data**—provides database access support
- **wfc.io**—provides file I/O support
- **wfc.util**—provides a set of basic utility classes
- **wfc.win32**—provides support for the Windows APIs

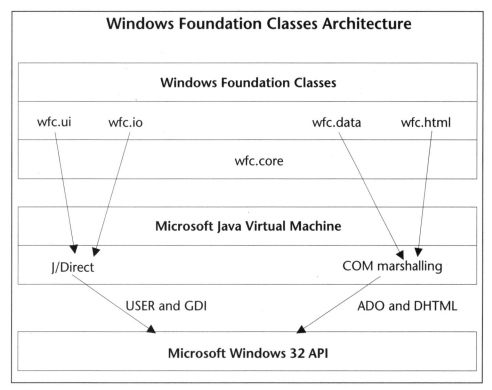

Figure 2.13   *WFC architecture*

We will not completely cover the WFC packages in this chapter, but we will create WFC examples demonstrating

- stand-alone Windows applications built with J++ 6.0 and WFC
- calling WIN32 API
- supporting DHTML with WFC

2.11 WFC event model

You use *delegates* when programming with the WFC class library. A delegate is a binding to a specific method of a specific object (not of a class). For example, if you want to process a mouse click event on a button control (or component), you specify that a specific method of a specific object in your program be called when a mouse click event happens in the button. For example, in the example developed in Section 2.14, we want to detect mouse down events in a control class **TicTacToeControl** when creating the application:

```
// Create event handler for mouse down events:
this.addOnMouseDown(
        new
MouseEventHandler(this.TicTacToeControl_MouseDown));
```

Notice that a specific method reference (using the object **this**) is used when constructing a new instance of class **MouseEventHandler**. The class **TicTacToeControl** (in Section 2.14) defines the method **TicTacToeControl_MouseDown** that is called whenever there is a mouse down event:

```
private void TicTacToeControl_MouseDown(Object sender,
MouseEvent e) {

  // Get mouse click X-Y location relative to the control:
  int y_mouse_loc = e.;
  int x_mouse_loc = e.;
  // Do something:
  //    ...

  // Force a redraw of this control:
  invalidate();
}
```

I don't think that the notation for using delegates is aesthetically appealing, but it does have the advantage of simplicity and efficiency. I prefer the use of inner classes and adapter classes in the AWT and AFC class libraries. However, the use of delegates does simplify WFC-based Java applications.

2.12   Integration of WFC and Web pages

The WFC classes are tightly integrated with the Internet Explorer HTML document object model (see Chapter 11). WFC provides both client- and server-side support for DHTML:

- Client-side applets used in DHTML documents have a simple interface to the DHTML document object model.

- Server-side Java programs using WFC can easily generate "raw" HTML to send back to Web clients.

Table 2.3 contained a simple example of using the **wfc.html** package, comparing it to using the **wfc.ui** package. Listing 2.10 shows another example of the use of DHTML in WFC.

Listing 2.10

```
// HTMLtest.java

import wfc.html.*;

public class HTMLtest extends DhModule
{
```

Listing 2.10 *(continued)*

```
public void documentLoad(Object sender, DhEvent p) {
  DhDocument doc = getDocument();
  DhButton button1 = new DhButton("Test DHTML event handler");
  button1.addOnClick( new DhEventHandler(this.onButton1Click) );
  doc.add(button1);
}

public void onButton1Click( Object sender, DhEvent e ) {
  DhDocument doc = getDocument();
  DhText t = new DhText("Event handled...");
  doc.newLine();
  doc.add(t);
}
}
```

Listing 2.11 shows the HTML file used to test the program in Listing 2.10.

Listing 2.11

```
<HTML>
  <BODY>
    Test the WFC Java example that uses package wfc.html<p>
    <OBJECT classid="java:HTMLtest" HEIGHT=90 WIDTH=90></OBJECT>
  </BODY>
</HTML>
```

Figure 2.14 shows the program in Listing 2.10 run inside IE 4.0 using the HTML file seen in Listing 2.11.

2.13 Using WFC for graphics

Windows programmers are used to using the GDI API. WFC provides a great interface to GDI: you can deal with GDI components like brushes and bitmaps at a high level, without having to handle memory alloca-

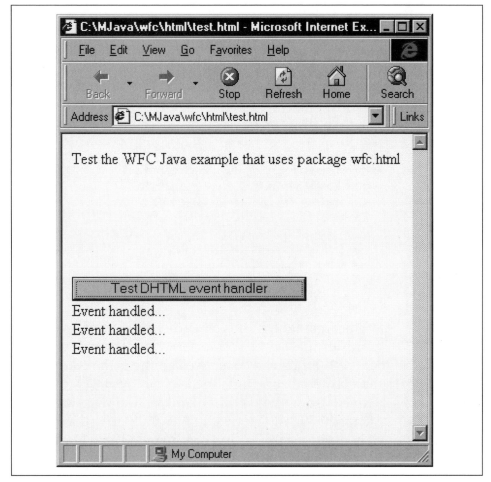

Figure 2.14   *HTML generated by the WFC **wfc.html** package*

tion, and so on. The first WFC class that you will use for graphics is, not surprisingly, called **Graphics**. The WFC **Form** class has a utility method for creating a graphics object relevant to a specific instance of the **Form** class; for example:

```
Graphics g = this.createGraphics();
```

An instance of the graphics class is the gateway through which we interface with the GDI API. Graphics operations through an instance of class **Graphics** only apply to the WFC control that was used to create the instance. The form class that you use for an application will probably need a special method to receive paint requests; the method signature for this method looks like this:

```
MyForm_paint(Object sender, PaintEvent e){
  e.graphics.setTextColor(Color.RED);
  e.graphics.setBackColor(Color.BLUE);
  e.graphics.setFont(new Font("Times New Roman", 14));
  e.graphics.drawString("test", new Point(30, 30));
  Pen pen = e.graphics.setPen(new Pen(Color(255,0,0),
  Pen.STYLE_DOT);
  e.graphics.drawLine(new Point(0, 0), new Point(25, 25));
}
```

The argument **e**, of type **PaintEvent**, contains a field **graphics** that is the instance of class **Graphics** created for the WFC control that received the paint event. Here, the class **MyForm** is defined in our application and is derived from the WFC **Form** class. If you are using Microsoft Visual J++ version 6.0, the IDE will automatically create a subclass of **Form** named **Form1**. (I usually rename this generated class to something more appropriate to my application.) The method **MyForm_paint** is registered to accept paint events by adding the following line of code to your program where you initialize the form:

```
this.addOnPaint(new PaintEventHandler(this.MyForm_paint));
```

The following objects are associated with a graphics object:

- **Brush**—used to fill enclosed surfaces with patterns, colors, and bitmaps

- **Font**—used to set properties for text drawn in a form
- **Pen**—used to draw lines and polygons in a form

The WFC classes automatically handle memory management for these objects. The following simple example shows how to draw an image file inside of a form:

```
Bitmap bitmap = new Bitmap("c:\\mjava\\demo\\mark.bmp");
private MyForm_paint(Object sender, PaintEvent e){
    e.graphics.drawImage(bitmap, new Point(0, 0));
}
```

Here, **MyForm** is the class name of a class in our application that we have derived from the WFC class **Form**. A paint event can be triggered at any time by invalidating a form; for example, in any method of a class derived from the WFC **Form** class:

```
this.invalidate();
```

The invalidate method, inherited from class **Form**, schedules a paint event.

2.14   Example WFC application

Listings 2.12 and 2.13 show a simple Windows application written in Java for the Windows platform. Listing 2.12 shows the definition of class **TicTacToeControl.java**, and Listing 2.13 shows the implementation of class **Form1** that contains a single instance of class **TicTacToeControl**. Figure 2.15 shows the UML class diagram for the example **TicTacToe** program.

Listing 2.12 shows the implementation of the **TicTacToeControl** class that encapsulates the data and behavior for either playing tic-tac-toe against the computer, playing against another player, or letting the computer

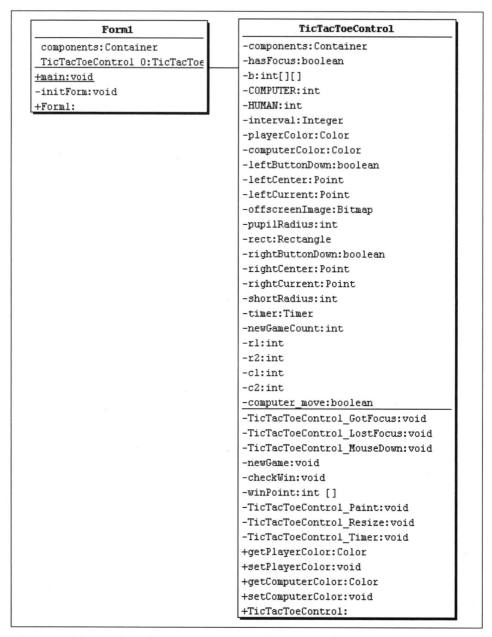

Figure 2.15 *UML class diagram created with TogetherJ modeling tool*

play against itself. If no move is made within 2 seconds for either side, the computer will automatically make a move for the side to play. A timer is used to time 2-second intervals. The control uses double buffering for graphics; all graphics calls are made to the offscreen bitmap (variable **offscreenImage**).

The class constructor calls the superclass **wfc.ui.Control** constructor and then calls the method **newGame** to set up parameters for a new game. Five event handlers are initialized in the following code:

```
// Create event handlers for events:
this.addOnPaint(new PaintEventHandler(this.TicTacToeControl_Paint));
this.addOnMouseDown(
new MouseEventHandler(this.TicTacToeControl_MouseDown));
this.addOnGotFocus(
      new EventHandler(this.TicTacToeControl_GotFocus));
this.addOnLostFocus(
      new EventHandler(this.TicTacToeControl_LostFocus));
this.addOnResize(new EventHandler(this.TicTacToeControl_Resize));
```

As described in Section 2.11, event handlers are set by specifying a specific method on a specific object; this specified method is called when the appropriate event occurs. The event handler method **TicTacToeControl_MouseDown** converts the coordinates of a mouse click event to the coordinates of the tic-tac-toe board, checks to see whose turn it is, and makes the indicated move. The method **TicTacToeControl_MouseDown** calls the method **invalidate** to force a repaint of the control (i.e., cause the method **TicTacToeControl_Paint** to be called). The method **newGame** simply zeros out the board (which is stored in the array **b**). The method **checkWin** checks for a win condition by either side. The method **winPoint** checks to see if there is an "instant win" point for a specified side (i.e., player or computer). The method **TicTacToeControl_Paint** simply examines the current board (stored in the variable **b**) and draws either blue or red circles for the player and computer pieces. The variables **r1**, **c1**, **r2**, and **c2** are used to calculate where to draw the lines on the tic-tac-toe board; these values are changed by the method **TicTacToeControl_Resize** if the control's window is resized. The method **TicTacToeControl_Timer** is called every 2-seconds if the player has not yet moved; this method will calculate a move for either the player or the computer. The inner class **ClassInfo** is used by the Microsoft Visual J++ 6.0 IDE for determining control properties.

Listing 2.12

```
//TicTacToeControl.java
//
// This example was derived from the Microsoft EyeControl.java
// example program for J++ 6.0 and WFC.
//
// Play tic-tac-toe against the computer.  If you do not move
// in 2 seconds, the computer chooses a random move for you.
//

import wfc.ui.*;
import wfc.core.*;
import wfc.app.*;

public class TicTacToeControl extends wfc.ui.Control
{
  private Container components = new Container();
  private boolean hasFocus;
  private int b[][] = new int[3][3];  // the board data

  private final int COMPUTER = 1;
  private final int HUMAN = 2;

  // The default update frequency is 2000ms
  private Integer interval = new Integer(2000);
```

```
private Color playerColor = wfc.ui.Color.BLUE;
private Color computerColor = wfc.ui.Color.RED;
private boolean leftButtonDown = false;
private Bitmap offscreenImage;
private Rectangle rect;
private Timer timer;

public TicTacToeControl() {
  super();
  newGame();
  setTabStop(true);
  setStyle(STYLE_OPAQUE, true);

  // The timer is used to check to see if the human has moved
  // within 2 seconds:
  timer = new Timer(components);
  timer.setInterval(interval.intValue());
  timer.addOnTimer (new EventHandler(this.TicTacToeControl_Timer));

  // Create event handlers for events:
  this.addOnPaint(new PaintEventHandler(this.TicTacToeControl_Paint));
  this.addOnMouseDown(
        new MouseEventHandler(this.TicTacToeControl_MouseDown));
  this.addOnGotFocus(
        new EventHandler(this.TicTacToeControl_GotFocus));
  this.addOnLostFocus(
        new EventHandler(this.TicTacToeControl_LostFocus));
  this.addOnResize(new EventHandler(this.TicTacToeControl_Resize));

  // the default size of our control is 128 x 128 pixels
  setBounds(0, 0, 128, 128);
  TicTacToeControl_Resize(null, null);
  timer.setEnabled(true);
}

private void TicTacToeControl_GotFocus(Object sender, Event e) {
  hasFocus = true;
  invalidate();
}
```

(continued)

Listing 2.12 *(continued)*

```java
private void TicTacToeControl_LostFocus(Object sender, Event e) {
  hasFocus = false;
  invalidate();
}

private void TicTacToeControl_MouseDown(Object sender, MouseEvent e) {
  // Make a move and force a repaint of the window:
  wfc.win32.Windows.SetFocus(getHandle());

  int deltaX = rect.width / 3;
  int deltaY = rect.height / 3;

  int r = e.y / deltaY;
  int c = e.x / deltaX;
  if (r > 2) r = 2;  if (c > 2) c = 2;
  if (computer_move) b[r][c] = COMPUTER;
  else               b[r][c] = HUMAN;

  computer_move = !computer_move;

  invalidate();
}

private void newGame() {
  for (int i=0; i<3; i++) {
    for (int j=0; j<3; j++) {
      b[i][j] = 0;
    }
  }
}

private void checkWin() {
  boolean won = false;
  boolean computerWin = true;
  // First, check the two diagonals:
  if (b[0][0] == b[1][1] && b[1][1] == b[2][2] &&
      b[0][0] != 0) {
    won = true;
    if (b[0][0]==HUMAN) computerWin = false;
  }
```

```
    if (b[2][0] == b[1][1] && b[1][1] == b[0][2] &&
        b[2][0] != 0) {
      won = true;
      if (b[2][0]==HUMAN) computerWin = false;
    }


    // Now check the rows:
    for (int row=0; row<3; row++) {
      if (b[row][0] == b[row][1] && b[row][1] == b[row][2] &&
          b[row][0] != 0) {
        won = true;
        if (b[row][0]==HUMAN) computerWin = false;
      }
    }
    // Now check the columns:
    for (int col=0; col<3; col++) {
      if (b[0][col] == b[1][col] && b[0][col] == b[2][col] &&
          b[0][col] != 0) {
        won = true;
        if (b[0][col]==HUMAN) computerWin = false;
      }
    }
  }

  private int [] winPoint(int sideToMove) {
    boolean won = false;
    boolean computerWin = true;
    // First, check the two diagonals:
    if (b[0][0] == b[1][1] && 0 == b[2][2] &&
        b[0][0] == sideToMove) {
      int [] ret = {2, 2};
      return ret;
    }
    if (b[2][2] == b[1][1] && 0 == b[0][0] &&
        b[2][2] == sideToMove) {
      int [] ret = {0, 0};
      return ret;
    }
    if (b[2][0] == b[1][1] && 0 == b[0][2] &&
        b[2][0] == sideToMove) {
      int [] ret = {0, 2};
```

(continued)

Listing 2.12 *(continued)*

```
    return ret;
  }
  if (b[0][2] == b[1][1] && 0 == b[2][0] &&
      b[0][2] == sideToMove) {
    int [] ret = {2, 0};
    return ret;
  }


  // Now check the rows:
  for (int row=0; row<3; row++) {
    if (b[row][0] == b[row][1] && 0 == b[row][2] &&
        b[row][0] == sideToMove) {
      int [] ret = new int[2];
      ret[0] = row;  ret[1] = 2;
      return ret;
    }
    if (b[row][2] == b[row][1] && 0 == b[row][0] &&
        b[row][2] == sideToMove) {
      int [] ret = new int[2];
      ret[0] = row;  ret[1] = 0;
      return ret;
    }
    if (b[row][2] == b[row][0] && 0 == b[row][1] &&
        b[row][2] == sideToMove) {
      int [] ret = new int[2];
      ret[0] = row;  ret[1] = 1;
      return ret;
    }
  }
  // Now check the columns:
  for (int col=0; col<3; col++) {
    if (b[0][col] == b[1][col] && 0 == b[2][col] &&
        b[0][col] == sideToMove) {
      int [] ret = new int[2];
      ret[0] = 2;  ret[1] = col;
      return ret;
    }
    if (b[2][col] == b[1][col] && 0 == b[0][col] &&
        b[2][col] == sideToMove) {
```

```
        int [] ret = new int[2];
        ret[0] = 0;   ret[1] = col;
        return ret;
      }
      if (b[2][col] == b[0][col] && 0 == b[1][col] &&
          b[2][col] == sideToMove) {
        int [] ret = new int[2];
        ret[0] = 1;   ret[1] = col;
        return ret;
      }
    }
  }
  return null;
}


private int newGameCount = -1;

private void TicTacToeControl_Paint(Object sender, PaintEvent e) {
  // Paint to offscreen offscreenImage.
  // When we are done bitBlt() offscreenImage to client area.
  Graphics g = offscreenImage.getGraphics();
  g.setPen(Pen.NULL);
  g.setBrush(e.graphics.getBrush());
  g.drawRect(rect);

  if (hasFocus)
    g.drawFocusRect(rect);

  g.setBrush(Brush.WHITE);
  g.setPen(Pen.BLACK);

  g.drawLine(0, r1, rect.width, r1);
  g.drawLine(0, r2, rect.width, r2);

  g.drawLine(c1, 0, c1, rect.height);
  g.drawLine(c2, 0, c2, rect.height);

  int deltaX = rect.width / 3;
  int deltaY = rect.height / 3;
  int widthX = deltaX / 5;
  int widthY = deltaY / 5;
```

(continued)

Listing 2.12 *(continued)*

```
for (int row=0; row<3; row++) {
  for (int col=0; col<3; col++) {
    if (b[row][col] == HUMAN) {
      g.setPen(new Pen(playerColor));
      g.setBrush(new Brush(playerColor));
      g.drawEllipse((col+1)*deltaX-widthX-deltaX/2 ,
                    (row+1)*deltaY-widthY-deltaY/2,
                    2*widthX ,
                    2*widthY);
    }
    if (b[row][col] == COMPUTER) {
      g.setPen(new Pen(computerColor));
      g.setBrush(new Brush(computerColor));
      g.drawEllipse((col+1)*deltaX-widthX-deltaX/2 ,
                    (row+1)*deltaY-widthY-deltaY/2,
                    2*widthX ,
                    2*widthY);
    }
  }
}
e.graphics.drawImage(offscreenImage, 0,0);
}

private int r1 = 35;
private int r2 = 65;
private int c1 = 35;
private int c2 = 65;

private void TicTacToeControl_Resize(Object sender, Event e) {
  rect = getBounds();
  rect.x = rect.y = 0;
  int deltaX = rect.width / 3;
  int deltaY = rect.height / 3;
  c1 = deltaX;
  c2 = deltaX + deltaX;
  r1 = deltaY;
  r2 = deltaY + deltaY;
  offscreenImage = new Bitmap(rect.width,rect.height);
}
```

```
private boolean computer_move = true;

private void TicTacToeControl_Timer(Object sender, Event e) {
  if (newGameCount < 0) {
    // First check for an instant win:
    int side = HUMAN; if (computer_move) side = COMPUTER;
    int [] win = winPoint(side);
    if (win != null) {
      b[win[0]][win[1]] = side;
      newGameCount = 3;
      invalidate();
      computer_move = !computer_move;
      return;
    }
    // Or, try to block an opponent win:
    side = HUMAN; if (!computer_move) side = COMPUTER;
    win = winPoint(side);
    if (win != null) {
      int side2 = HUMAN; if (computer_move) side2 = COMPUTER;
      b[win[0]][win[1]] = side2;
      invalidate();
      computer_move = !computer_move;
      return;
    }

    // random move:
    int r = -1; int c = -1;
    if (b[1][1] == 0) {
      r = 1; c = 1;
    } else {
    o1: for (int row=0; row<3; row++) {
        for (int col=0; col<3; col++) {
          if (b[row][col] == 0) {
            r = row; c = col;
            break o1;
          }
        }
      }
    }
    if (r == -1 && c == -1) {
```

(continued)

Listing 2.12 *(continued)*

```
      newGame();
    } else {
      if (computer_move) b[r][c] = COMPUTER;
      else                b[r][c] = HUMAN;
    }
    // Check for a win by either side:
    checkWin();
  } else {
    if (newGameCount == 0)  newGame();
  }
  newGameCount--;
  invalidate();
  computer_move = !computer_move;
}


public Color getPlayerColor()
{ return new Color(playerColor.getRGB()); }

public void setPlayerColor(Color c)
{ playerColor = new Color(c.getRGB()); }

public Color getComputerColor()
{ return new Color(computerColor.getRGB()); }

public void setComputerColor(Color c)
{ computerColor = new Color(c.getRGB()); }

public static class ClassInfo extends Control.ClassInfo  {
  public static final PropertyInfo computerColor =
  new PropertyInfo(TicTacToeControl.class,
      "computerColor",
      wfc.ui.Color.class,
      CategoryAttribute.Appearance,
      new DefaultValueAttribute(wfc.ui.Color.BLUE),
      new DescriptionAttribute("The color computer piece"));

  public static final PropertyInfo humanColor =
  new PropertyInfo(
      TicTacToeControl.class, "humanColor", wfc.ui.Color.class,
```

```
            CategoryAttribute.Appearance,
            new DefaultValueAttribute(wfc.ui.Color.RED),
            new DescriptionAttribute("The color human piece"));

    public void getProperties(IProperties props) {
        super.getProperties(props);
        props.add(computerColor);
        props.add(humanColor);
    }
  }
}
```

The class **Form1** is defined in Listing 2.13. The visual programming module in Microsoft Visual J++ 6.0 created this class. Class **Form1** has a static public method **main** so that it can run as a stand-alone application. An instance of class **TicTacToeControl** is allocated in the class. The constructor calls the method **initForm**; note that you should not rename the method **initForm** because it has special meaning to the Microsoft Visual J++ 6.0 visual programming module. The only (automatically generated) code in method **initForm** that requires some explanation is

```
    this.setNewControls(new Control[] { TicTacToeControl_0});
```

The method **setNewControls** is used to add an array of controls to a form all at one time. This expression is equivalent to:

```
    Control[] cntrls = new Control[1];
    cntrls[0] = TicTacToeControl_0;
    this.setNewControls(cntrls);
```

When you use the Microsoft Visual J++ 6.0 visual programming module, automatically generated code is rendered with a gray background; you should not edit automatically generated code.

Listing 2.13

```java
// Form1.java

import wfc.app.*;
import wfc.core.*;
import wfc.ui.*;

public class Form1 extends Form
{
  public Form1() {
    initForm();
  }

  public static void main(String args[]) {
    Application.run(new Form1());
  }

  TicTacToeControl TicTacToeControl_0 = new TicTacToeControl();

  private void initForm() {
    this.setBackColor(Color.CONTROL);
    this.setSize(new Point(150, 150));
    this.setTabIndex(-1);
    this.setTabStop(true);
    this.setText("Form1");
    this.setAutoScaleBaseSize(16);
    this.setClientSize(new Point(150, 150));
    TicTacToeControl_0.setLocation(new Point(5, 5));
    TicTacToeControl_0.setSize(new Point(128, 128));
    TicTacToeControl_0.setTabIndex(10);
    TicTacToeControl_0.setTabStop(true);
    TicTacToeControl_0.setText("TicTacToeControl_0");
    this.setNewControls(new Control[] {
                      TicTacToeControl_0});
  }
}
```

Figure 2.16 shows the sample **TicTacToe** program running as a stand-alone Windows application.

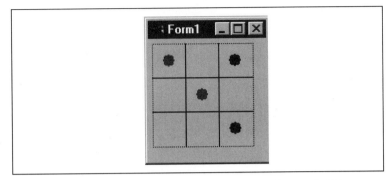

Figure 2.16   *The **TicTacToe** program uses the WFC API*

Implementation of an Internet News Browser Using AFC

In this chapter, we will design portable Java classes for accessing Internet newsgroups using the Network News Transfer Protocol (NNTP). These classes will be used to create a component class for adding to a tabbed-folder-based user interface. This new component will be wrapped as a stand-alone Java application at the end of this chapter. This same component will be wrapped as a JavaBean in Chapter 4 when we introduce JavaBean components. We will reuse the JavaBean newsreader at the end of Chapter 5 when we demonstrate how to convert JavaBeans to ActiveX components (this example will show you how the **NewsBean** JavaBean can be registered as an ActiveX component and used in Visual Basic, Visual C++, etc.).

The Java classes developed in this chapter use only the core Java API classes and the Microsoft AFC classes (which are written in Java and portable—see my Web site at *www.markwatson.com* for directions for patching the newest version of AFC to be portable). I have tested the material developed in this chapter for portability using

- Windows 95
- Windows NT
- Linux
- OS/2

The example programs developed in this chapter use NNTP. We want to separate the example classes for reading Internet newsgroups into two frameworks:

- Portable Java classes (**NewsServer** and **NewsArticleHeader**) that encapsulate the behavior of logging onto an NNTP server. These classes do not contain any user interface. The **NewsServer** class does contain a **public static void main** method for testing these two classes.

- The **NewsPanel** class that provides a user interface for accessing Internet newsgroups. The **NewsPanel** class uses the AFC class library.

3.1 Requirements for portable Java classes for using the NNTP protocol

The requirements for the **NewsServer** and **NewsArticleHeader** classes are the following:

- Encapsulate access to Internet newsgroups
- Support logging onto a specified NNTP server to start a session
- Support logging off of a specified NNTP server to end a session
- Support returning the starting and ending news article indices for a specified newsgroup
- Support retrieving a single news article header for a specified newsgroup and a specified article index
- Support retrieving the text of a single news article for a specified newsgroup and a specified article index

A fair amount of work will be required to write and debug the **NewsServer** class, so it will be useful to be able to test it "stand-alone" without a user interface. We will create a **public static main** method for testing the **NewsServer** class. The command file in **c:\mjava\ news\r.bat** will be used to test the **NewsServer** class.

3.2 Design of portable Java classes for using the NNTP protocol

It makes sense to completely encapsulate the behavior of interacting with an NNTP server in a single class because there are only a few well-defined operations that we perform on instances of this class; these operations are implemented as public methods for the following:

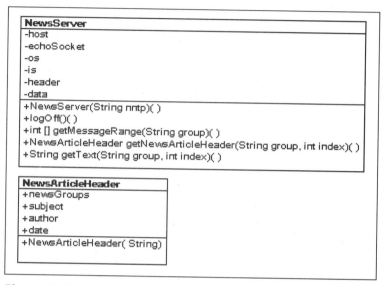

Figure 3.1 *UML class diagram for the portable Java classes for accessing Internet news servers. Public data and methods are prefaced with a + sign in UML class diagrams. Private data and methods are prefaced with a – sign.*

- A constructor that takes a single argument: the IP address of an NNTP server. This constructor automatically logs on to the NNTP server, setting up a session.

- Log off of the NNTP server to close a session.

- Return an array of integer message indices for a specified group.

- Return an instance of class **NewsArticleHeader** for a specified newsgroup and message index.

- Return the text of an article for a specified newsgroup and message index.

Figure 3.1 shows the UML class diagram for the classes **NewsServer** and **NewsArticleHeader**.

3.3   Implementation of portable Java classes for using the NNTP protocol

Listing 3.1 shows the implementation of the utility class **NewsArticleHeader**. The constructor for this class takes a string that is formatted header information returned from an NNTP server. The class constructor parses the header string and sets the values of the public class variables:

- **newsGroups**
- **subject**
- **author**
- **date**

Listing 3.1

```
// NewsArticleHeader.java
// Copyright 1997, Mark Watson. This software may
// be used without restriction in compiled form.

package com.markwatson.util;

import java.awt.*;
import java.util.*;
import java.io.*;
import java.net.*;

public class NewsArticleHeader // data of the header of an article
{
  public String newsGroups;
  public String subject = "";
  public String author = "";
  public String date = "";

  public NewsArticleHeader(String header) {
```

(continued)

Listing 3.1 *(continued)*

```
BufferedReader in;

try {
  in = new BufferedReader(new StringReader(header));
  while(in.ready()) {
    String line = in.readLine();
    if (line == null)  break;

    if(line.startsWith(".")) {
      if (line.startsWith("..")==false) {
        break;
      }
    }

    String lineLowerCase =line.toLowerCase();

    if(lineLowerCase.startsWith("subject:")) {
      subject = line.substring(8);
    }else if(lineLowerCase.startsWith("from:")) {
      author = line.substring(5);
    }else if(lineLowerCase.startsWith("newsgroups:")) {
      newsGroups = line.substring(11);
    }else if(lineLowerCase.startsWith("date:")) {
      date = line.substring(5);
    }
  }

  in.close();
}catch(IOException e) {
  System.err.println("Could not parse or read article header");
}
}
}
```

Listing 3.2 shows the implementation for the class **NewsServer**. This class contains a **public static void main** method that I found useful for testing the code in this class while I was writing it. The command file in **c:\mjava\news\r.bat** is used to test the **NewsServer**

> # *Design and implementation note*
>
> When I first designed and implemented the **NewsServer** class, I wrote the constructor so that it logged onto the NNTP server. Later, when I was using this class for creating a JavaBean in Chapter 4, I noticed that this behavior (i.e., immediately logging onto the NNTP server) increased the chances of losing the connection with the NNTP server because the connection could be made prematurely. I revisited the design and implementation of this class, adding the **logOn** and **logOff** methods. Now, the connection is made only when it is actually first used.

class. The class constructor requires a single **String** argument: the name (or IP address) of an NNTP server. The constructor simply stores the requested NNTP host name.

The private method **logOn** is responsible for making a connection to the specified NNTP server on port 119, which is the default port that NNTP servers use for socket connections to news-reading clients. The private method **connectionOK** is used in several places in the implementation of this class to check on the status of a connection. The method **requestData** has a single **String** argument: the command to send to the NNTP server. Possible commands are

- **quit**
- **group <group name>**

- head <message index>
- body <message index>

The method **requestData** calls the method **getData** after passing the desired command to the NNTP server. Method **getData** waits until the NNTP server returns a line of text, which it stores in the private class **String** variable **header**. Method **getData** then repetitively reads lines of text from the NNTP server until no more text is available.

The method **logOff** is used to break the connection with an NNTP server. Closing the socket connection breaks the connection.

The method **getMessageRange** requires a single string argument: the name of a newsgroup. This method returns an array of integers that are the message indices of all available messages. If there are no available messages in the specified group, then method **getMessageRange** returns **null**. The header is parsed to get the starting and ending message indices. The format of the header looks like

```
211 <group index> <starting index> <ending index>
```

The number 211 is a tag indicating that the line of text returned from the NNTP server is, in fact, a header.

The method **getNewsArticleHeader** has two arguments: the name of the desired newsgroup and the index of the message header to retrieve. The two commands are sent to the NNTP server that look like

- group <group name>
- head <message index>

The method **requestData** is called twice, once with each of these two requests. The method **requestData** calls the method **getData**, which sets the values of the two private class **String** variables:

- header
- data

The method **getNewsArticleHeader** constructs, and returns as its value, a new instance of class **NewsArticle-Header** from the **String** value stored in the variable **data**.

The method **getText** is very similar to the method **getNewsArticleHeader**, except that instead of passing the message

```
head <message index>
```

it passes the message

```
body <message index>
```

to the NNTP server. The method **getText** then simply returns as its value the **String** in the private class variable **data**.

Listing 3.2

```java
// NewsServer.java
// Copyright 1997, Mark Watson. This software may
// be used without restriction in compiled form.

package com.markwatson.util;

import java.awt.*;
import java.util.*;
import java.io.*;
import java.net.*;

public class NewsServer
{
  private String host;
  private Socket echoSocket = null;
  private DataOutputStream os = null;
```

(continued)

Listing 3.2 *(continued)*

```java
private BufferedReader is = null;
private String header;
private String data;

public static void main(String [] args) {
  System.out.println("You must be connected to the Internet.");
  if (args.length < 2) {
    System.out.println("Usage: NewsServer <host> <newsgroup>");
    System.exit(0);
  }
  NewsServer server = new NewsServer(args[0]);

  int [] range = server.getMessageRange(args[1]);
  if (range != null) {
    System.out.println("Message index range: " + range[0] +
                       " to " + range[1]);
    for (int i=range[0]; i<= range[1]; i++) {
      NewsArticleHeader header =
        server.getNewsArticleHeader(args[1], i);
      if (header != null) {
        System.out.println("Subject: " + header.subject +
                           ", author: " + header.author);
      }
      String body = server.getText(args[1], i);
      if (body != null) {
        System.out.println(body);
        System.exit(0);
      }
    }
  }
}

public NewsServer(String hostName)
{
  host = hostName;
}

private void logOn() {
  System.out.println("NewsServer.logOn()..");
  try {
```

```
    echoSocket = new Socket(host, 119);
    os = new DataOutputStream(echoSocket.getOutputStream());
    InputStreamReader ioreader =
      new InputStreamReader(echoSocket.getInputStream());
    is = new BufferedReader(ioreader);
  } catch (Exception e) {
    data = new String("Cannot log onto host: " + host);
    System.out.println("Cannot log onto host: " + host);
  }
  System.out.println("...connected to host OK");
  if (connectionOK()) {
    System.out.println("...connection is apparently OK");
    data = new String("connected to host: " + host);
  }
}

final private boolean connectionOK() {
  return echoSocket != null && os != null && is != null;
}

private void requestData(String cmd) {
  System.out.println(" ** NewsServer.requestData(" + cmd + ")...");
  if (connectionOK() == false)  logOn();
  data = new String();
  try {
    os.writeBytes(cmd+"\n");
    getData();
  } catch (IOException e) {
    // try reestablishing connection one time:
    try {
      logOn();
      os.writeBytes(cmd+"\n");
      getData();
      return;
    } catch (IOException e2) {
      data = new String("Error in sending command");
      System.out.println("Error in requestData(" + cmd +
                         "), exceptions:" + e + "\n" + e2);
    }
  }
  System.out.println(" ** leaving NewsServer.requestData(" +
```

(continued)

Listing 3.2 *(continued)*

```
                        cmd + ")");
  }

  public void logOff() {
    System.out.println("NewsServer.logOff()...");
    if(connectionOK()) {
      try {
        requestData("quit");
        os.close();
        is.close();
        echoSocket.close();
      } catch(IOException e) {
        data = new String("I/O failed on the conection to: " + host);
        System.out.println("...error logging off: " + e);
      }
    }
    System.out.println("...log off OK");
    echoSocket = null;
    os = null;
    is = null;
  }

  private void getData() {
    try {
      header = is.readLine();
      data = new String();
      while(is.ready()) {
        String s = is.readLine();
        System.out.println("NewsServer.getData(): from host: " + s);
        data = data + s + "\n";
      }

    } catch (Exception e) {
      System.out.println("NewsServer: error connecting: " + e);
      data = new String("I/O failed on the connection to: " + host);
      header = null;
    }
    System.out.println("  NewsServer.getData(): header=" + header +
                       "\n  data=" + data + "\n");
  }
```

```
public int[] getMessageRange(String group) {
  if (connectionOK() == false)  logOn();
  int range[] = new int[2];
  requestData("group " + group);
  logOff();
  if (header==null) {
    System.out.println("NewsServer.getMessageRange(" + group +
                       "): header is null");
  }
  if (header != null && header.startsWith("211")) {
    int index  = header.indexOf(' ', 4);
    int index2 = header.indexOf(' ', index + 1); // skip number field
    range[0] =
      (new Integer(header.substring(index + 1, index2))).intValue();
    int index3 = header.indexOf(' ', index2 + 1);
    range[1] =
      (new Integer(header.substring(index2 + 1, index3))).intValue();
    return range;
  } else {
    return null;
  }
}

public NewsArticleHeader getNewsArticleHeader(String group, int index) {
  System.out.println("NewsServer.getNewsArticleHeader(" + group +
                     ", " + index + ")...");
  if (connectionOK() == false)  logOn();
  header = null; data = null;
  requestData("group " + group);
  requestData("head " + index);
  logOff();
  if (header != null && header.startsWith("221")) {
    // article is available:
    return new NewsArticleHeader(data);
  }
  return null;
}

// Get the text of article:
public String getText(String group, int index) {
  if (connectionOK() == false)  logOn();
```

(continued)

Listing 3.2 *(continued)*

```
  header = null; data = null;
  requestData("group " + group);
  requestData("body " + index);
  logOff();
  if (header != null && header.startsWith("222")) {
    return data;
  }
  return null;
  }
}
```

The **NewsServer** class is written in portable Java; it should compile and run with any JDK 1.1 (or later) compiler and Java Virtual Machine.

3.4 Design of a Panel class for the newsreader user interface

In this section and in Section 3.5, we will use the material that we covered in Chapter 2 to build a reusable component (derived from the AFC class **UIPanel**) that encapsulates the user interface and behavior for browsing Internet newsgroups. Figures 3.2, 3.3, and 3.4 show the user interface that we will design in this section and implement in Section 3.5. Usually, when you are designing a user interface, you will probably sketch out the positions of the major components for each window or panel on a separate sheet of paper (or use a graphics drawing program). When I was designing the **News-Panel** class, I started by sketching out all four panels on paper, but in this section we will look at the final results (as captured screen shots) in Figures 3.2, 3.3, and 3.4.

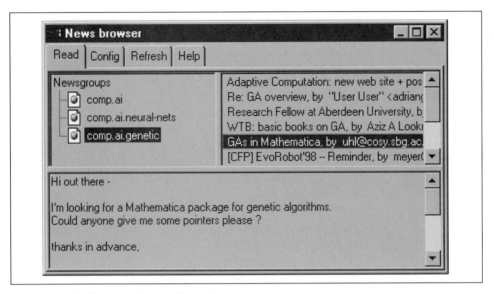

Figure 3.2 *Browse configured newsgroups*

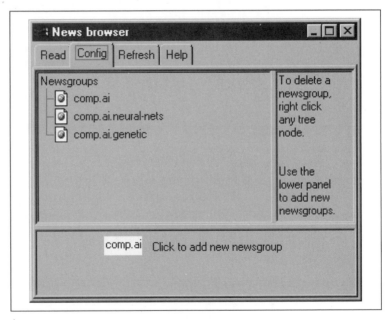

Figure 3.3 *Configure newsgroups*

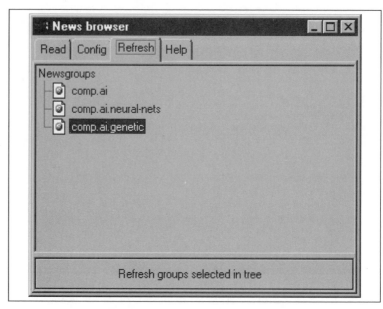

Figure 3.4 *Refresh selected newsgroup headers*

Designing and programming user interfaces

When I am designing and writing user interfaces, I use a Java Integrated Development Environment (IDE) about half the time; the rest of the time, I prefer to simply work with old-fashioned make files and use my favorite editor, Emacs. I like to use IDEs when designing and building complicated GUI components because most IDEs provide excellent visual programming environments. If a GUI component is fairly simple, I will often simply draw the desired interface on a piece of paper and code it up by hand. My favorite four Java IDEs are Borland's JBuilder (*www.borland.com*), Symantec's Café (*www.symantec.com*), Microsoft's J++ (patched to support JDK 1.1) (*www.microsoft.com/java*), and IBM's Visual Age for Java (*www.ibm.com/java*). All four of these IDEs are excellent; my selection usually depends on the preference of a particular consulting customer for their projects. For fast coding, I prefer keeping an Emacs window open with buffers for each source file. Since the Microsoft **jvc** Java compiler is so fast, I often simply use a **c.bat** command file that compiles all Java source files in the directory where I am working. An **r.bat** command file is useful for running a Java application after it is compiled. For fast coding, I like the combination of **jvc** and command files (both run from a DOS-style command window) with Emacs; on a Pentium-class PC, it usually only takes a few seconds to save a file, compile, and run my current application. For the development and maintenance of my commercial applications (see my Web site *www.markwatson.com*), I prefer to maintain a separate "clean" source tree that only contains my Java source files. I have separate directories for each product or project for building, using both make files and project files that use one or more IDEs.

The user interface that we will design will use a tabbed panel with four different views:

1. Browse configured newsgroups (seen in Figure 3.2)
2. Configure newsgroups (seen in Figure 3.3)
3. Refresh headers for selected (already configured) newsgroups (seen in Figure 3.4)
4. Online help (not shown)

The fourth panel ("Help") can be seen in Chapter 4, Figure 4.2. In Chapter 4, we will reuse the component for browsing newsgroups by wrapping it as a JavaBean.

3.5 Implementation of a Panel class for the newsreader user interface

Listing 3.3 shows the implementation of a new **Panel** class **NewsPanel** that provides a user interface for the network news utility classes. The class **ConfigFile** (shown in Listing 3.5) is used to save and reload configuration parameters from a disk file.

The **static int** variable **MAX_FETCH** is defined to have a value of 20. This limits the number of articles retrieved from a single newsgroup to a maximum of 20 articles. You may increase this limit.

The size of the news-browsing panel is defined by two **static int** variables: **WIDTH** and **HEIGHT**. You may change these values to make the panel larger or smaller.

A local utility class **NewsGroup** is defined at the end of Listing 3.3 and is used for storing newsgroup-specific data in an object. The variable **newsGroups** is an array of 20 objects of class **NewsGroup**. If you attempt to con-

Implementation note

The class **NewsPanel** contains a hard-coded array of 20 **NewsGroup** objects. This helps make the **NewsPanel** example class short and easy to implement but is probably not good coding style in general. A better alternative would be to make the variable **newsGroups** to be of type **Vector**, a class that supports increasing the number of contained objects at runtime. Each element added to a **Vector** could be fetched and coerced to the class **NewsGroup** before it is used. Another alternative implementation is to derive your own newsgroup collection class from class **Vector** and define your own methods for adding, removing, and accessing elements of type **NewsGroup**.

figure more than 20 newsgroups at one time, you will get a runtime error. The integer class variable **numNewsGroups** is used to count the current number of configured newsgroups.

The **NewsPanel** class constructor has no arguments. It creates a new instance of the AFC class **UITabViewer** and stores a reference to this object in the private class variable **tabViewer**. The class constructor then uses four private methods to set each of the **UIPanel** objects that are added to the tab viewer object:

- **initReadPanel**—creates the read panel using two instances of **UISplitViewer** and adds the top-level panel (which is the **UISplitViewer** object **entire**) to the tab viewer object stored in the class variable **tabViewer**. The class **ReadTree**, which is a subclass of **EventTree**, is defined and added to the split viewer object **top**.

- **initConfigPanel**—creates the configuration panel using two instances of **UISplitViewer** and adds the top-level panel (which is the **UISplitViewer** object **entire**) to the tab viewer object stored in the class variable **tabViewer**.

- **initRefreshPanel**—creates the newsgroup "refresh" panel using two instances of **UISplitViewer** and adds the top-level panel (which is the **UISplitViewer** object **entire**) to the tab viewer object stored in the class variable **tab-Viewer**. The class **RefreshTree**, which is a subclass of **EventTree**, is defined and added to the split viewer object **top**.

- **initHelpPanel**—creates a simple help screen using class **UIDrawText**.

We use the class **EventTree** that we developed in Chapter 2 three times in implementing the **NewsPanel** class. The three subclasses of **EventTree**, which we define as inner classes of **NewsPanel**, are

- **ReadTree**—This class is used to show a list of configured newsgroups. When a newsgroup node of the **ReadTree** object is clicked, the list object (member of class **UIList**) is filled with message headers that were collected from the NNTP news server the last time the selected newsgroup was "refreshed." The inner class **readListMouse-Listener** is used to handle mouse events for the **UIList** object. Clicking on a message header in the **UIList** object uses the **NewsServer** class to fetch the selected message body, which is displayed as text in the bottom panel (see Figure 3.2).

- **ConfigTree**—This class is used to show the newsgroups that have been added using the configuration panel.

- **RefreshTree**—This class is used to show the currently configured newsgroups. Clicking on a newsgroup node in this tree uses the **NewsServer** class to fetch up-to-date message headers from the NNTP server.

Listing 3.3 contains a fair amount of code. Figure 3.5 shows class diagrams for the classes defined in Listing 3.3.

Listing 3.3

```
// com.markwatson.news.NewsPanel
//
// This class implements a user interface for
// the NewsServer class.
//
// Copyright 1998 Mark Watson. Can be freely used
// in compiled form.

package com.markwatson.news;

import java.awt.*;
import java.net.URL;
import com.ms.ui.*;
import com.ms.ui.event.*;
import com.ms.fx.*;

import com.markwatson.util.*;

public class NewsPanel extends UIPanel {

  final static int MAX_FETCH = 20;
```

(continued)

Listing 3.3 *(continued)*

```java
private UITabViewer tabViewer;

private NewsGroup [] newsGroups = new NewsGroup[20];
int numNewsGroups = 0;

final static int WIDTH=512;
final static int HEIGHT=384;

public NewsPanel() {
  this(true);
}

public NewsPanel(boolean use_config_file) {

  setLayout(null);

  // Use an AFC tab viewer component:
  tabViewer = new UITabViewer();

  // build 4 news browser panels and insert into the tab viewer:
  initReadPanel();
  initConfigPanel();
  initRefreshPanel();
  initHelpPanel();

  // Use the class com.markwatson.util.ConfigFile to
  // access any preferences that have been written
  // to the file 'config.news':
  if (use_config_file) {
    try {
      ConfigFile cf = new ConfigFile("config.news");
      int count = 0;
      String s = cf.getLine(count++);
      numNewsGroups = Integer.parseInt(s);
      for (int i=0; i<numNewsGroups; i++) {
        s = cf.getLine(count++);
        // start by getting the newsgroup name:
        newsGroups[i] = new NewsGroup(s);
        readTree.addDocument(s);
        configTree.addDocument(s);
```

```
                refreshTree.addDocument(s);
                // read the number of headers stored for this newsgroup:
                s = cf.getLine(count++);
                int num = Integer.parseInt(s);
                System.out.println("Number of headers for " +
                                    newsGroups[i].name +
                                    " is " + num);
                newsGroups[i].numHeaders = num;

                // read the last header index stored for this newsgroup:
                s = cf.getLine(count++);
                num = Integer.parseInt(s);
                System.out.println("Last header index for " +
                                    newsGroups[i].name +
                                    " is " + num);
                newsGroups[i].lastIndex = num;

                for (int j=0; j<newsGroups[i].numHeaders; j++) {
                  // read the header string and message index:
                  newsGroups[i].headers[j] = cf.getLine(count++);
                  s = cf.getLine(count++);
                  newsGroups[i].headerIndex[j] = Integer.parseInt(s);
                }
              }
          } catch (Exception e) {
            System.out.println("Error reading config file: " + e);
            System.exit(1);
          }
        } else {
          numNewsGroups = 0;
        }

      add(tabViewer);
      tabViewer.setBounds(2, 2, WIDTH+8, HEIGHT+2);
      setValid(true);

  }

  public void save() {
    try {
      ConfigFile cf = new ConfigFile();
```

(continued)

Listing 3.3 *(continued)*

```
      cf.add(numNewsGroups);
      for (int i=0; i<numNewsGroups; i++) {
        cf.add(newsGroups[i].name);
        cf.add(newsGroups[i].numHeaders);
        cf.add(newsGroups[i].lastIndex);
        for (int j=0; j<newsGroups[i].numHeaders; j++) {
          cf.add(newsGroups[i].headers[j]);
          cf.add(newsGroups[i].headerIndex[j]);
        }
        cf.save("config.news");
      }
    } catch (Exception e) {
      System.out.println("Error writing 'config.news'");
    }
  }

  // inner class for implementing the read-news-tree:
  public class ReadTree extends com.markwatson.util.EventTree {

    public ReadTree() {
      super();
    }
    public ReadTree(String root) {
      super(root);
    }

    // define methods that are abstract in parent class:
    public void leftMouseClicked(String [] targets) {
      System.out.println("NewsPanel.ReadTree.leftMouseClicked()...");
      if (targets.length <1) return;
      System.out.println("...targets[0]=" + targets[0]);
      for (int i=0; i<numNewsGroups; i++) {
        if (targets[0].equals(newsGroups[i].name)) {
          // remove all items from readTitleList:
          for (int j=0; j<1000; j++) {
            try {
              readTitleList.remove(0);
            } catch (Exception e)      {  break;  }
          }
          for (int j=0; j<newsGroups[i].numHeaders; j++) {
```

```
                   readTitleList.add(newsGroups[i].headers[j]);
            }
         }
      }
   }
   public void rightMouseClicked(String [] targets) {
   }
   public void keyHit(char c) {
   }
}

protected ReadTree readTree;
private UIList readTitleList;
private UIDrawText readText;

private void initReadPanel() {

   // create tree for the top split viewer (left side):
   readTree = new ReadTree("Newsgroups");
   readTree.setMultiSelect(false);

   // create a list for the top viewer for showing article titles:
   readTitleList = new UIList();
   readTitleList.addMouseListener(new readListMouseListener());

   // create the top split viewer:
   UISplitViewer top =
      new UISplitViewer(readTree, readTitleList, 0, -45, true);

   // create the text viewing area:
   readText = new UIDrawText("test text\n1\n2\n3\n4\n5");

   // create the split viewer that covers the entire panel:
   UISplitViewer entire =
      new UISplitViewer(top, readText,
                        UISplitViewer.HORIZONTAL, -50, true);

   tabViewer.add("Read newsgroups", entire);
   entire.setBounds(1, 1, WIDTH, HEIGHT);
}
```

(continued)

Listing 3.3 *(continued)*

```
// inner class to handle mouse clicks for selection list
// (of news headers):
class readListMouseListener implements IUIMouseListener {
  public void mousePressed(UIMouseEvent me) {
  }
  public void mouseClicked(UIMouseEvent me) {
    int listIndex = readTitleList.getSelectedIndex();
    String s2 = readTree.getSelectedItem().getName();
    System.out.println("Index of clicked header = " + listIndex +
                       ", and readTree selection = " + s2);
    NewsServer server = new NewsServer(hostName);

    // find the index of this newsgroup:
    int index = 0;
    for (int i=0; i<numNewsGroups; i++) {
      if (newsGroups[i].name.equals(s2)) {
        index = i;
        break;
      }
    }

    System.out.println("group: " + s2 + ", index = " +
                       newsGroups[index].headerIndex[listIndex]);
    String s =
      server.getText(s2, newsGroups[index].headerIndex[listIndex]);

    System.out.println("fetched: " + s + "\n");
    readText.setValueText(s);
    server.logOff();
  }
  public void mouseReleased(UIMouseEvent me) {
  }
  public void mouseEntered(UIMouseEvent me) {
  }
  public void mouseExited(UIMouseEvent me) {
  }
}

// inner class for implementing the config-tree:
public class ConfigTree extends com.markwatson.util.EventTree {
```

```
public ConfigTree() {
  super();
}
public ConfigTree(String root) {
  super(root);
}

// define methods that are abstract in parent class:
public void leftMouseClicked(String [] targets) {
}
public void rightMouseClicked(String [] targets) {
  // delete the selected newsgroup:
  if (targets.length > 0) {
    // remove from local newsgroups list:
    for (int i=0; i<numNewsGroups; i++) {
      if (newsGroups[i].name.equalsIgnoreCase(targets[0])) {
        for (int j=i; j<numNewsGroups; j++) {
          newsGroups[j] = newsGroups[j+1];
        }
        numNewsGroups--;
        break;
      }
    }
    try {
      IUIComponent c = find(targets[0]);
      if (c != null) {
        c.setValid(true);
        this.remove(c);
      }
      this.setValid(true);
    }catch (Exception e) { }

    try {
      IUIComponent c = readTree.find(targets[0]);
      if (c != null) {
        c.setValid(true);
        readTree.remove(c);
      }
      readTree.setValid(true);
    } catch (Exception e) { }
```

(continued)

Listing 3.3 *(continued)*

```
    }
  }
  public void keyHit(char c) {
  }
}

protected ConfigTree configTree;
private UIEdit configEdit;
private UIPushButton configAddButton;

private void initConfigPanel() {

  // create tree for the top split viewer (left side):
  configTree = new ConfigTree("Newsgroups");
  configTree.setMultiSelect(false);

  // create some help text
  UIDrawText helpText = new UIDrawText("To delete a\n" +
                                       "newsgroup,\n" +
                                       "right click\n" +
                                       "any tree\n" +
                                       "node.\n\n\n" +
                                       "Use the\n" +
                                       "lower panel\n" +
                                       "to add new\n" +
                                       "newsgroups.");

  // create the top split viewer:
  UISplitViewer top = new UISplitViewer(configTree, helpText,
                                        0, -75, true);

  // create edit control and button for adding newsgroups:
  UIPanel p = new UIPanel();
  configEdit = new UIEdit("comp.ai");
  configEdit.setBackground(FxColor.white);

  configAddButton = new UIPushButton("Click to add new newsgroup");
  p.add(configEdit);
  p.add(configAddButton);
  configAddButton.addMouseListener(new configMouseListener());
```

```
    // create the split viewer that covers the entire panel:
    UISplitViewer entire =
      new UISplitViewer(top, p,
                        UISplitViewer.HORIZONTAL, -70,
                        true);

    tabViewer.add("Add and delete newsgroups", entire);
    entire.setBounds(0, 0, WIDTH, HEIGHT);
  }
  // inner class to handle config-add button mouse clicks:
  class configMouseListener implements IUIMouseListener {
    public void mousePressed(UIMouseEvent me) {   }
    public void mouseClicked(UIMouseEvent me) {
      // add the new newsgroup:
      configTree.addDocument(configEdit.getValueText());
      readTree.addDocument(configEdit.getValueText());
      refreshTree.addDocument(configEdit.getValueText());
      newsGroups[numNewsGroups++] =
        new NewsGroup(configEdit.getValueText());
    }
    public void mouseReleased(UIMouseEvent me) {   }
    public void mouseEntered(UIMouseEvent me) {   }
    public void mouseExited(UIMouseEvent me) {   }
  }

  // inner class for implementing the refresh-tree:
  public class RefreshTree extends com.markwatson.util.EventTree {

    public RefreshTree() {
      super();
    }
    public RefreshTree(String root) {
      super(root);
    }

    // define methods that are abstract in parent class:
    public void leftMouseClicked(String [] targets) {
    }
    public void rightMouseClicked(String [] targets) {
    }
```

(continued)

Listing 3.3 *(continued)*

```java
    public void keyHit(char c) {
    }
}

private RefreshTree refreshTree;
private UIPushButton refreshDeleteButton;
private UIEdit refreshEdit;
private UIPushButton refreshButton;

private void initRefreshPanel() {

    // create tree for the top split viewer (left side):
    // (multiselection option is the default, which is
    // what we want, so users can select multiple newsgroups
    // to refresh)
    refreshTree = new RefreshTree("Newsgroups");

    // create a list for the top viewer for showing article titles:
    refreshDeleteButton = new UIPushButton("Delete");

    // button to refresh groups selected in tree control:
    refreshButton =
      new UIPushButton("Refresh groups selected in tree");
    refreshButton.addMouseListener(new refreshMouseListener());

    // create the split viewer that covers the entire panel:
    UISplitViewer entire =
      new UISplitViewer(refreshTree, refreshButton,
                        UISplitViewer.HORIZONTAL, -85,
                        true);

    tabViewer.add("Refresh newsgroups", entire);
    entire.setBounds(0, 0, WIDTH, HEIGHT);
}

class refreshMouseListener implements IUIMouseListener {
    public void mousePressed(UIMouseEvent me) {
    }
    public void mouseClicked(UIMouseEvent me) {
        // Find all refreshTree items selected and refresh newsgroups:
```

```
IUIComponent [] selected = refreshTree.getSelectedItems();
if (selected == null)  return;
int num = selected.length;
for (int iii=0; iii<num; iii++) {
  UIComponent c = (UIComponent)selected[iii];
  String s = c.getName();
  System.out.println("Refreshing group " + s + " ...");
  // find the index of this newsgroup:
  int index = 0;
  for (int i=0; i<numNewsGroups; i++) {
    if (newsGroups[i].name.equals(s)) {
      index = i;
      System.out.println("  group is at index " + index);
      break;
    }
  }
  NewsServer server = new NewsServer(hostName);
  int [] range = server.getMessageRange(s);
  if (range != null) {
    int cutoff = 0;
    System.out.println("  range of group indices: " +
                      range[0] + " to " + range[1]);

    // First, we need to delete old newsgroup entries
    // that are outside of the range of available messages:
    for (int k=0; k<newsGroups[index].numHeaders; k++) {
      if (newsGroups[index].headerIndex[k] < range[0]) {
        for (int m=k; m<newsGroups[index].numHeaders-1; m++) {
          newsGroups[index].headerIndex[m] =
            newsGroups[index].headerIndex[m+1];
        }
        System.out.println("Deleting old header at index " + k);
        newsGroups[index].numHeaders -= 1;
        k--;
      }
    }

    if (newsGroups[index].lastIndex > range[0]) {
      System.out.println("Skipping message indices. lastIndex=" +
                        newsGroups[index].lastIndex +
                        ", range: " +
```

(continued)

Listing 3.3 *(continued)*

```
                            range[0] + " : " + range[1]);
        range[0] = newsGroups[index].lastIndex;
    }

    for (int i=range[0]; i<=range[1]; i++) {
        // see if we already have this header index:
        boolean skip = false;
        for (int k=0; k<newsGroups[index].numHeaders; k++) {
            if (newsGroups[index].headerIndex[k] == i) {
                skip = true;
                break;
            }
        }
        if (skip)                  continue;
        if (cutoff++ > MAX_FETCH)  break;

        try {
            NewsArticleHeader header =
                server.getNewsArticleHeader(s, i);
            newsGroups[index].lastIndex = i;
            if (header == null) {
                System.out.println("\nNull header at index " + i);
                continue;
            }
            String s2 = header.subject + ", by " + header.author;
            System.out.println("  adding article header: " + s2);
            int num_h = newsGroups[index].numHeaders;
            newsGroups[index].headers[num_h] = s2;
            num_h = newsGroups[index].numHeaders++;
            newsGroups[index].headerIndex[num_h] = i;
        } catch (Exception e) {
            System.out.println("Error while getting headers: " + e);
        }
    }
    }
    server.logOff();
    }
    save();
}
public void mouseReleased(UIMouseEvent me) {
}
```

```
  public void mouseEntered(UIMouseEvent me) {
  }
  public void mouseExited(UIMouseEvent me) {
  }
}


private void initHelpPanel() {

  // create the text viewing area:
  UIDrawText helpText =
    new UIDrawText("Use the 'config' panel to add and delete " +
                   "newsgroups.  Use the 'refresh' panel to\n" +
                   "fetch current message headers for selected " +
                   "newsgroups.  Use the 'read' panel to read\n" +
                   "articles (or messages) in selected newsgroups " +
                   "that have previously been configured\n" +
                   "and refreshed.\n");

  helpText.setSize(WIDTH, HEIGHT);

  tabViewer.add("Help", helpText);
  helpText.setBounds(1, 1, WIDTH, HEIGHT);
}

// Define the host name, and create get/set methods
// so that this class can function as a JavaBean
// and treat the host name as a JavaBean property:

private String hostName = "news.sedona.net";

// For later use as a JavaBean:
public void setHostName(String h) {
  hostName = h;
}
public String getHostName() {
  return hostName;
}

// Make the newsgroup array a JavaBean read-only property:
public NewsGroup [] getNewsGroups() {
```

(continued)

Listing 3.3 *(continued)*

```
    return newsGroups;
  }

}
```

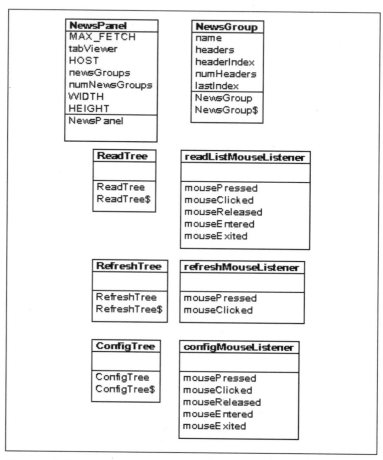

Figure 3.5 *Java classes defined in Listings 3.3 through 3.5. This UML class diagram, for brevity, shows only method names, not return type, visibility (e.g., private or public), and method arguments.*

> ## Design and implementation note
>
> The implementation of the **News-Group** class violates a principle of object-oriented development: encapsulation of private data inside an object, with access to private data through public access methods. Usually this is a good principle to follow. My rationale for simply making the **NewsGroup** class data public was to try to reduce the size of the **NewsPanel** example. I occasionally use "data only" classes like **NewsGroup** that only contain public data elements.

Listing 3.4 shows the implementation of the class **NewsGroup**, which is used to store information for a newsgroup. The **NewsGroup** class simply groups the data required to manage a specific Internet newsgroup in a single object. All class data items are public.

The class **NewsGroup** contains the following class data:

- **name**—the name of the newsgroup (e.g., **comp.ai.genetic**)
- **headers**—an array of strings used to store the message headers as they are fetched from an NNTP news server
- **numHeaders**—the number of message headers for this group that have been fetched from a news server
- **lastIndex**—the message (or article) index of the last message header fetched from a news server for this newsgroup

Listing 3.4

```java
// com.markwatson.news.NewsGroup.java

package com.markwatson.news;

class NewsGroup {
  public String name;
  public String [] headers;
  public int [] headerIndex;
  public int numHeaders;
  public int lastIndex;

  public NewsGroup() {
    name = "";
    numHeaders=0;
    headers = new String[300];
    headerIndex = new int[300];
    lastIndex = -1;
  }

  public NewsGroup(String a_name) {
    name = a_name;
    numHeaders = 0;
    headers = new String[300];
    headerIndex = new int[300];
    lastIndex = -1;
  }
}
```

Listing 3.5 shows the implementation of a useful utility class **ConfigFile** that reads text files, storing each line of the file as a string in an array of strings. The class contains the following public methods:

- **ConfigFile**—constructs an empty config file object
- **ConfigFile(String file_name)**—constructs a config file object by reading a specified text file, storing each line of the file in a separate string

- **add(String s)**—adds a new line to a config file object from a string
- **add(int i)**—adds a new line to a config file object by converting an integer value to a string
- **getNumberLines( )**—returns the number of lines in a config file object
- **getLine(int index)**—returns a string value for the line at a specified index
- **load(String file_name)**—clears the stored lines (if any) from a config file object and loads the lines from the specified file
- **save(String save_file)**—saves the lines in the config file object to a text file

Listing 3.5

```
// com.markwatson.util.ConfigFile.java
//
// You can use this class whenever you need to save and load
// application-specific parameters using local disk files.
//
// Copyright 1997, Mark Watson.  May be freely used in
// compiled form.
//

package com.markwatson.util;

import java.io.*;

public class ConfigFile {

  private String [] lines;
  private int numLines;

  public ConfigFile() {
    numLines = 0;
    lines = new String[50];
```

(continued)

Listing 3.5 *(continued)*

```java
  }

  public ConfigFile(String file_name) {
    load(file_name);
  }

  public void add(String s) {
    lines[numLines++] = new String(s);
  }

  public void add(int i) {
    lines[numLines++] = (new Integer(i)).toString();
  }

  public int getNumberLines() { return numLines;
  }

  public String getLine(int index) {
    if (index < 0 || index >= numLines) return "";
    System.out.println("getLine: " + lines[index]);
    return lines[index];
  }

  public void load(String file_name) {
    try {
      numLines = 0;
      lines = new String[50];
      FileInputStream ins = new FileInputStream(file_name);
      if (ins!=null) {
        BufferedReader in =
          new BufferedReader(new InputStreamReader(ins));
        try {
          while (true) {
            String s = in.readLine();
            if (s==null) break;
            if (s.length() > 0) {
              lines[numLines++] = new String(s);
            }
          }
        } catch (Exception e) { }
      }
```

```
      } catch (Exception e) { }
  }

  public void save(String file_name) {
    try {
      PrintWriter out =
        new PrintWriter(new BufferedWriter(new FileWriter(file_name)));
      for (int i=0; i<numLines; i++) {
        out.print(lines[i]);
        out.println();
      }
      out.close();
    } catch (Exception e) { }
  }
}
```

I have used the class **ConfigFile** in at least six separate Java programs that I have written. Hopefully, you will also find it useful.

3.6 Design of a stand-alone Java application for reading Internet news

Since we already have a component for reading Internet news, it is simple to "wrap" this component as a stand-alone Java application. We can derive a new class from the AFC class **UIFrame** and add the appropriate event handling code to terminate the application.

I like to design Java GUI components as **Panels** (or **UIPanels** if using AFC), designing separate wrapper classes to implement stand-alone Java applications. This dual-class implementation approach allows you to reuse the GUI component as a JavaBean, embed it directly in a container in new applications, and so on.

3.7 Implementation of a stand-alone Java application for reading Internet news

Figure 3.6 shows the class diagram for the **NewsFrame** class. The **NewsFrame** class contains a private instance of class **NewsPanel**. The **public static void main** method (so this class can run as a stand-alone Java application) initializes the application by

- creating a new instance of the **NewsFrame** class
- changing the background color and size of the **NewsFrame** object
- setting the visibility of the **NewsFrame** object to **true**

The **NewsFrame** constructor requires a string argument that it uses as the title for the frame window. The constructor initializes a new **NewsFrame** object by

- calling the **UIFrame** superclass constructor
- enabling window events
- creating a new instance of the class **NewsPanel**
- adding the new instance of the **NewsPanel** class to itself (the **NewsFrame** class is indirectly derived from the class **UIContainer** that provides the inherited **add** method)

The method **processEvent** is called automatically for any enabled events. Since we have enabled window events, the **processEvent** method will be called when the user closes the frame.

Listing 3.6 shows the implementation of the class **NewsFrame**. **NewsFrame** creates a visible window that contains an instance of class **NewsPanel**.

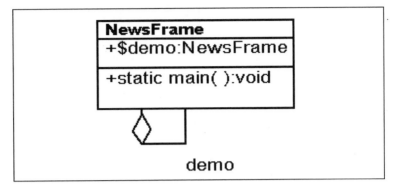

Figure 3.6 *UML class diagram for NewsFrame*

Listing 3.6

```java
// com.markwatson.apps.NewsFrame.java
//
// This class is a simple wrapper for the NewsPanel class
// that is used to create a stand-alone Java application.
//

package com.markwatson.apps;

import java.awt.*;
import java.net.URL;
import com.ms.ui.*;
import com.ms.ui.event.*;
import com.ms.fx.*;

import com.markwatson.util.*;
import com.markwatson.news.*;

public class NewsFrame extends UIFrame {
  public static void main(String args[]) {
    NewsFrame demo = new NewsFrame();
    demo.setBackground(FxColor.lightGray);
    demo.setSize(540,430);
    demo.setVisible(true);
  }
```

(continued)

Listing 3.6 *(continued)*

```java
private NewsPanel newsPanel;

public NewsFrame() {
  super("News browser");
  // enable window events so that we can handle window closing:
  enableEvents(AWTEvent.WINDOW_EVENT_MASK);

  //setLayout(new UIBorderLayout());
  newsPanel = new NewsPanel();
  add(newsPanel);
}
public void processEvent(UIEvent evt) { // JDK 1.1
  switch (evt.getID())  {
  case Event.WINDOW_DESTROY:
    System.out.println("Save config.news data before quitting.");
    newsPanel.save();
    System.exit(0);
  default:
    super.processEvent(evt);
  }
}

}
```

The **NewsFrame** class was simple to implement because it uses the **NewsPanel** class to implement both the behavior for browsing Internet newsgroups and the user interface required to select newsgroups and articles to read.

Introduction to JavaBeans

In the last chapter, we designed portable Java classes for accessing Internet newsgroups using the NNTP protocol. These classes were also used to create a **Panel** component class for adding a tabbed-folder-based user interface. This same **Panel** component will be wrapped as a JavaBean in this chapter after we introduce JavaBean components.

The Java classes developed in this chapter use only the core Java API classes and the Microsoft AFC classes (which are written in Java and portable; see my Web site at *www.markwatson.com* for help on patching AFC to make it portable). I have tested the material developed in this chapter for portability using

- Windows 95
- Windows NT
- Linux
- OS/2

The JavaBean developed in this chapter uses the Microsoft AFC class library. For comparison, the Java-Bean developed in Chapter 5 (that wraps the IE 4.0 HTML rendering ActiveX control) uses the standard AWT class library.

JavaBeans are used to package (in **JAR** files) one or more Java classes into a single reusable component. We will discuss both **JAR** and **CAB** archive files in Chapter 6. JavaBeans usually incorporate their own user interface, although some JavaBeans provide services that do not require a user interface. I usually package JavaBeans that I write so that they can be used both as a component in any container that can manage one or more JavaBean and so that they can be run as stand-alone applications (i.e., they contain a main class that contains a static **main** method). It is possible to package JavaBeans that can also be run as applets. We note that both the Netscape Communicator (versions 4.0 and above) and the Microsoft Internet Explorer (versions 4.0 and above) can run applets packaged in **JAR** files.

JavaBeans are used for both visual components (e.g., a graphing component or a text-editing component) and nonvisual applications like communications (Watson 1997).

Most JavaBeans have one or more *properties* that can be used to change both the appearance and runtime behavior of the JavaBean. Programmatically, it is almost trivial to add properties to a JavaBean; there are three steps:

1. Declare a variable as private for the property.

2. Write a public "get" method so that other classes can read the value of the property.

3. Optionally, write a "set" method so that other classes can change the value of the property.

A simple example is useful:

```
private String hostName = "localhost"
public Sring getHostName() { return hostName; }
public void setHostName(String h) { hostName=h; }
```

This is an important pattern: the get/set method names must be formed by capitalizing the first letter of the private variable name and then adding either "get" or "set" to form the method name. JavaBean containers (e.g., the BeanBox that is freely available in the JavaBean development kit at *java.sun.com*) provide a user interface for changing properties that have get/set methods associated with them.

4.1 Designing a JavaBean component for listing current news stories from Web news services

The design of the example JavaBean will be fairly simple since we will reuse the following Java classes that were developed in Chapter 3:

- **com.markwatson.util.NewsArticleHeader**
- **com.markwatson.util.NewsServer**
- **com.markwatson.util.NewsPanel**

Indeed, the **NewsPanel** class could be used as a simple JavaBean as is. However, we will augment the discussion of JavaBeans by designing and implementing a new class **NewsBean** that adds the following capabilities to the software developed in Chapter 3:

- Property and get/set methods for news server

4.2 Implementing a JavaBean component for listing current news stories from Web news services

Listing 4.1 shows the implementation of the class **News-Bean**. The implementation of this class is very simple since it uses the **NewsPanel** class developed in Chapter 3. This JavaBean has one property: **host**. In order for this property to be both read and write enabled, we define the methods:

- **public void setHost(String new_host_name)**
- **public String getHost( )**

Figure 4.1 shows the UML class diagram for **NewsBean**. As we see in Figure 4.1, the **NewsBean** class contains a **public static void main** method so that it can run as a stand-alone application or as a JavaBean component. The class **NewsBeanInfo** defines a **getIcon** method that is used by any IDE (like Borland's JBuilder or Symantec Café).

We call methods in the class **NewsPanel** for setting and retrieving the value of the private **NewsPanel** class variable **hostName**.

Listing 4.1

```
// com.markwatson.beans.NewsBean.java
//
// Copyright 1997, Mark Watson.
//

package com.markwatson.beans;

import java.net.*;
```

```
┌─────────────────────────────────────┐
│  ┌───────────────────────────────┐  │
│  │ NewsBean                      │  │
│  ├───────────────────────────────┤  │
│  │ -np:NewsPanel                 │  │
│  │ -host:String                  │  │
│  ├───────────────────────────────┤  │
│  │ +main( String):void {static}  │  │
│  │ +NewsBean(){constructor}      │  │
│  │ -reset():void                 │  │
│  │ +setHost( String):void        │  │
│  │ +getHost():String             │  │
│  └───────────────────────────────┘  │
│                                      │
│  ┌───────────────────────────────┐  │
│  │ NewsBeanInfo                  │  │
│  ├───────────────────────────────┤  │
│  │                               │  │
│  ├───────────────────────────────┤  │
│  │ +getIcon( int):java.awt.Image │  │
│  └───────────────────────────────┘  │
└─────────────────────────────────────┘
```

Figure 4.1   *UML class diagram for **NewsBean***

```java
import java.io.*;
import java.awt.*;
import java.awt.event.*;
import java.beans.*;

import com.ms.ui.*;
import com.ms.ui.event.*;

import com.markwatson.util.*;
import com.markwatson.news.*;

public class NewsBean extends UIPanel implements Serializable {

  public static void main(String args[]) {
    AppTestFrame demo =
      new AppTestFrame("Test NewsBean as a stand-alone application");
    demo.add(new NewsBean());
    demo.setSize(550,300);
    demo.setVisible(true);
  }

  public NewsBean() {
```

(continued)

Listing 4.1 *(continued)*

```
// Call superclass Panel constructor:
super();
// Call the 'reset' method to create the user interface
// components for the 'NewsBean' JavaBean:
reset();
}

private NewsPanel np = null;

// Create the 'NewsBean' JavaBean user interface:
private void reset() {
  np = new NewsPanel();
  //np.setSize(450, 320);
  add(np);
  np.setHostName(host);
}

private String host = "host.com";
public void setHost(String new_host) {
  host = new_host;
  if (np != null) np.setHostName(host);
}
public String getHost() {
  if (np != null) host = np.getHostName();
  return host;
}
}
```

Figure 4.2 shows the fourth panel of the news-browsing JavaBean.

Listing 4.2 shows the **BeanInfo** file for the **NewsBean** JavaBean. In Listing 4.2, we simply define two icons that can be used by JavaBean containers and JavaBean-enabled Java development environments (e.g., IBM Visual Age for Java, Borland JBuilder, and Symantec Café) to represent the JavaBean on a component palette.

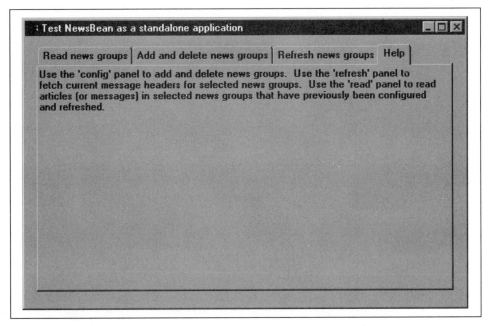

Figure 4.2   *The "Help" panel of the news-browsing JavaBean. The news-browsing panel was developed in Chapter 3.*

Listing 4.2

```
// NewsBeanInfo.java

package com.markwatson.beans;

import java.beans.*;

public class NewsBeanInfo extends SimpleBeanInfo {

  public java.awt.Image getIcon(int iconKind) {
    if (iconKind == BeanInfo.ICON_COLOR_16x16) {
      java.awt.Image img = loadImage("NewsIcon16.gif");
      return img;
    }
    if (iconKind == BeanInfo.ICON_MONO_32x32 ||
```

(continued)

Listing 4.2 *(continued)*

```
       iconKind == BeanInfo.ICON_COLOR_32x32 ) {
    java.awt.Image img = loadImage("NewsIcon32.gif");
    return img;
  }
  return null;
 }
}
```

If you add the **NewsBean** to a JavaBean-enabled Java development system, you should see either the file **NewsIcon16.gif** or **NewsIcon32.gif** on the available component palette or toolbar.

Javabean properties

The property **host** in the example shown in Listing 4.1 is a little contrived. Typically, properties are used for controlling both the appearance and the behavior of JavaBeans. This JavaBean example is also unusual because the **NewsBean** is not self-contained: we store detailed information on configured newsgroups in a local file **config.news** instead of as Java properties. Still, the example makes practical sense because you might want to build a Java application that supported newsgroup browsing; when you add the JavaBean component to your application, you might want to configure the news server host via the JavaBean **host** property. When an end user runs your Java application, her newsgroup settings are stored in a file that is located in the same directory as the application.

4.3 Using the JavaBean component for listing current news stories from Web news services

Figure 4.3 shows the **NewsBean** JavaBean running inside a test frame as a stand-alone application. When I package either a stand-alone Java application or a JavaBean component, I use the **JAR** archive file format (which we will cover in Chapter 6) to package all the files necessary to run the application or component in a single file.

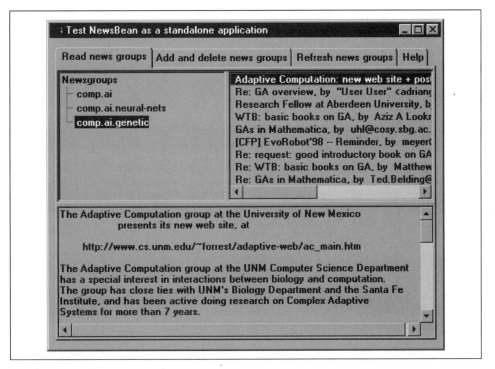

Figure 4.3   *Testing the NewsBean*

It is also possible to store text files in a **JAR** file and read the contents of the enclosed text file as if it were a separate local file. Listing 4.3 shows some example code for reading the file **test.dat** from the **JAR** file that contains the JavaBean.

Listing 4.3

```
private void readFileInJAR() {
    // look for a file named 'test.dat' in the current JAR file:
    try {
      InputStream ins =
        ClassLoader.getSystemResourceAsStream("test.dat");

      if (ins==null) {
        System.out.println("readConfig(): failed to open " +
                          'test.dat' in JAR file");
      } else {
        BufferedReader in =
            new BufferedReader(new InputStreamReader(ins));
        try {
          while (true) {
            String s = in.readLine();
            if (s==null) break;
            System.out.println("line in test.dat: " + s);
        } catch (Exception e2) { }
      }
    } catch (Exception e) {
      System.out.println("Could not find 'test.dat' in JAR file");
    }
}
```

Listing 4.4 shows a **makefile** that can be used for creating a JavaBean. The program **nmake.exe**, which ships with the Microsoft Java SDK 3.0 (or later), reads the commands in the file **makefile** and builds a JavaBean.

CHAPTER 4

Listing 4.4

```
newsbean.jar:
    jvc /g /cp %CLASSPATH% -d ..\classes *.java
    cd ..\classes
    jar cfm newsbean.jar <<manifest.tmp
com\markwatson\beans\*.class com\markwatson\util\ConfigFile.class
com\markwatson\news\*.class
    copy newsbean.jar ..\javabean
    erase newsbean.jar

Name: ../classes/com/markwatson/beans/NewsBean.class
Java-Bean: True

<<
```

Listing 4.5 shows the command file **c.bat** (also located in the directory **c:\mjava\javabean**) that processes the **makefile** (using **nmake.exe**) and moves the generated JAR file to the current directory (**c:\mjava\javabean**). Note that **nmake.exe** by default looks for a file named **makefile** in the directory where it is run.

Listing 4.5

```
nmake
copy ..\classes\newsbean.jar
erase ..\classes\newsbean.jar
```

The JavaBean **newsbean.jar** will probably not be particularly useful, but I generate it as an example of producing a JavaBean that contains a manifest file of all files encapsulated in the JavaBean. If you want to write JavaBeans, you can download for free the JavaSoft Bean Development Kit (BDK) and a JavaBean tutorial from Sun's Java Web site (*java.sun.com*).

Using ActiveX Components in Java Programs

It might seem like Java and ActiveX components are competing technologies, but if you are programming in Java specifically for the Windows 95/NT platforms, then incorporating existing ActiveX components in your Java programs makes a lot of sense. In this chapter, we will use the ActiveX component that is used in the Internet Explorer version 4.0. Specifically, we will encapsulate the code for using the IE 4.0 ActiveX control in a JavaBean; using the Java class developed in this chapter, you will be able to add the full functionality of the IE 4.0 HTML rendering engine by adding a few lines of code to your Java programs. Figure 5.1 shows the IE 4.0 ActiveX control inside the JavaBean **BrowserBean** that is developed in Section 5.1.

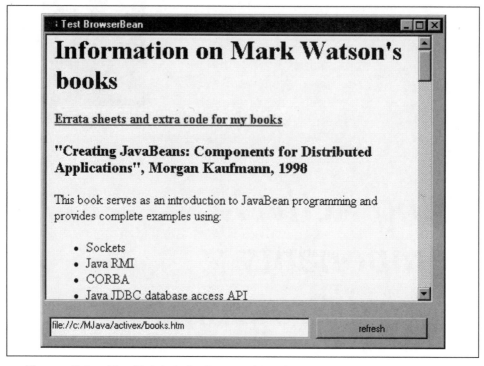

Figure 5.1   *The IE 4.0 ActiveX control inside a JavaBean component*

It is also fairly easy to wrap your Java code as an ActiveX component. We will finish this chapter with a short example that will show you how to do this.

I suggest a specific strategy for using ActiveX and Component Object Model (COM) programming techniques with Java. Since we understand that our code that directly uses ActiveX and COM will not be portable to non-Windows platforms, it is important to put an "abstraction layer" around Windows-specific code. This abstraction layer, or so-called wrapper, will allow us to later, if required, port applications to standard Java platforms by reimplementing the code on the inside of the abstraction layer. For example, in this chapter, we will write a small wrapper around Windows-specific code for using the IE 4.0 HTML rendering ActiveX control. This is an attractive thing for Windows programmers to do: it will allow us to render HTML documents inside our Java applications by adding just a couple of lines of Java code. Also, since we use an abstraction layer, or wrapper, if an application needs to be ported to a non-Windows platform, then you could reimplement the HTML rendering code inside of the wrapper by using the JavaSoft HTML rendering class that ships with the Java Foundation Classes (JFC). You might not want to use the JFC HTML rendering engine on Windows platforms because (at least at the time I wrote this chapter in October 1997) the IE 4.0 ActiveX HTML control is much faster and fuller featured than the JFC HTML rendering Java classes.

5.1 How to access ActiveX controls in Java programs

ActiveX controls are Microsoft's component technology. You can program ActiveX controls in many languages; for example:

- Microsoft Visual Basic
- Microsoft Visual C++
- Java, using the tools supplied with the Java SDK (version 2.0 or later)
- Borland's Delphi

So, if you are programming specifically for the Windows platform (and for the Intel CPU), you have a wide range of programming tools for writing ActiveX controls. Even better yet, hopefully you can find useful ActiveX controls that someone else wrote, and incorporate them into your Microsoft platform-specific Java applications.

There are two Java packages supplied with the Java SDK that are used for integrating Java and ActiveX:

- **com.ms.activeX**—used for ActiveX and JavaBean integration with Microsoft Windows–specific Java programs
- **com.ms.com**—used for low-level Java and COM integration

You can read rather detailed documentation for these two Microsoft Java packages in the online documentation that ships with the Java SDK (click on the "Java & Native Code" link).

In general, if you have an ActiveX control that you want to use in a Java application, you must perform the following steps:

- Run the program **jactivex** on the ActiveX control to generate a Java wrapper for the ActiveX control.
- Use the generated Java class as though it is a native Java class (although the original ActiveX control must be installed on your computer at runtime).

For example (from the Microsoft documentation), if you have an ActiveX control **fooX** that has methods **fooMethod1** and **fooMethod2**, then you can generate a Java wrapper by running

```
jactivex fooX
```

You can then use this Java wrapper in your Java programs; for example:

```
import fooX.*;
import java.awt.*;

class testFooX extends Panel {

    public testFooX() {
```

```
                          // create the control
                          fooX x = new fooX();
                          //add the control to the layout
                          add("Center", x);
                     }

                     public callActiveX(int methodIndex) {
                        if (methodIndex == 1) x.fooMethod1();
                        if (methodIndex == 2) x.fooMethod2();
                     }
                }
```

This is a little tedious, but it is easier than completely re-creating the functionality of an existing ActiveX control in pure Java. In the next section, we will take advantage of the fact that Microsoft has wrapped the IE 4.0 **WebBrowser** ActiveX control in a separate package, **com.ms.ie**.

5.2 Wrapping the Internet Explorer 4.0 ActiveX control as a JavaBean

In this section, we take advantage of the fact that Microsoft has already wrapped the IE 4.0 **WebBrowser** ActiveX control in a separate package, **com.ms.ie**. This saves us from having to run the **jactivex** utility.

Listing 5.1 shows how simple it is to use the class **BrowserBean** in your own Java applications.

Listing 5.1

```
Frame f = new Frame("Test BrowserBean");
BrowserBean bb =
    new BrowserBean("file://c:/MJava/activex/books.htm");
```

(continued)

Listing 5.1 *(continued)*

```
f.add("Center", bb);
f.setSize(501, 400);
f.setVisible(true);
bb.setURL("file://c:/MJava/activex/books.htm");
```

The class **BrowserBean** is derived from the AWT **Panel** class. This browser component can only be activated by calling **setURL** after the container of the browser component is visible.

The class **BrowserBean** implements three Java interfaces:

- **com.ms.activeX.ActiveXControlListener**— derived from the interface **java.util.EventListener**. This interface has one method **controlCreated** that is called after an ActiveX control is created. In the **BrowserBean** class, implementing the **ActiveXControlListener** interface requires us to implement the method **controlCreated** (which does nothing in the **BrowserBean** class, but it is still required).

- **com.ms.ie.WebBrowserEventListener**—defines the required methods for using the IE 4.0 **WebBrowser** ActiveX control. Unfortunately, the entire package **com.ms.ie** is not documented; however, the Java SDK sample program **Jbrowser.java** is detailed enough to allow us to use this useful Java package. This interface defines 17 methods that must be defined in the class **BrowserBean**:
  - **StatusTextChange**
  - **TitleChange**
  - **ProgressChange**
  - **DocumentComplete**

- CommandStateChange
- DownloadBegin
- DownloadComplete
- PropertyChange
- BeforeNavigate2
- NewWindow2
- NavigateComplete2
- OnQuit
- OnVisible
- OnToolBar
- OnMenuBar
- OnFullScreen
- OnTheaterMode
- **Serializable**—allows the **BrowserBean** class to function as a JavaBean.

All of the methods in interface **com.ms.ie.Web-BrowserEventListener** are "stubbed out" in the class **BrowserBean**. You can subclass **BrowserBean**, adding new versions of the methods defined in this interface, if your Java application requires special handling of any events that cause the methods in this interface to be called.

If the **BrowserBean** class is used as a JavaBean, the following properties can be used:

- **width**—the desired width of the **BrowserBean** component
- **height**—the desired height of the **BrowserBean** component
- **showRefreshButton**—a Boolean flag that indicates if the refresh button should be visible

The **public static void main** method allows the **BrowserBean** class to run as a stand-alone Java application. Notice that the method **main** calls the **BrowserBean** method **setURL** after the frame containing the sample **BrowserBean** is made visible. The parent container of an instance of class **BrowserBean** must be visible before **setURL** is called, or a runtime error will occur.

The **BrowserBean** class has two constructors:

- **BrowserBean( )**—creates a new browsing component without an initial URL document set

- **BrowserBean(String initialURL)**—creates a new browsing component with an initial URL document set

Both class constructors perform the following initialization:

- Create a new instance of **com.ms.ie.WebBrowser**.

- Add a **WebBrowserEventListener** for receiving notification of events like download begin, download complete, and so on.

- Add an **ActiveXControlListener** for receiving notification of the control creation event.

- Create a new panel and add the **WebBrowser** ActiveX control.

- Add the refresh button, if desired.

The **BrowserBean** class contains one inner class for handling mouse events for the refresh button: **browserMouseListener**. This class can access the public **setURL** method of the outer class (i.e., of class **BrowserBean**).

The example implemented in Listing 5.2 is derived from the Microsoft example program **Jbrowser** that is included in the **Samples** directory of the Java SDK (thanks to the authors of this example).

Listing 5.2

```
// BrowserBean.java
//
// This example uses the com.ms.ie.WebBrowser control from the
// Internet Explorer, version 4.0.  This example is
// derived from the Microsoft example file 'JBrowser.java'
//

package com.markwatson.ms.activex;

import java.awt.*;
import java.awt.event.*;
import java.io.*;
import java.beans.*;

import com.ms.activeX.*;
import com.ms.com.Variant;

import com.markwatson.util.*;

public class BrowserBean extends Panel implements
ActiveXControlListener, com.ms.ie.WebBrowserEventListener, Serializable
{
  // The ActiveXControlFromIE4 object:
  private com.ms.ie.WebBrowser ActiveXControlFromIE4 = null;
  protected TextArea urlText = null;
  // JavaBean properties:
  private int width = 500;
  public int getWidth() { return width; }
  public void setWidth(int w) { width = w; }
  private int height = 330;
  public int getHeight() { return height; }
  public void setHeight(int h) { height = h; }
  private boolean showRefreshButton = true;
  public boolean getShowRefreshButton() { return showRefreshButton; }
  public void setShowRefreshButton(boolean b) { showRefreshButton = b; }

  // static main for TESTING:
  public static void main(String[] args)
  {
```

(continued)

Listing 5.2 *(continued)*

```
  Frame f = new Frame("Test BrowserBean");
  BrowserBean bb =
    new BrowserBean("file://c:/MJava/activex/books.htm");
  f.add("Center", bb);
  f.setSize(501, 400);
  f.setVisible(true);
}

public BrowserBean() {
  this("");
}

public BrowserBean(String initialURL)  {
  setLayout(null);
  setBackground(Color.lightGray);
  ActiveXControlFromIE4 = new com.ms.ie.WebBrowser();
  ActiveXControlFromIE4.addWebBrowserEventListener(this);
  ActiveXControlFromIE4.addActiveXControlListener(this);

  // Add the ActiveX com.ms.ie.WebBrowser control
  Panel p = new Panel();
  p.add(ActiveXControlFromIE4);
  ActiveXControlFromIE4.setBounds(1, 4, width - 20, height);
  p.setBounds(1, 1, 500, 330);
  p.setVisible(true);
  add(p);

  if (showRefreshButton) {
    setBounds(0,0,width+1,height+30);
    Button b = new Button("refresh");
    b.setBounds((width*2)/3 + 5, height+10,
                width - (width*2)/3 - 30, 25);
    b.addMouseListener(new browserMouseListener());
    add(b);
    urlText = new TextArea(initialURL);
    urlText.setBounds(7, height+10, (width*2)/3 - 10, 25);
    add(urlText);
  } else {
    setBounds(0,0,width+1,height+10);
  }
```

```
    ActiveXControlFromIE4.setVisible(true);
    setVisible(true);
}

//
// Public method for setting a new URL to display:
//
public void setURL(String url) {
    ActiveXControlFromIE4.Navigate(url, null, null, null, null);
}

//
//      ActiveXControlListener interface:
//
public void controlCreated(Object target)  {  }

//
//      com.ms.ie.WebBrowserEventListener interface:
//

public void StatusTextChange(String text)  {  }

public void TitleChange(String new_title) {  }

public void ProgressChange(int pos, int range) {  }

public void DocumentComplete(Object pDisp, Variant URL) {  }

public void CommandStateChange(int Command, boolean Enable) {  }

public void DownloadBegin() {  }

public void DownloadComplete() {  }

public void PropertyChange(String szProperty) {  }

public void BeforeNavigate2(Object pDisp, Variant URL, Variant Flags,
          Variant TargetFrameName, Variant PostData,
          Variant Headers, boolean[] Cancel)
{
```

(continued)

Listing 5.2 *(continued)*

```
   }

   public void NewWindow2(Object[] ppDisp, boolean[] Cancel) {   }

   public void NavigateComplete2(Object pDisp, Variant URL)  {   }

   public void OnQuit()  {   }

   public void OnVisible(boolean Visible) {   }

   public void OnToolBar(boolean ToolBar) {   }

   public void OnMenuBar(boolean MenuBar) {   }

   public void OnStatusBar(boolean StatusBar)  {   }

   public void OnFullScreen(boolean FullScreen)  {   }

   public void OnTheaterMode(boolean TheaterMode)  {   }

   //
   //       Inner class to handle refresh button events:
   //

   class browserMouseListener implements MouseListener {
     public void mousePressed(MouseEvent me) {
     }
     public void mouseClicked(MouseEvent me) {
       System.out.println("mouse click");
       setURL(urlText.getText());
       ActiveXControlFromIE4.setBounds(0, 0, 480, 320);
     }
     public void mouseReleased(MouseEvent me) {   }
     public void mouseEntered(MouseEvent me)  {   }
     public void mouseExited(MouseEvent me)   {   }
   }
}
```

The class **BrowserBean** is very useful for easily adding
HTML viewing capabilities to your Java programs.

5.3 Example of writing an ActiveX control in Java

Both JavaBeans and ActiveX controls are component models. Almost everyone agrees that component-level programming makes sense for several reasons:

- Components are a larger module of code than classes.

- Components can both encapsulate complex internal behavior and provide a user interface.

- Many programming development systems support visual programming by plugging together components.

The Microsoft Java SDK contains a tool, **javareg**, for packaging JavaBean components as ActiveX controls. The **javareg** program registers Java classes as COM objects in the Windows registry database.

Listing 5.3 shows a very simple JavaBean that we will use to demonstrate wrapping a JavaBean as an ActiveX control. The class **TestBean** extends the **Panel** class and implements the **Serializable** interface. The class itself is very simple because the **TestBean** only includes one component: a static text field of class **Label**. We enable mouse events for the **TestBean** class by calling the inherited (from class **java.awt.Component**) method **enableEvents**.

Listing 5.3

```
// TestBean.java
//
// This example is used to show how to package a
// JavaBean as an ActiveX control.
//
```

(continued)

Listing 5.2 *(continued)*

```java
package com.markwatson.ms.activex;

import java.awt.*;
import java.awt.event.*;
import java.io.*;
import java.beans.*;


public class TestBean extends Panel implements Serializable
{
  // JavaBean properties:
  private int width = 280;
  public int getWidth() { return width; }
  public void setWidth(int w) { width = w; }
  private int height = 80;
  public int getHeight() { return height; }
  public void setHeight(int h) { height = h; }

  // static main for TESTING:
  public static void main(String[] args)
  {
    Frame f = new Frame("TestBean");
    TestBean bb =
      new TestBean();
    f.add("Center", bb);
    f.setSize(bb.getWidth() + 15, bb.getHeight() + 35);
    f.setVisible(true);
  }

  private Label label;

  public TestBean()  {
    setLayout(null);
    setBackground(Color.red);
    enableEvents(AWTEvent.MOUSE_EVENT_MASK);
    label = new Label("Mouse clicked 0 times in panel");
    label.setBounds(1, 4, width - 8, height / 3);
    add(label);
    setVisible(true);
```

```
   }

  protected void processMouseEvent(MouseEvent e)  {
    if((e.getID()) == MouseEvent.MOUSE_PRESSED) {
      doClick();
    }
  }

  public void doClick() {
    label.setText("Mouse clicked " + ++clicks + " times in panel");
  }

  protected int clicks = 0;

}
```

The class **TestBean** is derived from the standard Java class **java.awt.Panel**; I could have also implemented this example using AFC. Figure 5.2 shows the **TestBean** running as a stand-alone Java application.

It is fairly easy to add this **TestBean** to Visual Basic applications. The file **c:\mjava\activex\register.bat** can be used to register this class as an ActiveX control:

```
javareg /register /control
/class:com.markwatson.ms.activex.TestBean
/codebase:c:\mjava\classes /typelib:TestBean.tlb
```

The command file **register.bat** does not set a specific unique ID for the **TestBean** component, so the **javareg**

Figure 5.2   *The class **TestBean** running as a stand-alone Java application*

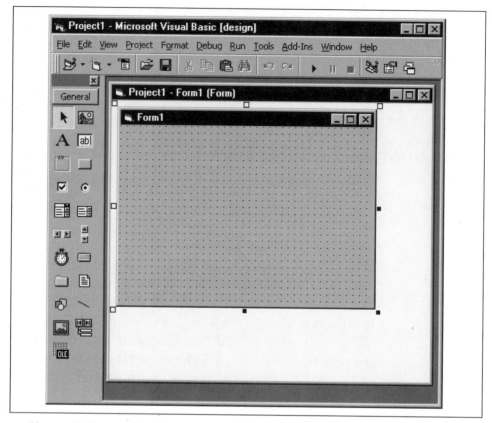

Figure 5.3 *Starting a new project in Visual Basic*

program supplies a new unique ID. The file **c:\mjava\
activex\unregister.bat** can be used to unregister the
ActiveX control:

```
javareg /unregister /control
/class:com.markwatson.ms.activex.TestBean
/codebase:c:\mjava\classes /typelib:TestBean.tlb
```

You should run the **unregister.bat** command file
before rerunning the **register.bat** command file. This
will avoid multiple ActiveX controls that are registered
with the same name but different unique IDs.

Figures 5.3 through 5.6 show how to use the **TestBean**
JavaBean in Visual Basic applications. Figure 5.3 shows

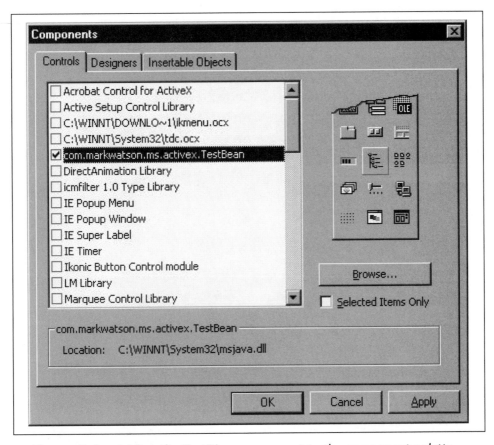

Figure 5.4   *Adding the **TestBean** component to the component palette*

the Visual Basic application after creating a new project for a stand-alone application. Note that the component palette on the left side of the application window shows only the standard (default) components.

Figure 5.4 shows the dialog box for adding components to the component palette. You use the **Projects** menu and select the **Components** menu option. In Figure 5.4, I have added a component labeled **com.markwatson.ms.activex.TestBean**.

Figure 5.5 shows the Visual Basic application window after adding a **TestBean** component to the project's

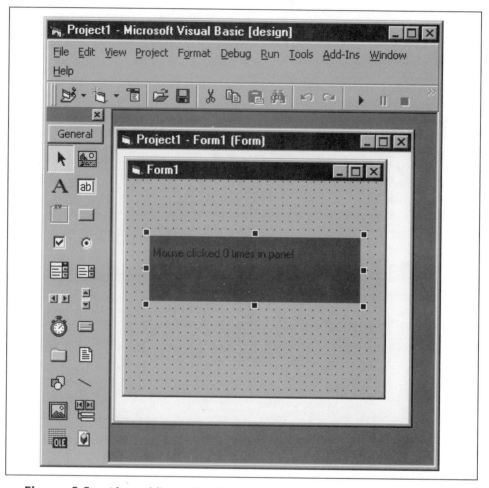

Figure 5.5 *After adding a **TestBean** component to the project's form*

form. Note that the **TestBean** component appears in the lower right corner of the component palette as a default icon (a three-dimensional box).

Figure 5.6 shows a stand-alone Windows application that was created with Visual Basic. This application contains a **TestBean** component.

By using **javareg**, we have taken a Java component and packaged it for use as an ActiveX component. We

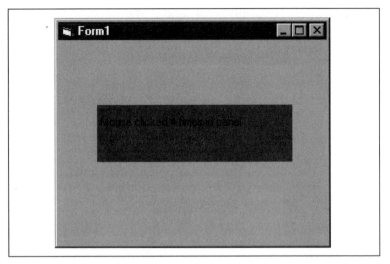

Figure 5.6 *Running the stand-alone application created with Visual Basic*

did not have to do any extra work for handling event processing in this (Java-built) ActiveX component. We used the **enableEvents** method that is inherited from the **java.awt.Component** class and defined a typical **processMouseEvent** method that is called for all mouse events that occur inside the **TestBean**.

5.4 Using WFC with the Internet Explorer 4.0 ActiveX control

We used the Internet Explorer 4.0 ActiveX control in Section 5.2 in a JavaBean. In this section, we will wrap the same control in a small Java application using the WFC class libraries.

Listing 5.4 shows the class **Form1** that was generated automatically by the J++ (version 6) IDE. The following

160   Using ActiveX Components in Java Programs

two lines of code are executed when the button on
Form1 is clicked:

```
aURL = edit1.getText();
webBrowser1.Navigate(aURL, null, null, null, null);
```

The text typed in the edit field **edit1** is retrieved and
passed to the **Navigate** method of the IE 4.0 HTML rendering control.

Listing 5.4

```
// Form1.java

import wfc.app.*;
import wfc.core.*;
import wfc.ui.*;

public class Form1 extends Form
{
  private void Fetch_click(Object sender, Event e)
  {
    if (sender == Fetch) {
      aURL = edit1.getText();
      webBrowser1.Navigate(aURL, null, null, null, null);
    }
  }

  public Form1()
  {
    // Required for Visual J++ Form Designer support
    initForm();
  }

  private String aURL;

  public static void main(String args[])
  {
    Application.run(new Form1());
  }
```

```
/**
 * NOTE: The following code is required by the Visual J++ form
 * designer.  It can be modified using the form editor.  Do not
 * modify it using the code editor.
 */

Container components = new Container();
shdocvw.WebBrowser.WebBrowser webBrowser1 =
   new shdocvw.WebBrowser.WebBrowser();
Edit edit1 = new Edit();
Button Fetch = new Button();

private void initForm()
{
  ResourceManager resources = new ResourceManager(this, "Form1");
  this.setBackColor(Color.CONTROL);
  this.setLocation(new Point(0, 0));
  this.setSize(new Point(479, 259));
  this.setTabIndex(-1);
  this.setTabStop(true);
  this.setText("Form1");
  this.setAutoScaleBaseSize(13);
  this.setClientSize(new Point(471, 232));
  webBrowser1.setLocation(new Point(10, 40));
  webBrowser1.setSize(new Point(450, 180));
  webBrowser1.setTabIndex(0);
  webBrowser1.setTabStop(false);
  webBrowser1.setOcxState((AxHost.State)resources.getObject(
          "webBrowser1_ocxState"));
  edit1.setBackColor(Color.WINDOW);
  edit1.setCursor(Cursor.IBEAM);
  edit1.setLocation(new Point(10, 10));
  edit1.setSize(new Point(330, 20));
  edit1.setTabIndex(1);
  edit1.setTabStop(true);
  edit1.setText("edit1");
  Fetch.setLocation(new Point(350, 10));
  Fetch.setSize(new Point(110, 20));
  Fetch.setTabIndex(3);
  Fetch.setTabStop(true);
```

(continued)

Listing 5.4 *(continued)*

```
    Fetch.setText("Fetch");
    Fetch.addOnClick(new EventHandler(this.Fetch_click));
    this.setNewControls(new Control[] {
      Fetch,
        edit1,
        webBrowser1});
  }
  // NOTE: End of form designer support code

  public static class ClassInfo extends Form.ClassInfo
  {
    // TODO: Add your property and event infos here
  }
  protected void onResize(Event p1)
  {
    super.onResize(p1);
    Rectangle r = this.getClientRect();
    Point p = new Point(r.width, r.height);
    webBrowser1.setClientSize(p);
  }
}
```

Building the application shown in Listing 5.4 was fairly simple. I selected the "Windows application" option when creating a new project. A blank form (class **Form1**) was automatically created. I used the "Customize toolbox" option, using the "ActiveX Control" tab to add the "WebBrowser" IE 4.0 control to the tool palette. I painted the IE 4.0 control onto **Form1**, added a button and a text field, and then added the event handling code for passing the contents of the text field to the IE 4.0 control. Figure 5.7 shows the program in Listing 5.4 compiled and linked as a stand-alone Windows application.

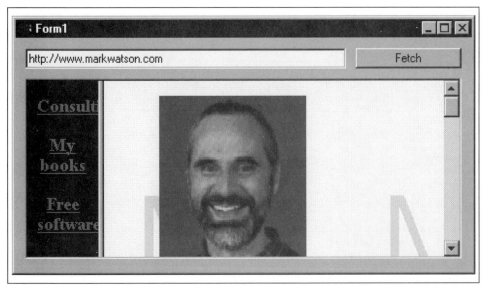

Figure 5.7   *Figure 5.7 A stand-alone Java/Windows application built using J++ (version 6) and the WFC class libraries*

Using Applets with CAB and JAR Archives

Although most of my Java programming is for creating either stand-alone Java applications or JavaBean components, Java applets are also useful for placing client-side applications directly in Web documents. In this chapter, we will develop a simple Java applet that uses Microsoft's recommended technique of using a separate applet implementation class that is embedded in a **UIApplet** class. We will then see how we can speed up applet loading by placing applet class files in either a Microsoft format **CAB** archive file or a Sun/JavaSoft format **JAR** archive file. The IE 4.0 supports both **CAB** and **JAR** archive file formats. The Netscape Communicator (version 4 and later) supports **JAR** archive files.

6.1 A simple example Java applet

Listing 6.1 shows the implementation of a very simple Java applet that can serve as a design and implementation template for any applets that you write using the AFC. The public class **TestApplet** is derived from the AFC class **AwtUIApplet**. The constructor for the **TestApplet** class simply runs the constructor for the superclass **AwtUIApplet**, passing an instance of the class **TestAppletImplementation**, which is also defined in Listing 6.1. Figure 6.1 shows the UML class diagram for **TestApplet**.

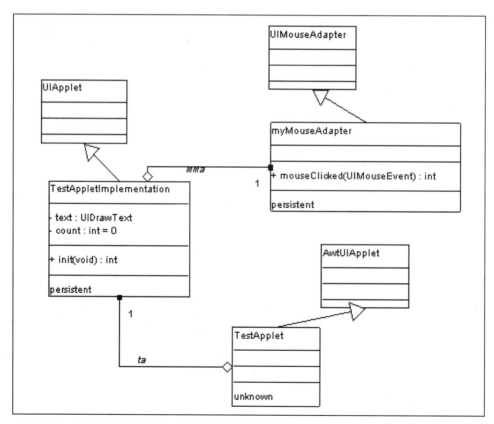

Figure 6.1   *UML class diagram for **TestApplet***

The class **TestAppletImplementation** is derived from **UIApplet** and contains two components:

- A push button that uses the inner class **myMouseAdapter** to handle events
- A label that displays the number of times that the mouse has been clicked inside of the applet

Listing 6.1

```
// com.markwatson.applets.TestApplet.java
//
// This simple example applet demonstrates using a bridge
// class that is derived from the class AwtUIApplet, with
// a separate implementation class.  The use of a bridge
// class is recommended in the online AFC documentation
// that ships with the Microsoft Java SDK 3.0.
//

package com.markwatson.applets;

import com.ms.ui.*;
import com.ms.ui.event.*;
import com.ms.fx.*;

public class TestApplet extends AwtUIApplet { // bridge
  public TestApplet ()    {
    super (new TestAppletImplementation ());
  }
}

class TestAppletImplementation extends UIApplet { // implementation
  public void init()  {
    setLayout(new UIBorderLayout(25, 25));
    setBackground(new FxColor(130,225,255));
    UIPushButton b =
      new UIPushButton("Click me!", UIPushButton.RAISED);
    b.setFont(new FxFont("Dialog", FxFont.BOLD, 18));
```

(continued)

Listing 6.1 *(continued)*

```
    b.setForeground(new FxColor(255,0,0));
    b.addMouseListener(new myMouseAdapter());
    add(b, "CENTER");
    text = new UIDrawText("Button has been clicked   0 times");
    text.setFont(new FxFont("Dialog", FxFont.PLAIN, 14));
    add(text, "SOUTH");
  }
  private UIDrawText text;
  private int count = 0;
  class myMouseAdapter extends UIMouseAdapter {
    public void mouseClicked(UIMouseEvent me) {
      text.setValueText("Button has been clicked " +
                    ++count + " times");
    }
  }
}
```

Listing 6.2 shows a simple HTML file (**c:\mjava\ applets\test.html**) that can be used to run the test applet inside IE 4.0. We use the **codebase** applet parameter to specify that the directory **..\classes** (or **c:\mjava\classes**) is searched for the applet's class files.

Listing 6.2

```
<HTML>
  <BODY>
    <APPLET
      codebase="..\classes"
      code="com.markwatson.applets.TestApplet.class"
      width=205 height=80>
    </APPLET>
  </BODY>
</HTML>
```

Figure 6.2 shows a screen shot of the test applet running inside IE 4.0.

Figure 6.2   *The test applet running inside IE 4.0*

6.2 Packaging an applet in a CAB archive file

Packaging your applet class files inside a **CAB** archive file will speed up loading your Web pages. This speedup is most noticeable if your applet contains many individual class files, since a single socket connection with a Web server can retrieve all of the files required to run a complex applet. The applet in this example consists of only three class files:

- **TestApplet.class**
- **TestAppletImplementation.class**
- **TestAppletImplementation$myMouseAdapter.class**

The file **c:\mjava\make_cab.bat** contains a command file to build a **CAB** file for the applet in the directory **c:\mjava\applets**. You must compile this applet first by typing the following in a Windows 95 or NT DOS-style window:

```
c:
cd \mjava\applets
c.bat
cd \mjava
make_cab.bat
```

Listing 6.3 shows the file **c:\mjava\make_cab.bat**. The program **cabarc.exe** is in the directory **c:\SDK-Java.30\Bin\PackSign**. The option **n** creates a new **CAB** file. The second argument is the name of the **CAB** file being created. List all files to be included in the **CAB** file after the **CAB** file name.

Listing 6.3

```
cabarc n test.cab classes\com\markwatson\applets\*.class
```

6.3 Using a CAB archive file on a Web page

The HTML file **c:\mjava\test_cab.html** can be double-clicked to run the example applet (seen in Listing 6.1) for the **CAB** file in IE 4.0 (assuming that IE 4.0 is your default browser). Listing 6.4 shows the HTML file **c:\mjava\test_cab.html** that can be used to test the **CAB** file that we just made.

Listing 6.4

```
<HTML>
  <BODY>
    <APPLET code="com.markwatson.applets.TestApplet.class"
      width=205 height=80>
    <PARAM NAME="cabbase" VALUE="test.cab">
    </APPLET>
  </BODY>
</HTML>
```

The **CAB** file is specified inside of a **<PARAM>** HTML tag by specifying the attribute name "**cabbase**".

6.4   Packaging an applet in a JAR archive file

Packaging your applet class files inside a **JAR** archive file will speed up loading your Web pages. This speedup is most noticeable if your applet contains many individual class files.

The file **c:\mjava\make_jar.bat** contains a command file to build a **JAR** file for the applet in the directory **c:\mjava**. You must compile this applet first by typing the following in a Windows 95 or NT DOS-style window:

```
c:
cd \mjava\applets
c.bat
cd \mjava
make_jar.bat
```

Listing 6.5 shows the contents of the command file **c:\mjava\make_jar.bat**.

Listing 6.5

```
jar cvf test.jar classes\com\markwatson\applets\*.class
```

The **jar.exe** program is not included with the Microsoft Java SDK. However, it is included with most commercial Java development systems (e.g., Borland JBuilder, Symantec Café, and IBM Visual Age for Java). The **jar.exe** file is also available for free by downloading Sun/JavaSoft's Java Development Kit (JDK) from the Web site *java.sun.com*.

6.5 Using a JAR archive file on a Web page

The HTML file **c:\mjava\test_jar.html** can be double-clicked to run the example applet for the **JAR** file in either IE 4.0 or Netscape Communicator (version 4 or later). Listing 6.6 shows the HTML file **c:\mjava\test_jar.html**.

Listing 6.6

```
<HTML>
  <BODY>
    <APPLET code="com.markwatson.applets.TestApplet.class"
      ARCHIVE="test.jar"
      width=205 height=80>
    </APPLET>
  </BODY>
</HTML>
```

The **ARCHIVE** parameter inside the **<APPLET>** HTML tag specifies which **JAR** file to search for the class **TestApplet.class**.

Extensible Markup Language (XML) and the Channel Definition Format (CDF)

I have been interested in hypertext since 1985 and have read several good books on nonlinear text (Barret 1985; Barret 1989; Berk and Devlin 1991). The 1990s brought us the World Wide Web (I have had my own public Web page since April 1994), and life has never been the same for people who use computers to communicate and find information. Still, the Web, based on HTML, is far from a perfect solution for sharing information. HTML and the current Web have several problems:

- There is no way to annotate other people's work.

- HTML is not a good medium for publishing changing data (although the combination of Web servers, databases, and CGI programs that generate HTML on the fly have been useful).

- HTML is not a good medium for managing data. (HTML is, however, great for displaying data.)

Certainly, extensions to HTML (e.g., scripting with JavaScript/JScript and the document object model with stylesheets) have continually improved the ability to display data in HTML-based documents. A new development, the Extensible Markup Language (XML), provides an extensible tool for organizing and maintaining data that will work well with HTML. At the time that I am writing this chapter (March 1998), the World Wide Web consortium has approved the use of XML, and it is in the process of standardization. At this time, Microsoft and Netscape have slightly different Document Object Models (DOM) for naming HTML components; this naming is important so that scripting languages (see Chapter 11) can refer to specific parts of a Web document. Both Netscape and Microsoft have promised to become compatible with whatever DOM standard that the World Wide Web consortium approves.

The combination of a standard DOM, standard HTML, the widespread use of a newly standardized XML, and standard scripting languages (both Netscape's JavaScript and Microsoft's JScript are compatible supersets of the evolving standard) will make distributed, collaborative applications for exchanging and sharing information easier to write and to maintain. The effect of the standardization of Web technologies on all of our lives in the near and distant future is hard to predict accurately, but the effect will be profound.

The Channel Definition Format (CDF) was designed to improve the organization of all information assets at a Web site. CDF uses the syntax, and is an extension, of the XML. Both CDF and XML appear to be similar to

HTML; however, unlike HTML, CDF and XML are extensible languages that support metadata for defining structured data and to specify content type.

In this chapter, we will develop three examples:

- Encoding data as XML documents for communication between Java applications and for saving data to local disk files

- A tree-style browser for XML documents that uses the **EventTree** class that was developed in Chapter 2

- A stand-alone server application that delivers CDF-formatted documents to the IE 4.0 Web browser

There are several freely available parsers for XML. In this book we will use one made available by Microsoft. Microsoft has also provided a built-in XML in their latest Java Virtual Machine and supporting class libraries. For the purposes of this chapter, I prefer to use Microsoft's older XML parser for the following reasons:

- It is available in source code form at Microsoft's Web site and is included with this book (in slightly modified form) in the directory **\Mjava\ms\xml_parser**.

- It has a generous reuse license (please read Microsoft's software license agreement, included in the directory **\Mjava\ms\xml_parser**, before incorporating this parser in your software applications).

There are several good sources for information about XML and CDF on the Internet:

- *www.w3.org/XML/*—the World Wide Web consortium's Web site for XML

- *www.microsoft.com/xml*—Microsoft's Web site for XML

Both of these sites provide links for other XML sources on the Web.

7.1 Overview of XML

XML allows us to add metadata to the data in documents. Metadata defines the data type and semantics of data elements. An XML document contains a single element. Any element can contain zero or more nested elements. XML documents look like HTML documents, but we will see that their structure is more precise, and they can be arbitrarily extended by adding new element types, where an element is always represented by beginning and ending tags. For example, an element named **NAME** would start with the beginning tag <**NAME**> and end with the ending tag </**NAME**>.

For example, Listing 7.1 (from the file **cust.xml** provided with the Microsoft Java XML parser) shows an XML document that contains the top-level element **CUSTOMERS**. The top-level element contains two subelement tags, both with the value **CUSTOMER**. A **CUSTOMER** element contains tags **NAME**, **DATE**, and **ORDERS**. The **NAME** element contains tags **LASTNAME** and **FIRSTNAME**, and so on. The indentation seen in

XML data is tree-structured

Like its predecessor, the Standard Generalized Markup Language (SGML), XML documents are inherently tree structures. The single top-level element in an XML document is the root of the tree. The correspondence between XML documents and their tree structure will become more apparent after we design, develop, and run the XML browser in Sections 7.2 and 7.3.

Listing 7.1 is arbitrary, but it is, in general, a good idea to indent each nested tag/element level.

Listing 7.1

```
<CUSTOMERS>
  <CUSTOMER>
    <NAME>
      <LASTNAME>Bosworth</LASTNAME>
      <FIRSTNAME>Adam</FIRSTNAME>
    </NAME>
    <DATE>March 17, 1997</DATE>
    <ORDERS>
      <ITEM>
        <NAME>Number, the Language of Science</NAME>
        <AUTHOR>Danzig</AUTHOR>
        <PRICE>5.95</PRICE>
      </ITEM>
      <ITEM>
        <NAME>Tales of Grandpa Cat</NAME>
        <AUTHOR>Wardlaw, Lee</AUTHOR>
        <PRICE>6.58</PRICE>
      </ITEM>
    </ORDERS>
  </CUSTOMER>

  <CUSTOMER>
    <NAME>
      <LASTNAME>Layman</LASTNAME>
      <FIRSTNAME>Andrew</FIRSTNAME>
    </NAME>
    <DATE>March 17, 1997</DATE>
    <ORDERS>
      <ITEM>
        <NAME>Evolution of Complexity in Animal Culture</NAME>
        <AUTHOR>Bonner</AUTHOR>
        <PRICE>5.95</PRICE>
      </ITEM>
      <ITEM>
        <NAME>When We Were Very Young</NAME>
        <AUTHOR>Milne, A. A.</AUTHOR>
```

(continued)

Listing 7.1 *(continued)*

```
        <PRICE>12.50</PRICE>
      </ITEM>
    </ORDERS>
  </CUSTOMER>
</CUSTOMERS>
```

XML is really a subset of the Standard Generalized Markup Language (SGML). SGML and XML documents are self-describing and extensible. XML documents are actually easier to parse because XML does not support "missing tags"; for example, the following is legal HTML:

```
<HTML>
  <H1>Heading 1
  <H1>Heading 2</H1>
</HTML>
```

XML and artificial intelligence

XML might be one of the most important technologies for enabling artificial intelligence (AI). AI applications of natural language processing of text and data mining require a potentially huge amount of labor because they must deal with natural language text and data stored in a variety of formats.

XML will make information extraction much easier because there will be standard Data Type Documents (DTDs) to store specific types of data. The metadata stored in XML tags will make it less expensive to develop data extraction software (and software agents).

Notice that the first beginning **<H1>** tag does not have a matching ending **</H1>** tag: the HTML parser must be able to figure this out from context. The following has matching start-end tags and is legal both as HTML and XML:

```
<HTML>
  <H1>Heading 1</H1>
  <H1>Heading 2</H1>
</HTML>
```

7.1.1 The Microsoft XML parser is written in Java

There are many freely available XML parsers. We will use an XML parser written by Microsoft for all of the examples in this book. This parser is available in source code form (see the CD-ROM) and uses several Java interfaces and classes to access the structured elements in XML documents.

The **Element** interface represents individual items (or elements) in XML documents. There are seven types of elements, the most commonly used being **Document** and **Element**. Classes that implement the **Element** interface are also containers for other objects that implement the **Element** interface. The **Document** class implements the **Element** interface and is used to represent a single XML document.

Figure 7.1 shows the UML class diagram (with all methods) for the **Document** and **Element** classes. The Microsoft XML parser contains 19 classes (see the directory **c:\mjava\ms\xml_parser**).

Figure 7.2 shows the UML class diagram for the **SampleReader** class, which opens an XML document as a local file (we will also access XML documents by URLs). The sample program prints a formatted listing of all elements in a document. The method **SampleReader.doTree** is called with a reference to any object that is an element and recursively calls itself for processing nested elements.

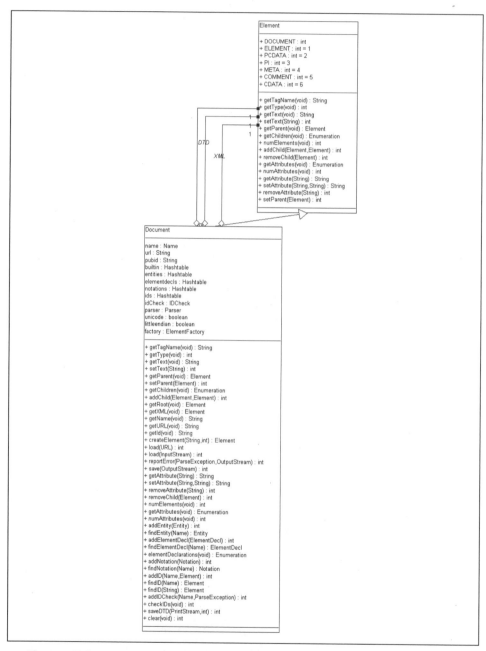

Figure 7.1   *UML class diagram for the **Document** and **Element** classes*

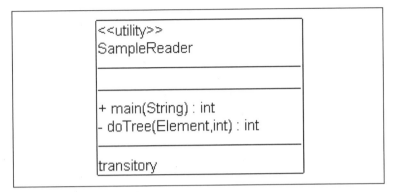

Figure 7.2 *UML class diagram for* **SampleReader**

Listing 7.2 shows the implementation of the class **SampleReader**. The method **main** gets an XML file name or URL containing an XML document from the command line argument and constructs a new **SampleReader** object. The **SampleReader** class constructor requires a single argument: a string containing either a URL or a file name. The constructor creates a valid URL reference, creates a new instance of the class **com.ms.xml.Document**, and uses the **Document** class **load** method to create a tree-structured representation of the XML document. In this tree structure, the **Document** object is the root of the tree, and objects of class **com.ms.xml.Element** are the tree nodes and tree leaves (i.e., nodes that do not contain children). After the **load** method constructs the tree, the **SampleReader** class method **doTree** traverses the tree, printing out an indented representation of the original XML document. The **doTree** method is fairly simple. It has two arguments: an instance of class **Element** and a depth parameter. Each time the method **doTree** calls itself recursively, it increases the depth parameter by one; this allows the **doTree** method to properly indent tags and content. The **doTree** method calls itself recursively whenever the **Element** object that it is currently processing contains children.

Listing 7.2

```java
// SampleReader.java

import com.ms.xml.ParseException;
import com.ms.xml.Document;
import com.ms.xml.Element;
import com.ms.xml.Attribute;

import java.util.Enumeration;
import java.io.*;
import java.io.PrintStream;
import java.net.*;

class SampleReader
{
  public static void main(String args[]) {
    if (args.length<1) {
      System.out.println("Need to specify an XML file name...");
      System.exit(1);
    }
    new SampleReader(args[0]);
  }

  public SampleReader () {
    System.out.println("Error: called SampleReader () constructor");
    System.exit(1);
  }

  public SampleReader (String fileName) {

    URL url = null;
    try {
      url = new URL(fileName);
    } catch (MalformedURLException ex) {
      File f = new File(fileName);
      try {
        String path = f.getAbsolutePath();
        path.replace('\\', '/');
        url = new URL("file:///" + path);
      } catch (MalformedURLException e) {
        System.out.println("Cannot create URL for: " + fileName);
        System.exit(0);
      }
```

```
  }

  Document d = new Document();
  try {
    d.load(url);
  } catch (ParseException e) {
    d.reportError(e, System.out);
  }
  // Get all of the elements recursively:

  Element e = d.getRoot();
  int depth = 0;
  doTree(e, depth);
}

private void doTree(Element e, int depth) {
  if (e==null) return;
  if (e.getTagName()==null) return;
  for (int i=0; i<depth; i++) System.out.print(" ");
  System.out.println("<" + e.getTagName() + "> " + e.getText());
  Enumeration attributes = e.getAttributes();
  if (attributes!=null) {
    for (int i=0; i<depth+2; i++) System.out.print(" ");
    System.out.println("Attributes:");
    while (attributes.hasMoreElements()) {
      Attribute a = (Attribute)attributes.nextElement();
      for (int i=0; i<depth+4; i++) System.out.print(" ");
      System.out.println(a.getName() + " ");
    }
  }

  Enumeration enum = e.getChildren();
  while (enum.hasMoreElements()) {
    Element e2 = (Element)enum.nextElement();
    if (e2!=null) {
      doTree(e2, depth+1);
    }
  }
  for (int i=0; i<depth; i++) System.out.print(" ");
  System.out.println("</" + e.getTagName() + ">");
  }
}
```

The method **SampleReader.doTree** is a good implementation template for using the Microsoft XML parser for processing XML documents. The method **doTree** performs a depth-first recursive traversal of the tree-structured XML document, starting at a specified element in the document.

Listing 7.3 shows the output of running the **SampleReader** program, parsing the **cust.xml** file seen in Listing 7.1.

Listing 7.3

```
C:\MJava\XML>java SampleReader cust.xml

<CUSTOMERS> Bosworth Adam March 17, 1997 Number, the Language of Science
Danzig 5.95 Tales of Grandpa Cat Wardlaw, Lee 6.58 Layman Andrew March 17,
1997 Evolution of Complexity in Animal Culture Bonner 5.95 When We Were Very
Young Milne, A. A. 12.50
 <CUSTOMER> Bosworth Adam March 17, 1997 Number, the Language of Science
Danzig 5.95 Tales of Grandpa Cat Wardlaw, Lee 6.58
  <NAME> Bosworth Adam
   <LASTNAME> Bosworth
   </LASTNAME>
   <FIRSTNAME> Adam
   </FIRSTNAME>
  </NAME>
  <DATE> March 17, 1997
  </DATE>
  <ORDERS> Number, the Language of Science Danzig 5.95 Tales of Grandpa Cat
Wardlaw, Lee 6.58
   <ITEM> Number, the Language of Science Danzig 5.95
    <NAME> Number, the Language of Science
    </NAME>
    <AUTHOR> Danzig
    </AUTHOR>
    <PRICE> 5.95
    </PRICE>
   </ITEM>
   <ITEM> Tales of Grandpa Cat Wardlaw, Lee 6.58
    <NAME> Tales of Grandpa Cat
```

```
    </NAME>
    <AUTHOR> Wardlaw, Lee
    </AUTHOR>
    <PRICE> 6.58
    </PRICE>
   </ITEM>
  </ORDERS>
 </CUSTOMER>
<CUSTOMER> Layman Andrew March 17, 1997 Evolution of Complexity in Animal
Culture Bonner 5.95 When We Were Very Young Milne, A. A. 12.50
  <NAME> Layman Andrew
   <LASTNAME> Layman
   </LASTNAME>
   <FIRSTNAME> Andrew
   </FIRSTNAME>
  </NAME>
  <DATE> March 17, 1997
  </DATE>
  <ORDERS> Evolution of Complexity in Animal Culture Bonner 5.95 When We
Were Very Young Milne, A. A. 12.50
    <ITEM> Evolution of Complexity in Animal Culture Bonner 5.95
    <NAME> Evolution of Complexity in Animal Culture
    </NAME>
    <AUTHOR> Bonner
    </AUTHOR>
    <PRICE> 5.95
    </PRICE>
   </ITEM>
    <ITEM> When We Were Very Young Milne, A. A. 12.50
    <NAME> When We Were Very Young
    </NAME>
    <AUTHOR> Milne, A. A.
    </AUTHOR>
    <PRICE> 12.50
    </PRICE>
   </ITEM>
  </ORDERS>
 </CUSTOMER>
</CUSTOMERS>

C:\MJava\XML>
```

Is this all there is to XML?

Well, no. There are two types of XML documents: *well formed* and *valid*. Listing 7.1 is an example of a well-formed XML document. Valid XML documents have two additional elements: an XML declaration and the specification of a DTD for the document. An XML document must obey the DTD to be valid. A DTD specifies legal tags and can optionally specify rules for the type of data that can be stored in tags. We will not use DTDs in this book, but when we use CDF documents, which are also well-formed XML documents, we will specify an XML declaration.

We see in Listing 7.3 that the **SampleReader** program prints out all of the text associated with an element starting on the same line as the beginning element tag. Some text wraps to new lines. We use the method **Element.getText( )**, which returns a list of the text for a tag, followed by the text for all nested tags. Notice that the **getText( )** method performs a depth-first search of nested elements; text returned from the **getText( )** method is ordered by this depth-first search.

7.2   Design of a Java browser for XML documents

In Listing 7.1, we saw how easy it is to read an XML document, create a **Document** object, and traverse the tree structure of the document. In this section, we will design a Java applet that can be used to browse XML documents, hiding subelements or showing hidden subelements by clicking on a tree display with a mouse.

The following steps are required for displaying an XML document in tree form:

- Create a new Java application frame.
- Create an instance of **UITree** (or a subclass of **UITree**) in the application frame.
- Use a depth-first walk of the specified XML document (similar to the class **SampleReader** seen in Listing 7.2) to find each nested element in the document.
- Create a new node in the display tree for each nested XML element.

Figure 7.3 shows the UML class diagram for **XMLBrowser**.

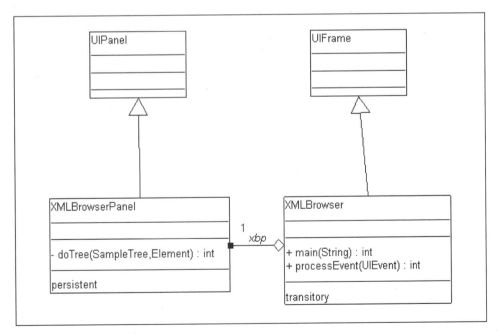

Figure 7.3   *UML class diagram for **XMLBrowser***

7.3 Implementation of a Java browser for XML documents

This example is very simple to implement because we use the tree component defined in the file **c:\mjava\demo\SampleTree.java** that we developed in Chapter 2. The **XMLBrowser** class, seen in Listing 7.4, is derived from the AFC class **UIFrame**. The constructor for **XMLBrowser** has two required arguments:

- A frame/window title
- The file name or URL for an XML document

The constructor for class **XMLBrowser** creates an instance of the class **XMLBrowserPanel** (which is implemented as a local class in Listing 7.4). The constructor for the class **XMLBrowserPanel** creates a top-level instance of the class **SampleTree** and then recursively walks the specified XML document, adding subtrees (also of class **SampleTree**) to the top-level **SampleTree** for each nested element in the specified XML document.

Listing 7.4

```
// XMLBrowser.java
//
// Derived from a few examples from Microsoft.
//

package com.markwatson.xml;

import com.ms.xml.*;
import com.markwatson.util.*;
import com.markwatson.demo.SampleTree;

import java.util.Enumeration;
```

```java
import java.io.*;
import java.io.PrintStream;
import java.net.*;

import java.awt.*;
import java.net.URL;
import com.ms.ui.*;
import com.ms.ui.event.*;
import com.ms.fx.*;

public class XMLBrowser extends UIFrame
{
  public static void main(String args[])
  {
    if (args.length < 1) {
      System.out.println("Requires an arg: XML file name");
      System.exit(1);
    }
    try {
      XMLBrowser uiframe = new XMLBrowser(args[0],
              args[0]);
      uiframe.setBackground(FxColor.lightGray);
      uiframe.setSize(180, 250);
      uiframe.setVisible(true);
    }
    catch (Exception e) { e.printStackTrace(); }
  }

  public XMLBrowser(String str, String xml_file) {
    super (str);
    enableEvents(AWTEvent.WINDOW_EVENT_MASK);
    setLayout(new UIBorderLayout(0, 0));
    setFont(new Font("Dialog", Font.BOLD, 12));
    XMLBrowserPanel xbp = new XMLBrowserPanel(xml_file);
    add("Center", xbp);
    xbp.setVisible(true);
  }

  public void processEvent(UIEvent evt) { // JDK 1.1
    switch (evt.getID()) {
    case Event.WINDOW_DESTROY:
```

(continued)

Listing 7.4 *(continued)*

```java
      System.exit(0);
    default:
      super.processEvent(evt);
    }
  }
}

class XMLBrowserPanel extends UIPanel {

  XMLBrowserPanel(String xml_file)  {
    SampleTree tv;

    setLayout(new UIBorderLayout());

    tv = new SampleTree(xml_file);

    URL url = null;
    try {
      url = new URL(xml_file);
    } catch (MalformedURLException ex) {
      File f = new File(xml_file);
      try {
        String path = f.getAbsolutePath();
        path.replace('\\', '/');
        url = new URL("file:///" + path);
      } catch (MalformedURLException e) {
        System.out.println("Cannot create URL for: " + xml_file);
        System.exit(0);
      }
    }

    Document d = new Document();
    try {
      d.load(url);
    } catch (ParseException e) {
      d.reportError(e, System.out);
    }
    // Get all of the elements recursively:
```

```
    Element e = d.getRoot();
    int depth = 0;
    doTree((SampleTree)tv, e);

    add(new UIScrollViewer(tv), "Center");
  }

private void doTree(SampleTree root, Element e) {
  if (e==null) return;
  if (e.getTagName()==null) return;
  if (root==null) return;
  SampleTree tv = new SampleTree(e.getTagName());
  if (e.numElements() < 2) tv.add(e.getText());

  Enumeration enum = e.getChildren();
  while (enum.hasMoreElements()) {
    Element e2 = (Element)enum.nextElement();
    doTree(tv, e2);
  }
  root.add(tv);
  }
}
```

The implementation of the **XMLBrowser** class was fairly simple because we used three existing assets:

- The **SampleTree** class developed in Chapter 2
- Microsoft's XML parser
- The logic for the **doTree** method (modified from Listing 7.2)

Figure 7.4 shows the **XMLBrowser** class used as a stand-alone application.

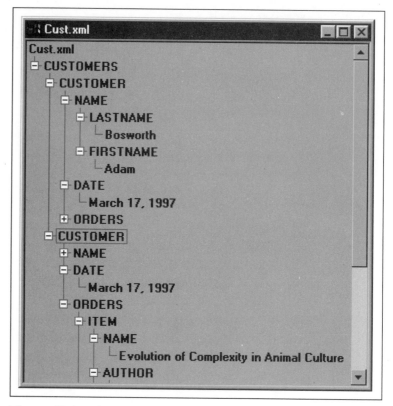

Figure 7.4   *The XMLBrowser*

7.4 Overview of CDF

The Channel Definition Format is based on XML. Like
XML-based documents, CDF-based documents are inherently tree-structured (actually, named tags allow a more
general graph structure). CDF allows developers of Web
content to specify metadata indicating which parts of the
document should be searched by Internet search engines
and for customized document viewers to customize
delivery and presentation of information based on the
viewer's preferences.

The Web site *www.microsoft.com/xml* contains a wealth of information on both XML and CDF. George Young, with Microsoft, has written two good tutorials on creating CDF documents, which are available online at Microsoft's XML Web site. I recommend that you read these two tutorials and other CDF-related material at Microsoft's Web site since the material in this chapter deals more with Java programs that use XML and CDF rather than serving as a complete tutorial on manually creating CDF documents.

7.5 Example CDF document

We have seen that XML documents are similar to HTML documents with two exceptions:

- Beginning tags must have a matching ending tag.
- You may "make up" new tag names to represent new element types.

CDF documents are proper XML documents. Listing 7.5 shows a simple CDF document, which is in the file **c:\mjava\xml\text.xml**, that is also a valid XML document. The IE 4.0 now contains a built-in XML parser that is used to parse CDF documents. The API for this parser is documented at Microsoft's Web site *www.microsoft.com/xml*, and is recommended if you are processing XML documents in programs written in C++. The first line in Listing 7.5 is referred to as an XML declaration that specifies which version of XML is used to encode this document.

Listing 7.5

```
<?XML Version="1.0"?>
<CHANNEL HREF="http://127.0.0.1:9090/chan1.htm">
```

(continued)

Listing 7.5 *(continued)*

```
    <ABSTRACT>This is a simple channel</ABSTRACT>
    <TITLE>Mark's Channel</TITLE>
    <ITEM HREF="http://127.0.0.1:9090/chan2.htm">
      <ABSTRACT>First item for Mark's channel</ABSTRACT>
      <TITLE>Title for first sample channel item</TITLE>
    </ITEM>
</CHANNEL>
```

As we see in Listing 7.5, the top-level element in a CDF document is a **CHANNEL**. A **CHANNEL** element contains at least the following three nested elements:

- An **ABSTRACT** element indicating what type of information is available in the channel

- A **TITLE** element that will appear in the IE 4.0 channel menu if the channel is installed in IE 4.0

- One or more **ITEM** elements that specify elements that may be selected from the channel for viewing

Stylesheets for XML documents

The World Wide Web Consortium (*www.www.org*) is currently approving the final specifications for both XML and the Extensible Stylesheet Language (XSL). An XSL file specifies information that indicates how to render (or display) XML documents. ArborText is a developer of both SGML and XML tools. If you want to write your own XSL files, you can download the **XSLStyler** program for free from their Web site (*www.arbortext.com*).

You probably already use channels in IE 4.0. If not, you might want to get on the Internet now and try installing a few channels in the IE 4.0 before working through the Java programming example in this chapter that creates channel data.

Listing 7.6 shows the HTML file **c:\mjava\xml\ chan1.htm** that is referenced in the CDF file shown in Listing 7.5.

Listing 7.6

```
<HTML>
  <HEAD>
    <TITLE>chan1 info</TITLE>
  </HEAD>
  <BODY>
    This is the HTML page for channel
    <B>chan1</B>
  </BODY>
</HTML>
```

Listing 7.7 shows the HTML file **c:\mjava\xml\ chan2.htm** that is referenced in the CDF file shown in Listing 7.5.

Listing 7.7

```
<HTML>
  <HEAD>
    <TITLE>chan2 info</TITLE>
  </HEAD>
  <BODY>
    This is the HTML page for the first channel
    <B>ITEM</B>
  </BODY>
</HTML>
```

We will use the channel file seen in Listing 7.5 and the HTML files seen in Listings 7.6 and 7.7 for testing our

CDF-enabled Web server that we will implement in Section 7.6. CDF is one of the first commercial uses of XML. I believe that the widespread use of XML for document preparation and distribution will enable a new generation of software tools both for interactively browsing information sources and for automated software agents that will find information that we are likely to be interested in.

7.6   Implementing a customized CDF Web server in Java

One of the most compelling uses for the Java programming language is for server-side applications. Although Java gained its initial popularity for allowing Web developers to write client-side applets, Java's support for automatic garbage collection, multiple threading, exception handling, and strong network programming library support make Java arguably the most efficient development language (in terms of software development time) for network applications. In this section, we will develop an example Web server that also supports sending CDF document streams back to the IE 4.0 Web browser.

The example CDF-enhanced Web server seen in Listing 7.8 uses port number 9090 (by default) for accepting socket connections from Web browsers. Sun's Java Web Server also uses port 9090 by default, so you will want to change the default if you run the Java Web Server on the same machine. For developing and testing the CDF-enhanced Web server, implemented as class **XMLServer** in Listing 7.8, I simply run both **XMLServer** as a stand-alone Java application and IE 4.0 on the same computer, using the following base URL to access the **XMLServer**: *127.0.0.1:9090*.

The IP address 127.0.0.1 always refers to the local computer; the URL specifies that the IE 4.0 browser will attempt to open a socket connection with a Web server at port 9090, instead of the default port 80.

The **XMLServer** functions as a typical Web server. For example, referring to the URL *127.0.0.1:9090/test.html* causes the **XMLServer** to look for a file **test.html** in the directory in which it is run and returns the contents of the file to the IE 4.0 browser. The **XMLServer** supports multiple simultaneous connections from different browsers. In addition to "normal Web server behavior," the **XMLServer** processes URLs of the form: *127.0.0.1:9090/XML?* in a special way. Any characters following "XML?" in the URL are passed to the method **processXML**. The method **processXML** returns a string value that is returned to the Web browser.

Figure 7.5 shows the UML class diagram for the **XMLServer** class.

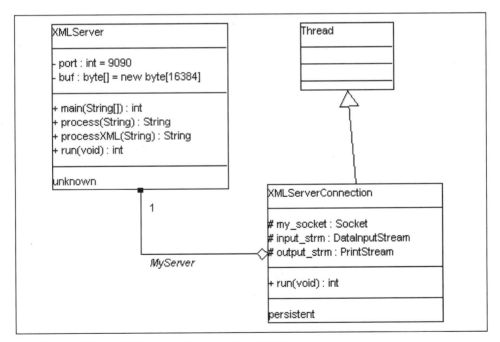

Figure 7.5   *UML class diagram for **XMLServer***

Troubleshooting IP problems on your development machine

If you are having problems getting a connection when you specify a URL like *127.0.0.1:9090* under Windows 95, either of the following two procedures will probably make things work:

- Edit the file **\Windows\hosts** and add your machine name with the address 127.0.0.1.

- Connect to the Internet through a dial-up service provider. See if the examples work while you are connected.

Actually, just adding your machine name to **\Windows\hosts** should do the trick. Here is my **\Windows\hosts** file:

```
127.0.0.1          localhost
127.0.0.1          colossus
```

Note that "colossus" is my machine name.

The implementation of class **XMLServer** has a simple default **processXML** method; however, for your applications, you will want to subclass **XMLServer**, providing your own application-specific version of **processXML**. In Chapter 9, we will reuse the **XMLServer** class by deriving a new class that accesses data in relational databases, wraps the data in XML, and returns it to an applet.

There are two classes defined in Listing 7.8:

- The **XMLServer** class can be run as a stand-alone Java application and both functions as a "normal" Web server and can be subclassed to provide (server) application-specific behavior for your distributed Internet applications that require CDF support.
- The **XMLServerConnection** class runs in a separate thread for each new client connection to an **XMLServer** object.

The class **XMLServer** is meant to be subclassed for your applications. Specifically, you will want to override the method

```
Public String processXML(String command)
```

If the **XMLServer** receives a URL request of the form

127.0.0:9060/XML?a_command

then the string after the question mark ("a_command" in this example) is passed as the argument to the method **processXML**. All URL requests not containing the string "XML?" are treated as normal URLs.

Listing 7.8

```
// XMLServer.java
//
// This class implements a Web server that both
// functions as a "normal" Web server and has
// hooks for special processing of XML data
// stream requests.
```

(continued)

Listing 7.8 *(continued)*

```java
//
// Copyright 1998, by Mark Watson.  This software
// may be freely used in compiled form, but the
// source code may not be distributed without
// permission.
//

package com.markwatson.xml;

import java.io.*;
import java.util.*;
import java.net.*;

public class XMLServer {

  static public void main(String [] args) {
    if (args.length > 0) {
      new XMLServer(Integer.parseInt(args[0]));
    } else {
      new XMLServer();
    }
  }

  protected int port - 9090;

  public XMLServer(int p) {
    port - p;
    run();
  }

  public XMLServer() {
    run();
  }

  // allocate a buffer once only:
  private byte [] buf - new byte[16384];

  // Callback from XMLServerConnection class:
  public String process(String command) {
    System.out.println("XMLServer.process(" + command + ")");
```

```java
    int index = -1;

    // Check for a special "XML?" command in the URL:
    index = command.indexOf("XML?");
    if (index == -1) index = command.indexOf("xml?");
    if (index > -1) {
      String c = command.substring(index+4);
      index = c.indexOf(" ");
      c = c.substring(0,index);
      return processXML(c);
    }

    // Check for a "GET /"
    index = command.indexOf("GET /");
    if (index > -1) {
      String file_name = command.substring(5);
      index = file_name.indexOf(" ");
      file_name = file_name.substring(0,index);
      File f = new File(file_name);
      int num = 0;
      try {
        FileInputStream in = new FileInputStream(f);
        num = in.read(buf, 0, 16384);
      } catch (Exception e) { }
      if (num>0) return new String(buf, 0, num);
      else       return "<HTML><BODY>Error, bad URL " +
                   "(XMLServer)</BODY></HTML>";
    }

    // Return an HTML data stream containing an error message
    return "<HTML><HEAD><TITLE>XMLServer error</TITLE>" +
      "</HEAD>\n<BODY>Unknown <B>XMSserver</B> command</BODY></HTML>";
  }


  // Override this method in your applications
  public String processXML(String command) {
    System.out.println("processXML(" + command + ")");
    String s = "<HTML><BODY><B>Response from stub " +
      "XMLServer.processXML()</B><p><p>" +
```

(continued)

Listing 7.8 *(continued)*

```
      "You should subclass <B>XMLServer</B>, overriding this " +
      "method, adding your own XML processing code." +
      "<p>XML processing request:<P><pre>\n" +
      command + "\n</pre>" +
      "</BODY></HTML>";
    return s;
  }

  public void run() {
    ServerSocket serverSocket;
    try {
      serverSocket = new ServerSocket(port, 2000);
    } catch (IOException e) {
      System.out.println("XMLServer: " + e);
      return;
    }

    try {
      while (true) {
        Socket socket = serverSocket.accept();
        new XMLServerConnection(this, socket);
      }
    } catch (IOException e) {
      System.out.println("Error: new socket connection: " + e);
    } finally {
      try {
        serverSocket.close();
      } catch (IOException e) {
        System.out.println("I/O exception: " + e);
      }
    }
  }
}
```

Listing 7.9 shows the implementation of the class **XMLServerConnection**, which is used by instances of class **XMLServer** to manage incoming socket connections.

Listing 7.9

```
// XMLServerConnection.java
//
// A connection class used by instances of XMLServer
//
// Copyright 1998, by Mark Watson.  This software
// may be freely used in compiled form, but the
// source code may not be distributed without
// permission.
//

package com.markwatson.xml;

import java.io.*;
import java.util.*;
import java.net.*;

// Utility class to manage socket connections:

public class XMLServerConnection extends Thread {
  protected transient Socket my_socket;
  protected transient DataInputStream input_strm;
  protected transient PrintStream output_strm;
  protected transient XMLServer MyServer;

  public XMLServerConnection(XMLServer server,
                             Socket client_socket) {
    MyServer = server;
    my_socket = client_socket;
    try {
      input_strm  = new DataInputStream(my_socket.getInputStream());
      output_strm = new PrintStream(my_socket.getOutputStream());
    }
    catch (IOException io_exception) {
      try { my_socket.close(); } catch (IOException io_ex2) {  };
      System.err.println("Exception: getting socket streams " +
        io_exception);
      return;
    }
    // Start the thread (i.e., call method 'run'):
```

(continued)

Listing 7.9 *(continued)*

```
    this.start();
    System.out.println("XMLServerConnection is set up.");
  }

  public void run() {
    String input_buf;
    String s_ret = "";
    try {
      while (true) {
          input_buf = input_strm.readLine();
          if (input_buf == null) break;
          //System.out.println("web browser request: " + input_buf);
          if (input_buf.indexOf("GET") > -1 ||
              input_buf.indexOf("XML") > -1 ||
              input_buf.indexOf("xml") > -1)
            {
              s_ret = MyServer.process(input_buf);
            }
          if (input_buf.length() < 2) {
              output_strm.print(s_ret);
              output_strm.flush();
              System.out.println("response:\n" + s_ret);
              break;
          }
      }
    }
    catch (Exception exception) { }
    finally {
      try {
        my_socket.close();
      }
      catch (Exception exception) { };
    }
  }
}
```

You can run the **XMLServer** by typing

```
cd c:\mjava\xml
jview com.markwatson.xml.XMLServer
```

Figures 7.6 through 7.9 show screen shots of the IE 4.0 browser while interacting with the **XMLServer** Java application that is seen in Listing 7.8.

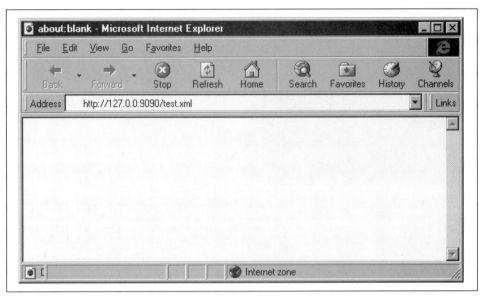

Figure 7.6   *The IE 4.0 Web browser has just requested the URL test.html from a Web server running on the local machine and listening to port 9090. IE 4.0 is waiting for a response.*

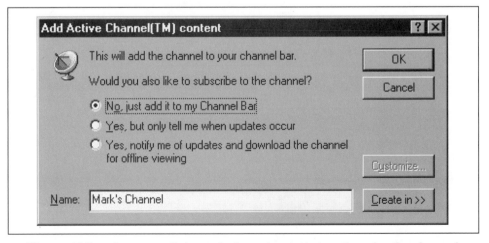

Figure 7.7   *A pop-up dialog asks for subscription options for the channel created by the **XMLServer** example. Here, we do not use the default option but click on "No, just add it to my Channel Bar".*

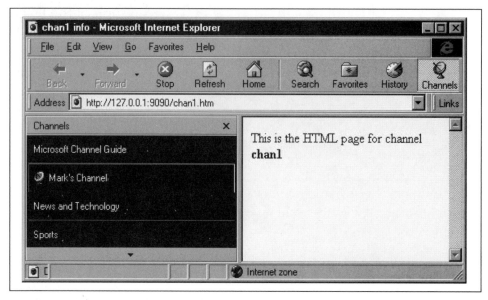

Figure 7.8   *After IE 4.0 has asked the user for channel installation options, it displays the channel menu frame showing all installed channels. Notice that the new channel "Mark's Channel," which has been delivered from the **XMLServer**, is now visible and available for viewing.*

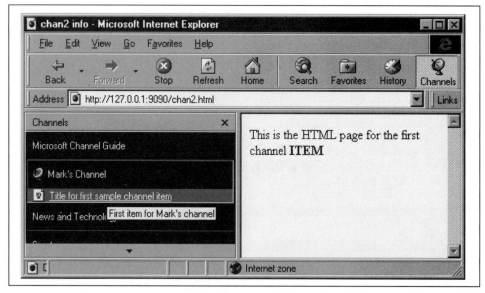

Figure 7.9   *The user has selected the first item in "Mark's Channel."*

Custom Desktop/WebTop in Java

One of the great things about the Internet Explorer 4.0 is the optional ActiveX desktop. This allows you to customize your personal desktop by adding Java applets and ActiveX controls. In this chapter, we will take two different approaches to customizing the desktop (or WebTop):

- We will develop a Java class framework that includes a class for "taking over" the entire desktop and a Java class that is used for wrapping JavaBean, applets, and Java applications into "dockable" components. We will implement these classes, then quickly construct a sample custom desktop/WebTop that contains components for text editing and reading Internet newsgroups (yes, we are reusing the newsreader Java class library again!).

- We will provide an example of adding Java components to the standard Microsoft ActiveX desktop.

If you are adventurous, you can have fun experimenting with different desktop designs. The classes developed in this chapter might also be a useful jumping-off point for developers of networked thin client workstations.

8.1 Taking over the desktop

We will design and implement a simple class, **DesktopFrame**, that is derived from the AFC class **UIFrame**. An instance of class **DesktopFrame** covers the entire desktop and serves as a Java application platform. A **DesktopFrame** is divided into two parts: a menu bar along the left edge and a large work space.

Figure 8.1 shows the UML class diagram for the classes **DeskTopFrame** and the mouse event handling inner class **myButtonMouseAdapter**.

The method **addApplication** requires two parameters: a string containing a menu item name and a component that will be made visible on the desktop when the menu item name is clicked with the mouse. The class **DesktopFrame** uses two private class variables for maintaining the desktop and applications:

- **applications**—an array of **UIComponent** objects used to store references to all components that have been added to the desktop with the method **addApplication**

- **names**—an array of strings for the menu items

Listing 8.1 shows the implementation of the **DesktopFrame** class.

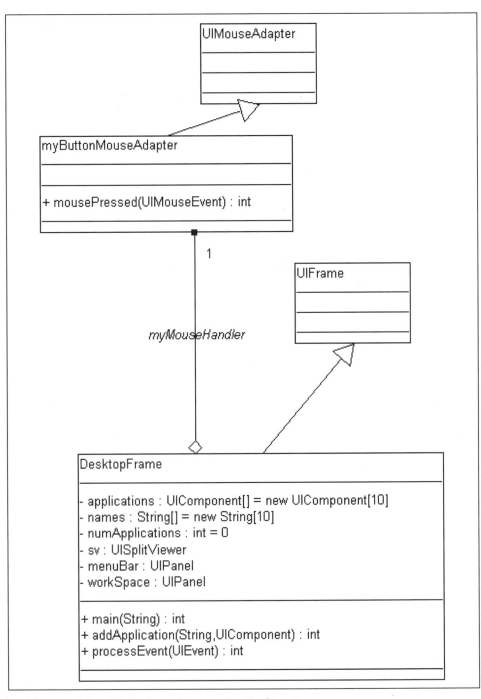

Figure 8.1   *UML class diagram for **DesktopFrame***

Listing 8.1

```java
// com.markwatson.util.DesktopFrame.java
//
// An example application platform that supplies
// a menu list and a work area.
//


package com.markwatson.util;

import java.awt.*;
import com.ms.ui.*;
import com.ms.ui.event.*;
import com.ms.fx.*;

import com.markwatson.news.*;

public class DesktopFrame extends UIFrame {

  public static void main(String args[]) {
    DesktopFrame f = new DesktopFrame("");
    f.setBounds(-11, -25, 1100, 910);
    // add two dummy applications for testing:
    UIEdit et = new UIEdit("Back up hard disk\n" +
                           "Answer Email\n" +
                           "Take out trash\n");
    f.addApplication("To do list", et);
    NewsPanel np = new NewsPanel();
    f.addApplication("Newsreader", np);
    f.setVisible(true);
  }

  public DesktopFrame(String str) {
    super (str);
    enableEvents(AWTEvent.WINDOW_EVENT_MASK);
    setFont(new Font("Dialog", Font.BOLD, 12));
    menuBar = new UIPanel();
    menuBar.setBackground(FxColor.lightGray);
    workSpace = new UIPanel();
    menuBar.setBackground(FxColor.white);
    workSpace.setLayout(new UIVerticalFlowLayout());
```

```
    menuBar.setLayout(new UIVerticalFlowLayout());
    UIDrawText te = new UIDrawText(" Menu");
    te.setFont(new FxFont("Helvetica", 0, 18));
    menuBar.add(te);
    UIDrawText txt = new UIDrawText("Work space");
    txt.setFont(new FxFont("Helvetica", 0, 18));
    workSpace.add(txt);
    UISplitViewer sv = new UISplitViewer(menuBar, workSpace,
                                          0, -12, true);

    add(sv);
  }

  private UIComponent applications [] = new UIComponent[10];
  private String names [] = new String[10];
  private int numApplications = 0;

  public void addApplication(String name, UIComponent app) {
    names[numApplications] = name;
    applications[numApplications++] = app;
    UIPushButton b = new UIPushButton(name);
    myMouseHandler = new myButtonMouseAdapter();
    b.addMouseListener(myMouseHandler);
    menuBar.add(b);
    b.setVisible(true);
    app.setVisible(false);
    workSpace.add(app);
  }

  private myButtonMouseAdapter myMouseHandler;
  private UISplitViewer sv;
  private UIPanel menuBar;
  private UIPanel workSpace;

  class myButtonMouseAdapter extends UIMouseAdapter {
    public void mousePressed(UIMouseEvent me) {
      String button_name = ((UIText)(me.getSource())).getName();
      for (int i=0; i<numApplications; i++) {
        if (names[i].equals(button_name)) {
          System.out.println("Match at " + i);
```

(continued)

Listing 8.1 *(continued)*

```
        applications[i].setVisible(true);
        //workSpace.add(applications[i]);
      } else {
        applications[i].setVisible(false);
      }
    }
  }
}

public void processEvent(UIEvent evt) { // JDK 1.1
  switch (evt.getID())  {
  case Event.WINDOW_DESTROY:
    System.exit(0);
  default:
    super.processEvent(evt);
  }
 }
}
}
```

How to hide the Windows 95 and NT 4.0 desktop menu bar

Depending on how you configure your system, your Windows 95 or Windows NT 4.0 desktop menu bar (or task bar) might still be visible when running the example program in Listing 8.1. If you want your custom Java desktop to hide the standard desktop menu bar, right mouse click on a blank area of the menu bar and choose the "Properties" option. Disable the option "Always on top".

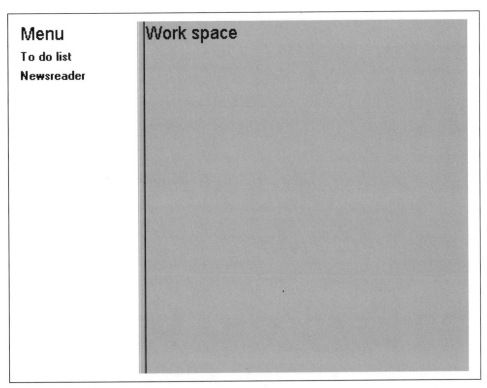

Figure 8.2   *DesktopFrame using the example "applications" defined in List-*
ing 8.1. No applications have been activated.

Figures 8.2, 8.3, and 8.4 show the class **Desk-topFrame**. Figure 8.2 shows the program in Listing 8.1 running. No "applications" have been selected from the menu bar panel on the left-hand side of the figure. As seen in Listing 8.1, we specified that the background color of the menu bar panel is white and the background color of the work space panel is light gray.

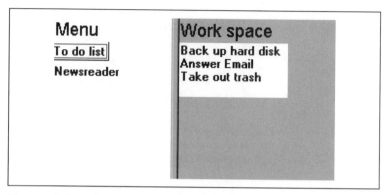

Figure 8.3 *The **DesktopFrame** after clicking on the "To do list" menu bar item. This figure only shows the upper left-hand corner of the **DesktopFrame**.*

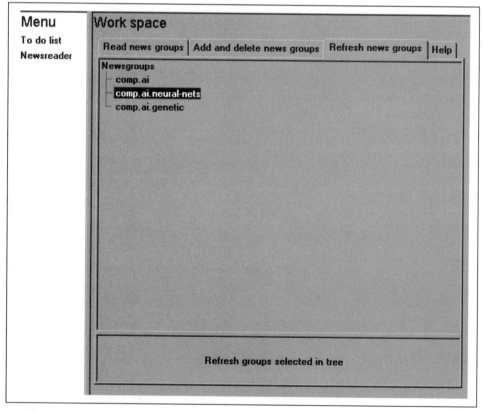

Figure 8.4 *The **DesktopFrame** after clicking on the "Newsreader" menu bar item*

Programming project—supporting icon menu items

The **DesktopFrame** class supports only text labels for menu items. However, these menu items are implemented as instances of the class **UIPushButton**. When you construct a new **UIPushButton** object, you can specify either a text label or an image. Derive a new class **IconDesktopFrame** that allows menu items to be specified as text labels or images. You will also need to modify the method **myButtonMouse-Adapter.mousePressed** that detects which menu item is selected with the mouse.

8.2 Adding Java applets to the Microsoft Active Desktop

In the last section, we developed a simple Java class that can be used on any Java platform to create custom desktops. In this section we demonstrate how to add Java applets to the Microsoft Active Desktop.

Assuming that you have the Active Desktop option installed, it is simple to add either your own components or prepackaged channels to your desktop. Channels are implemented using CDF and XML (see Chapter 7). Adding a component requires the following steps:

- Right mouse click on the Active Desktop and select the menu option "Active Desktop -> Customize my Desktop...".

- You should now see the standard Windows 95 or Windows NT 4 "Display Properties" dialog box, and the tab "Web" should be selected.

- Click the button "New". If you are asked if you want to see Microsoft's gallery of Active Desktop components, then click "No".

- You should now see a dialog box labeled "New Active Desktop Item". Enter the URL **c:\mjava\applets\test.html** and then click the "OK" button.

- You should now see the "Display Properties" dialog box, and the URL **c:\mjava\applets\test.html** should now be listed. Click the "Apply" button.

- Close the "Display Properties" dialog box and move the new component to a blank location on your desktop.

Do you have the Active Desktop option installed?

Having the Internet Explorer version 4.0 (or later) installed is a prerequisite for running many of the example programs in this book. If you want to experiment with the software in this section, you must also install the Active Desktop option for IE 4.0. You can do this by opening the "Control panel" and selecting "Add/Remove Programs". Select "Microsoft Internet Explorer 4.0" and click "Add/Remove"; then select the "Install Windows Active Desktop Component" option. You will have to be connected to the Internet in order to have the Active Desktop components downloaded from Microsoft's Web site.

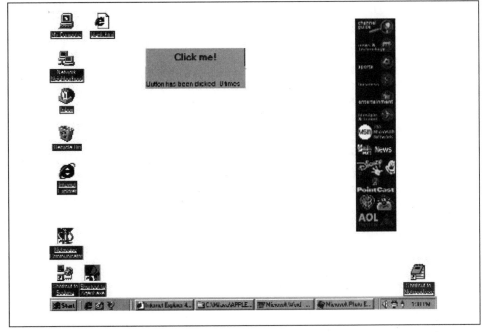

Figure 8.5   *Image of the Active Desktop with the test applet from Chapter 6 installed. The default Active Desktop menu bar is visible along the right-hand side of the screen.*

Figure 8.5 shows the **TestApplet** that we developed in Chapter 6 installed on the Active Desktop.

We see from this example that we can add any content to the Active Desktop that can be displayed in the IE 4.0 Web browser, including HTML, ActiveX components, and Java applets. When we start to design new Java applications, we seem to have several design choices that affect the usability, portability, and the look and feel of the application:

- Do we want to use the portable Java AWT user interface classes (most portable), the JavaSoft JFC user interface classes (portable but must be installed on client platform), or the Microsoft AFC classes (may be portable but must be installed on client platform)?

- Most client applications require access to some data source to be useful (e.g., a database, remote stock quote system, etc.). How do we separate user interface from data collection and data storage software components?

The first design decision is tough. When programming for the Windows platform, using the AFC makes our Java applications look like standard Windows 95/NT applications. Using AFC will probably affect the portability of our applications, however.

The second design decision is especially important when we realize that Java applets added to our Active Desktop will not, in general, have access to local disk files, and so on, because of the Java security model. The inability of Java applets to access local files is not necessarily bad because it encourages us to create multiple-tier application architectures in which we separate user interface, data collection, and data storage components. We will look at a complete example of a three-tier application in Chapter 9.

Three-Tier Application Example

At the end of Chapter 8 we showed how to install our Java applets in Microsoft's Active Desktop. One problem that we will have with these applets is that they will not be able to access local files and databases because of Java's security model. We will address this problem in this chapter by developing a three-tier application with three separate components: user interface (a Java applet), separate data collection agent (a subclass of the **XMLServer** developed in Chapter 7), and a separate data source (a local Microsoft Access database).

The Java applet will call a new class **DBXMLServer** that wraps database query information as a series of XML elements. XML tag names will be the database column names returned from a query. The **DBXMLServer** class will be created by subclassing the **XMLServer** class, with an ODBC-based database interface added. The middle layer pulls data from the Access database, wraps it as XML, and passes it to the applet for rendering. The

DBXMLServer class uses the standard Java database access API JDBC. I developed and tested the **DBXMLServer** class using Sun/JavaSoft's JDK, available from the Web site *java.sun.com*.

9.1 Design of the three-tier system

The three-tier system consists of the following components:

- Java applet serves as a user interface for retrieving information from a database
- Modified **XMLServer** (from Chapter 7), which accepts database queries from the applet, accesses a relational database to obtain query information, and wraps the retrieved data as a well-formed XML data stream that is returned to the applet
- A relational database (we will use Microsoft Access in this chapter)

Figure 9.1 shows a UML class diagram for the user interface applet implemented as class **ViewXML**. The class **ViewXML** will use a separate implementation class **ViewXMLImplementation**, similar to the example applet in Chapter 6. The applet will contain several visual components:

- Title
- Push button for fetching all available names from a remote database
- List that is used for displaying all names retrieved from a remote database
- Text area that is used to display, as an XML document, all information for a person selected from the list component

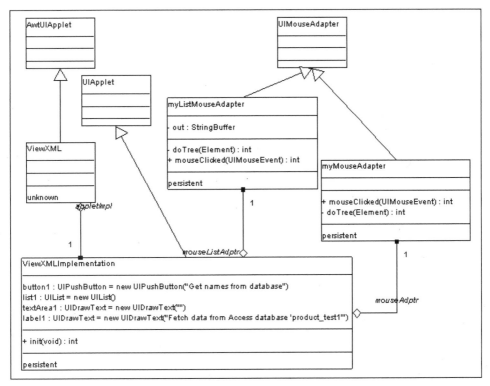

Figure 9.1   *UML class diagram for ViewXML*

The class **ViewXMLImplementation** uses two inner classes, **myListMouseAdapter** and **myMouseAdapter**, to handle mouse events for the list component and the push button component. Both of these inner classes must process well-formed XML document data streams. Both inner classes implement a private method **doTree** that recursively processes an XML document. Note that both **doTree** methods are similar to the method with the same name in the **SampleReader** class that we developed in Chapter 7.

Figure 9.2 shows a UML class diagram for the **DBInterface** class. The public API for the **DBInterface** class is simple. There are public static methods:

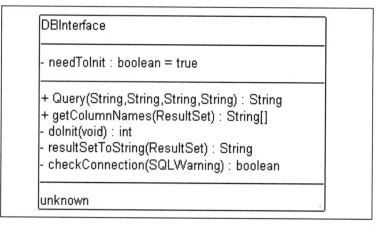

Figure 9.2   *UML class diagram for* **DBInterface**

- **Query**—queries a specified database given an SQL query string, a URL containing the JDBC/ODBC driver and database source name, database account name, and database password. The query results are returned as a **String** containing well-formed XML elements (one element for each query row returned from the SQL query).

- **getColumnNames**—returns column heads.

Figure 9.3 shows a UML class diagram for the **DBXMLServer** class, derived from the **XMLServer** class developed in Chapter 7. The **DBXMLServer** class only requires two methods to be defined:

- **main**—This public static method allows instances of this class to run as stand-alone Java applications.

- **processXML**—This method has one argument, a **String** passed to the Web server; this method returns a **String** containing a well-formed XML document.

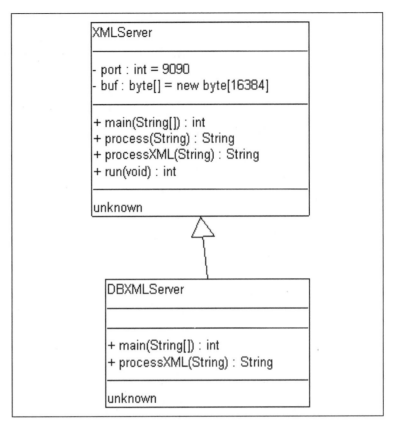

Figure 9.3   *UML class diagram for **DBXMLServer***

9.2 Implementation of the three-tier system

Listing 9.1 shows the user interface for the database query applet implemented as class **ViewXML**. The class **ViewXML** is derived from the AFC class **AwtUIApplet**; the constructor for **ViewXML** creates a new instance of the applet implementation class **ViewXMLImplementation** and passes this instance to the constructor for class **AwtUIApplet**.

We see a useful Java coding trick in Listing 9.1. In setting up the user interface, we specify a **null** layout manager for the applet (or container), add each component to the container, and then use the **setBounds** method to precisely specify the position and size of the component inside the container. You must call **setBounds** for each component after adding each component to the container.

Listing 9.1

```java
// com.markwatson.xml.threetier.ViewXML.java
//
// Example applet that accesses the DBXMLServer
//
// Copyright 1998, Mark Watson. This program
// may be reused without restriction.
//

package com.markwatson.xml.threetier;

import java.io.*;
import java.net.*;

import com.ms.xml.ParseException;
import com.ms.xml.Document;
import com.ms.xml.Element;
import com.ms.xml.Attribute;

import java.util.Enumeration;

import com.ms.ui.*;
import com.ms.ui.event.*;
import com.ms.fx.*;

public class ViewXML extends AwtUIApplet { // bridge
  public ViewXML()    {
    super(new ViewXMLImplementation());
  }
}
```

```
class ViewXMLImplementation extends UIApplet {

  UIPushButton button1 = new UIPushButton("Get names from database");
  UIList list1 = new UIList();
  UIDrawText textArea1 = new UIDrawText("");
  UIDrawText label1 =
  new UIDrawText("Fetch data from Access database 'product_test1'");

  public void init() {
    System.out.println("in init()");
    setLayout(null);
    label1.setFont(new FxFont("Dialog", FxFont.BOLD, 15));
    label1.setBackground(new FxColor(130,225,255));
    add(label1);
    label1.setBounds(14, 14, 372, 30);
    button1.addMouseListener(new myMouseAdapter());
    button1.setBackground(new FxColor(180,225,85));
    add(button1);
    button1.setBounds(13, 53, 152, 71);
    list1.setBackground(new FxColor(140,15,255));
    list1.addMouseListener(new myListMouseAdapter());
    UIScrollViewer vs = new UIScrollViewer(list1);
    add(vs);
    list1.setBounds(1, 1, 200, 71);
    vs.setBounds(172, 53, 214, 71);
    textArea1.setBackground(new FxColor(160,225,205));
    add(textArea1);
    textArea1.setBounds(14, 136, 372, 147);
  }

  class myMouseAdapter extends UIMouseAdapter {

    private void doTree(Element e) {
      if (e==null) return;
      if (e.getTagName()==null) return;
      System.out.println("<" + e.getTagName() + "> " + e.getText());
      if (e.getTagName().equalsIgnoreCase("NAME")) {
        list1.add(new UIText(e.getText()));
      }
```

(continued)

Listing 9.1 *(continued)*

```
      Enumeration enum = e.getChildren();
      while (enum.hasMoreElements()) {
        Element e2 = (Element)enum.nextElement();
        if (e2!=null) {
          doTree(e2);
        }
      }
    }

    public void mouseClicked(UIMouseEvent me) {
      System.out.println("mouse pressed");
      String fileName = "http://127.0.0.1:9090/XML?allnames";
      try {
        URL url = null;
        try {
          url = new URL(fileName);
        } catch (MalformedURLException ex) {
          File f = new File(fileName);
          try {
            String path = f.getAbsolutePath();
            path.replace('\\', '/');
            url = new URL("file:///" + path);
          } catch (MalformedURLException e) {
            System.out.println("Cannot create URL for: " + fileName);
            System.exit(0);
          }
        }
        Document d = new Document();
        try {
          d.load(url);
        } catch (ParseException e) {
          d.reportError(e, System.out);
        }
        // Get all of the elements recursively:
        Element e = d.getRoot();
        int depth = 0;
        doTree(e);
      } catch (Exception e) {
        System.out.println("Exception: " + e);
      }
```

```java
    }
}

// Handle mouse click events from the name selection list:
class myListMouseAdapter extends UIMouseAdapter {

  private StringBuffer out;

  private void doTree(Element e) {
    if (e==null) return;
    if (e.getTagName()==null) return;
    if (e.getTagName().equals("DBDATA") == false &&
        e.getTagName().equals("NAMEQUERY") == false) {
      out.append("    <" + e.getTagName() + ">" +
                 e.getText() +
                 "</" + e.getTagName() + ">\n");
    }
    Enumeration enum = e.getChildren();
    while (enum.hasMoreElements()) {
      Element e2 = (Element)enum.nextElement();
      if (e2!=null) {
        doTree(e2);
      }
    }
  }

  public void mouseClicked(UIMouseEvent me) {
    String item_name = ((UIText)(me.getSource())).getName();
    System.out.println("mouse pressed: " + item_name);
    out = new StringBuffer("<" + item_name + ">\n");

    String fileName = "http://127.0.0.1:9090/XML?name=" +
      item_name + "*";
    try {
      URL url = null;
      try {
        url = new URL(fileName);
      } catch (MalformedURLException ex) {
        File f = new File(fileName);
        try {
```

(continued)

Listing 9.1 *(continued)*

```
        String path = f.getAbsolutePath();
        path.replace('\\', '/');
        url = new URL("file:///" + path);
      } catch (MalformedURLException e) {
        System.out.println("error: URL: "+ fileName);
        System.exit(0);
      }
    }
    Document d = new Document();
    try {
      d.load(url);
    } catch (ParseException e) {
      d.reportError(e, System.out);
    }
    // Get all of the elements recursively:
    Element e = d.getRoot();
    int depth = 0;
    doTree(e);
  } catch (Exception e) {
    System.out.println("Exception: " + e);
  }
  textArea1.setValueText(
                  new String(out.append(("</" +
                                      item_name +
                                      ">\n"))));
    }
  }
}
```

Listing 9.2 shows a database interface class **DBInterface** that uses the JDBC/ODBC Java class libraries. The **DBXMLServer** class (shown in Listing 9.3) will use this class. The **DBInterface** class was tested with the JavaSoft JDK 1.1 (or later) runtime system. You can download Sun/JavaSoft's JDK from *java.sun.com*. The database access utility class **DBInterface** only supports querying (i.e., reading) databases; you can download a version of **DBInterface** from my Web site (see *www.markwatson.com/umlbook.html*) that supports querying and database modification.

Listing 9.2

```java
// DBInterface.java
//
// Static class for easy access to
// ODBC-compliant databases via JDBC.
//
// Copyright Mark Watson, 1997
//
// Note on URL specifying database driver:
// If you install the JavaSoft JDK 1.1, and
// set up ODBC, use the driver url="jdbc:odbc:XXX"
// where XXX is the name of the database as
// defined when you run the ODBC control panel
// (in Windows 95/NT).

package com.markwatson.xml.threetier;

import java.rmi.*;
import java.rmi.server.UnicastRemoteObject;

import java.sql.*;

public class DBInterface
{
  // url=database driver name + database name
  static public String Query(String a_query, String url,
                        String user_id, String passwd) {
    System.out.println("\n\n++++++++++++++++++++++++\nQuery: " +
                    a_query + "\nurl=" + url);
    String results = "";

    try {

      doInit();

      // Connect to the JDBC driver:
      Connection con =
        DriverManager.getConnection(url, user_id, passwd);
      checkConnection(con.getWarnings()); // connection OK?
```

(continued)

Listing 9.2 *(continued)*

```
    Statement stmt = con.createStatement();

    // Submit a query:
    ResultSet rs = null;
    try {
      rs = stmt.executeQuery(a_query);
    } catch (SQLException se) {
      System.out.println("NO result set");
    }

    if (rs != null) {
      // Display all columns and rows from the result set
      results = resultSetToString(rs);

      // Close the result set
      rs.close();
    }

    // Close the statement
    stmt.close();

    // Close the connection
    con.close();
  }
  catch (SQLException ex) {
    while (ex != null) {
      System.out.println("SQL error message:  " + ex.getMessage());
      ex = ex.getNextException();
      System.out.println("");
      results = ex.getMessage();
    }
  }
  catch (java.lang.Exception ex) {
    ex.printStackTrace();
    results = ex.getMessage();
  }
  System.out.println("DBInterface.Select() results: " + results);
  return results;
}
```

```java
public static String [] getColumnNames(ResultSet rs_local)
    throws SQLException
{
  ResultSetMetaData rsmd = rs_local.getMetaData ();
  // Get the number of columns in the result set
  int numCols = rsmd.getColumnCount ();
  String s[] = new String[numCols];
  // Display column headings
  for (int i=1; i<=numCols; i++) {
    s[i-1] = new String(rsmd.getColumnLabel(i));
  }
  return s;
}


static private boolean needToInit = true;

static private void doInit() {
  if (needToInit) {
    try {
      // Load the JDBC driver
      Class.forName("sun.jdbc.odbc.JdbcOdbcDriver");
      // uncomment for debug printout:
      //DriverManager.setLogStream(System.out);
    } catch (Exception e) {
      System.out.println("Could not set up JDBC: " + e);
    }
    needToInit=false;
  }
}



// This method wraps data as multiple XML elements, so
// whoever gets the query information must wrap the
// returned XML stream in an enclosing XML element:

static private String resultSetToString(ResultSet rs)
    throws SQLException
{
  int i;
  String [] colNames = getColumnNames(rs);
```

(continued)

Listing 9.2 *(continued)*

```
StringBuffer outputText = new StringBuffer();
int numCols = rs.getMetaData().getColumnCount();
boolean more = rs.next();
while (more) {
  outputText.append("  <DBDATA>\n");
  for (i=1; i<=numCols; i++) {
    outputText.append("    <" + colNames[i-1] + ">");
    outputText.append(rs.getString(i));
    outputText.append("</" + colNames[i-1] + ">\n");
  }
  outputText.append("  </DBDATA>\n");
  if (i!=numCols)  outputText.append("\n");
  more = rs.next();
}
return new String(outputText);
}

static private boolean checkConnection(SQLWarning warning)
    throws SQLException  {
      boolean ret = false;
      if (warning != null) {
        System.out.println("\n *** Warning ***\n");
        ret = true;
        while (warning != null) {
          System.out.println("Message " + warning.getMessage());
          warning = warning.getNextWarning();
        }
      }
      return ret;
}
}
```

Listing 9.3 shows the implementation of the **DBXMLServer** class. The implementation of this class is very simple because it derives most of its behavior from its base class **XMLServer**. The method **processXML** is overridden from the base class implementation to provide the following behavior:

- Define the URL for the JDBC/ODBC driver and data source.

- Define the data source database account name.

- Define the data source database account password.

- Test for two options: return "allnames" in the database, or look for a request that begins with "name=". Build an appropriate SQL query for the request and call the static method **DBInterface.Query** to return a string containing zero or more XML elements; this list of elements is wrapped in a set of opening/closing XML tags.

Listing 9.3

```
// DBXMLServer.java
//
// This class implements a Web server that both
// functions as a "normal" Web server and has
// hooks for special processing of XML data
// stream requests.
//
// Copyright 1998, by Mark Watson.  This software
// may be freely used in compiled form, but the
// source code may not be distributed without
// permission.
//

package com.markwatson.xml.threetier;

import java.io.*;
import java.util.*;
import java.net.*;

import com.markwatson.xml.*;
import com.markwatson.db.tools.*;

class DBXMLServer extends XMLServer{
```

(continued)

Listing 9.3 *(continued)*

```java
static public void main(String [] args) {
  if (args.length > 0) {
    new DBXMLServer(Integer.parseInt(args[0]));
  } else {
    new DBXMLServer();
  }
}


public DBXMLServer(int p) {
  port = p; // inherited from base class XMLServer
  run();
}


public DBXMLServer() {
  run();    // inherited from base class XMLServer
}

// Override method from base class XMLServer:
public String processXML(String command) {

  String url    = "jdbc:odbc:product_test1";
  String user_id = "Admin";
  String passwd = "sammy";

  // Look for allnames command:
  if (command.equalsIgnoreCase("allnames")) {
    // use JDBC to access test database:
    String s = DBInterface.Query("SELECT Name from NameTable",
                                 url, user_id, passwd);
    System.out.println("query result=" + s);

    return "<ALLNAMES>\n" + s + "\n</ALLNAMES>\n";

  }

  int index = command.indexOf("name=");
  if (index == -1) {
    String s = "<HTML><BODY><B>Response from " +
      "DBXMLServer.processXML()</B><p><p>" +
```

```
        "Illegal request: \n<pre>\n" +
        command + "\n</pre>" +
        "</BODY></HTML>";
      return s;
    }

    int index2 = command.indexOf("*");
    String requested_name = command.substring(index + 5, index2);
    requested_name.trim();
    System.out.println("Name requested from DB=" + requested_name);
    // use JDBC to access test database:
    String s =
      DBInterface.Query("SELECT * from NameTable WHERE Name = '" +
      requested_name + "'",
      url, user_id, passwd);
    System.out.println("query result=" + s);

    return "<NAMEQUERY>\n" + s +
      "\n</NAMEQUERY>";

  }
}
```

Figure 9.4 shows the user interface applet. The XML that is received from the **DBXMLServer** application is read as a text stream and used to create an instance of the class **com.ms.xml.Document**. We recursively parse the **Document** object to build the display shown in the text area at the bottom of the applet. For the purposes of this applet, we could have simply displayed the text of the XML data stream, but we implemented the applet using Microsoft's Java XML parser to serve as another example of processing XML tags and data.

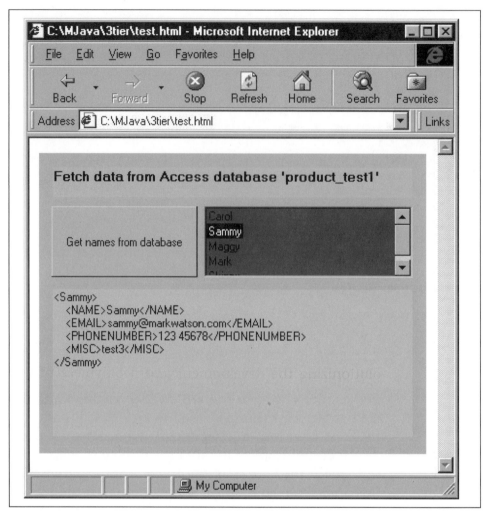

Figure 9.4 *The ViewXML applet after retrieving data from an instance of class DBXMLServer*

Game Library Using Direct3D

The Java programming language and platform are revolutionizing the development and deployment of distributed software. I believe that the huge "twitch" game market (based on game consoles and PCs) will continue to grow, but the largest market growth will eventually be in distributed games and entertainment experiences. With steady improvements in runtime performance, Java is well positioned to be a language of choice for writing distributed entertainment software.

JavaSoft has recently released the specification for the Java3D API that will provide a cross-platform solution to real-time 3D graphics. Microsoft has also released a beta API for Java bindings of their DirectX libraries. The Microsoft Java API for DirectX is specific to the Windows environment. We will use the DirectX and Direct3D libraries for the examples developed in this chapter.

10.1 Requirements of a game library

The purpose of the game library designed and implemented in this chapter is to provide a rather simple toolkit so that you can start to play with Direct3D without initially getting too deep into the COM interface to Direct3D and DirectX. This chapter is by no means a thorough treatment of the Java binding for DirectX and Direct3D. However, the Java APIs used to implement the game library will be discussed in detail, so you will be gently introduced to a rather broad topic.

If you have programmed DirectX applications in C or C++, then you will have a pleasant surprise: it is much easier to use the Java API for DirectX (and programs are much shorter).

The DirectX libraries for Java can be downloaded for free from Microsoft's Web site (they are included with the Java SDK 3.0, but you will also want to download the 5 megabytes of DirectX and Direct3D documentation). The DirectX libraries include

- DirectDraw—low-level drawing utilities using an abstract model for graphics hardware
- Direct3D—medium-level library for displaying 3D objects
- Direct3DRM—retained-mode high-level library that makes it fairly simple to load 3D models and display them (built using Direct3D)
- DirectInput—abstraction for all input devices
- DirectSound—abstraction for sound hardware and a high-level API to play sounds

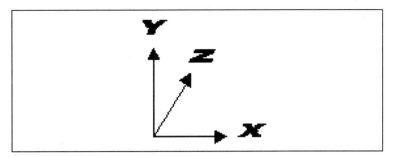

Figure 10.1 *Left-handed coordinate system used in DirectX. The positive z-axis is into the page.*

This chapter demonstrates the relative ease of generating a simple 3D game world using Java and the Direct3D retained-mode library.

We will primarily use Direct3D retained mode (Direct3DRM) in this simple example. The retained-mode libraries provide scene management and moving object management functions.

If you have never programmed 3D graphics before, it will initially be difficult to visualize the position and spatial orientation of objects. Direct3D uses a left-handed coordinate system, as seen in Figure 10.1.

By default, we look down the positive z-axis away from the origin; here the positive z-axis points into the page. (This is a left-handed coordinate system.) For the example, we will place two rotating spheres (one predominately blue and the other brown) in orbit in the x-z plane. We initially position ourselves at $x = 0$, $y = 0$, and $z = -14$ (looking by default down the positive z-axis, toward the origin $x = y = z = 0$).

If you have never used Microsoft's COM model or DirectX before, you need to learn a few new terms:

- COM—Component Object Model. COM objects are accessed via interfaces (which are largely abstracted away in the Java API).

- U-V coordinates—a coordinate system used to map textures onto three-dimensional objects (not required in our example since the texture wrapping is specified in the **ncube1.x** and **ncube2.x** files).

- 3D transformations—matrix arithmetic used to move, rotate, and size objects and to move the viewing position and orientation.

- Retained mode—adds scene management and object management functionality to the underlying Direct3D library.

We access the native Windows libraries for the Direct3D retained mode through the interfaces for a few objects:

- **Direct3dRMDevice**—visual display destination for rendering a scene.

- **Direct3dRMFrame**—used for positioning one or more objects within a scene. We attach visual objects (or a viewpoint) to a frame; move or rotate the frame and all attached objects move or rotate.

- **Direct3dRMViewport**—defines how a 3D scene is rendered (or mapped) to a 2D Java frame.

There are other objects used in Direct3D (eventually, you should read the excellent Direct3D documentation that is included with the DirectX developers' kit) that we do not use in this simple example (e.g., lights).

We will design several classes to make it easier to write simple games with Direct3D:

- **Game**—encapsulates setting up DirectX/Direct3D, serves as a container for instances of class **GameObject**, and implements a simple simulation engine that moves each contained instance of **GameObject** every game cycle

- GameObject—has shape and texture
- GameData—is a container class for all instances of **GameObject** and contains data for maintaining the state of the player's viewpoint
- GameEngine—runs a separate work thread to move objects and to update the graphics display

10.2 Implementation of a game library using Direct3D

Figure 10.2 shows the top-level class diagram for the generic game library. The following classes seen in Figure 10.2 belong to the generic game library:

- Game
- GameEngine
- GameData
- GameObject

Listing 10.1 shows the implementation of the **Game-Data** class. A single **GameData** object represents the data for a specific game. A fixed array **gameObjects** of instances of class **GameObject** is managed. In the test game developed in this chapter, we will derive a new class **PlanetGameObject** from the class **GameObject**. The **GameData** object used in the test game holds references to the planet game objects in the array **gameObjects**. The **GameData** member variables **rx**, **ry**, **rz**, and **rtheta** are used for calculating changes in viewing angle/orientation and **keydown** for keeping track of which keyboard keys are currently in a down state.

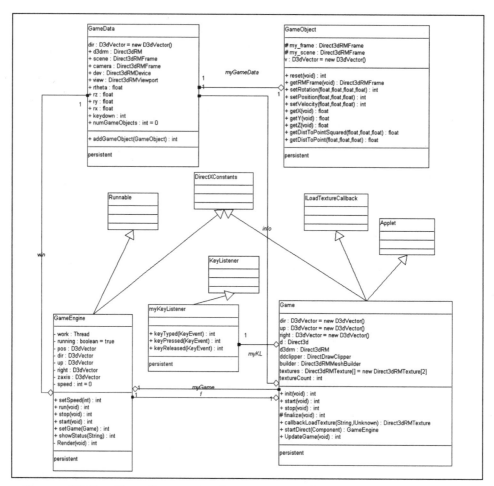

Figure 10.2   *Class diagram for the Java game classes*

Listing 10.1

```
// GameData.java
//


package com.markwatson.d3d;

import com.ms.com.*;
import com.ms.awt.*;
```

```
import com.ms.awt.peer.*;
import com.ms.directX.*;

public class GameData
{
  D3dVector dir = new D3dVector();
  public Direct3dRM d3drm;
  public Direct3dRMFrame scene;
  public Direct3dRMFrame camera;
  public Direct3dRMDevice dev;
  public Direct3dRMViewport view;
  public float rx,ry,rz,rtheta;
  public int keydown;
  public GameObject gameObjects[];
  public int numGameObjects = 0;
  public final static int MAX = 5;
  public void addGameObject(GameObject go) {
    if (numGameObjects < MAX-1) {
      gameObjects[numGameObjects++] = go;
    }
  }

  public GameData() {
    gameObjects = new GameObject[MAX];
  }
}
```

Listing 10.2 shows the implementation of the **Game** class. This class is derived from the **applet** class. **Game** is an abstract class; to use it, you must derive a new class from **Game** that defines the following methods:

- **protected void finalize( );**

- **public Direct3dRMTexture callbackLoad-Texture(String name, IUnknown a);**

- **public GameEngine startDirect(Component c);**

- **public void UpdateGame( )**

The file **TestGame.java** (Listing 10.6) shows how these four methods are defined for a sample game. The member variable **info** (of class **GameData**) is used for the current data for a game. The member variable **gameEngine** (of class **GameEngine**, see Listing 10.4) is used to manage the runtime performance of the game. Since instances of classes derived from the abstract **Game** class are Java applets, the game setup is performed in the **init** method. The **init** method performs the following initialization:

- Creates a key listener object to manage keyboard input
- Creates a new instance of class **GameEngine** using the factory method **startDirect** (this is an abstract method)
- Sets the game variable in the **GameEngine** object to this applet
- Requests input focus for this applet

The key listener class **MyKeyListener** handles keyboard events by modifying game engine parameters:

- Speed of the viewing location (i.e., the perspective shown in the game applet window)
- The viewing orientation angles

The **GameEngine** object runs in its own thread, so once speed and viewing angle parameters are set using the keyboard, the game simulation runs with these settings until new keyboard events trigger changes to the speed and viewing angles.

Listing 10.2

```
// Game.java
//

package com.markwatson.d3d;
```

```java
import java.awt.*;
import java.applet.*;
import java.util.Vector;
import java.awt.event.*;
import com.ms.com.*;
import com.ms.directX.*;
import com.ms.ui.*;
import com.ms.ui.event.*;

abstract public class Game extends Applet
implements DirectXConstants, ILoadTextureCallback {
  GameEngine gameEngine = null;
  D3dVector dir = new D3dVector();
  D3dVector up = new D3dVector();
  D3dVector right = new D3dVector();
  GameData info;

  private myKeyListener myKL;

  public void init() {
    myKL = new myKeyListener();
    addKeyListener(myKL);
    gameEngine = startDirect(this);
    gameEngine.setGame(this);
    requestFocus();
  }

  public void start() {
    gameEngine.start();
  }

  public void stop() {
    gameEngine.stop();
  }

  class myKeyListener implements KeyListener {
    public void keyTyped(KeyEvent ke) {
      if (ke.getKeyChar() == 'q')  System.exit(0);
      if (ke.getKeyChar() == 'Q')  System.exit(0);
    }
```

(continued)

Listing 10.2 *(continued)*

```java
public void keyPressed(KeyEvent ke) {
    gameEngine.win.camera.getOrientation(gameEngine.win.scene,
            dir, up);
    gameEngine.win.d3drm.vectorCrossProduct(right, up, dir);

    int key = ke.getKeyCode();

    if (key >= KeyEvent.VK_0 && key <= KeyEvent.VK_9) {
        gameEngine.setSpeed((int)(key - KeyEvent.VK_0));
    }

    switch(key) {
    case KeyEvent.VK_DOWN:
        gameEngine.win.keydown |= 0x1;
        gameEngine.win.rtheta = 0.01F;  // speed to rotate
        gameEngine.win.rx     = right.x;  // axis to rotate about
        gameEngine.win.rz     = right.z;
        break;

    case KeyEvent.VK_UP:
        gameEngine.win.keydown |= 0x2;
        gameEngine.win.rtheta = 0.01F;
        gameEngine.win.rx     = -right.x;
        gameEngine.win.rz     = -right.z;
        break;

    case KeyEvent.VK_LEFT:
        gameEngine.win.keydown |= 0x10;
        gameEngine.win.rtheta = 0.01F;
        gameEngine.win.ry     = -up.y;
        break;

    case KeyEvent.VK_RIGHT:
        gameEngine.win.keydown |= 0x20;
        gameEngine.win.rtheta = 0.01F;
        gameEngine.win.ry     = up.y;
        break;
    }
}
```

```
public void keyReleased(KeyEvent ke) {
  int key = ke.getKeyCode();
  switch(key) {
  case KeyEvent.VK_DOWN:
    gameEngine.win.keydown &= ~0x1;
    gameEngine.win.rtheta = 0.0F;  // speed to rotate
    gameEngine.win.rx     = 0.0f;  // axis to rotate about
    gameEngine.win.rz     = 0.0f;
    break;
  case KeyEvent.VK_UP:
    gameEngine.win.keydown &= ~0x2;
    gameEngine.win.rtheta = 0.0F;
    gameEngine.win.rx     = 0.0F;
    gameEngine.win.rz     = 0.0F;
    break;

  case KeyEvent.VK_Q:
  case KeyEvent.VK_ESCAPE:
    System.exit(0);
    break;

  case KeyEvent.VK_LEFT:
    gameEngine.win.keydown &= ~0x10;
    gameEngine.win.rtheta = 0.0F;
    gameEngine.win.ry     = 0.0f;
    break;
  case KeyEvent.VK_RIGHT:
    gameEngine.win.keydown &= ~0x20;
    gameEngine.win.rtheta = 0.0F;
    gameEngine.win.ry     = 0.0f;
    break;
  }
 }
}


// Four abstract methods that subclasses need to define for
// specific games:
```

(continued)

Listing 10.2 *(continued)*

```
abstract protected void finalize();

abstract public Direct3dRMTexture callbackLoadTexture(String name,
            IUnknown a);

abstract public GameEngine startDirect(Component c);

// called once per loop from GameEngine:
abstract public void UpdateGame();
}
```

Listing 10.3 shows the implementation of the class **GameObject**. This class encapsulates many of the details for dealing with Direct3D objects. An instance of class **GameObject** (or more likely, an instance of a class derived from the **GameObject** class) is stored in an array in a **GameData** object and also maintains a reference to the **GameData** container in the member variable **myGameData**. This reference to the **GameData** container is used for referencing the scene member data for class **GameData**. The constructor for class **GameObject** reads a local file containing three-dimensional mesh data that describes the shape of a game data object and color texture information. There are also methods for setting the position, speed, and rotation of a game object. Two additional methods make it easy to interact with other game objects:

- **getDistToPoint**—returns the distance to a point in game space
- **getDistToPointSquared**—returns the square of the distance to a point in game space

Listing 10.3

```java
// GameObject.java
//

package com.markwatson.d3d;

import com.ms.com.*;
import com.ms.awt.*;
import com.ms.awt.peer.*;
import com.ms.directX.*;

class GameObject {
  protected Direct3dRMFrame my_frame;
  protected Direct3dRMFrame my_scene;
  protected GameData myGameData = null;
  public GameObject(GameData gameData, String model_file,
                    ILoadTextureCallback cb)
  {
    System.out.print("Entered GameObject(...," + model_file + ")\n");
    my_scene = gameData.scene;
    my_frame = gameData.d3drm.createFrame(gameData.scene);
    myGameData = gameData;
    reset();
    System.out.print("..before creating a mesh builder..\n");
    Direct3dRMMeshBuilder builder = gameData.d3drm.createMeshBuilder();
    if (builder==null) System.out.print("NULL builder!\n");
    System.out.print("..before loading file..\n");
    builder.loadFromFileByPos(model_file, 0, 0,
                              (ILoadTextureCallback)cb, null);
    builder.setColorRGB(0.8F, 0.8F, 0.8F);
    System.out.print("..before adding mesh builder..\n");
    my_frame.addVisualMeshBuilder(builder);
  }
  public void reset() {
    if (myGameData==null) return;
    my_frame.setRotation(myGameData.scene, 0.0F, 0.0F, 0.0F, 0.0F);
    my_frame.setPosition(myGameData.scene, 0.0F, 0.0F, 0.0F);
  }

  // expose the private RMFrame object to provide access for
  // special effects (e.g., fog) through Direct3dRMFrame class API:
  public Direct3dRMFrame getRMFrame() {
```

(continued)

Listing 10.3 *(continued)*

```java
    return my_frame;
}
// Low-level position, etc. methods:
public void setRotation(float x, float y, float z, float angle) {
  my_frame.setRotation(my_scene, x, y, z, angle);
}
public void setPosition(float x, float y, float z) {
  my_frame.setPosition(my_scene, x, y, z);
}
public void setVelocity(float vx, float vy, float vz) {
  my_frame.setVelocity(my_scene, vx, vy, vz, 0);
}

D3dVector v = new D3dVector();

public float getX() {
  my_frame.getPosition(my_scene, v);
  return v.x;
}
public float getY() {
  my_frame.getPosition(my_scene, v);
  return v.y;
}
public float getZ() {
  my_frame.getPosition(my_scene, v);
  return v.z;
}
public float getDistToPointSquared(float x, float y, float z) {
  my_frame.getPosition(my_scene, v);
  return (v.x-x)*(v.x-x) + (v.y-y)*(v.y-y) + (v.z-z)*(v.z-z);
}
public float getDistToPoint(float x, float y, float z) {
  my_frame.getPosition(my_scene, v);
  return (float)Math.sqrt((v.x-x)*(v.x-x) + (v.y-y)*(v.y-y) + (v.z-
        z)*(v.z-z));
}


}
```

Listing 10.4 shows the implementation of the class **GameEngine**. This class maintains its own execution thread that runs separately from the main game applet. The class constructor requires two arguments:

- An integer thread priority
- A reference to an instance of class **GameData**

When the work thread is started, the method **run** is called. Method **run** has an interesting behavior: it loops continually, updating game state (e.g., position of all game objects), but it checks the real-time clock and limits itself to performing these calculations to a time interval not less than approximately 33 milliseconds. The **run** method is also responsible for requesting the Direct3D system to re-render and display the game view in the applet window.

Listing 10.4

```
// GameEngine.java
//

package com.markwatson.d3d;

import java.awt.*;
import java.applet.*;
import com.ms.com.*;
import com.ms.awt.*;
import com.ms.awt.peer.*;
import com.ms.directX.*;

class GameEngine implements Runnable, DirectXConstants
{
  private Thread work; // work thread
  private boolean running = true;

  public GameData win;
```

(continued)

Listing 10.4 *(continued)*

```
private D3dVector pos;
private D3dVector dir;
private D3dVector up;
private D3dVector right;
private D3dVector zaxis;

private int speed = 0;
public void setSpeed(int s) { speed = s; }

public GameEngine(int p, GameData info) {

  win = info;
  work = new Thread(this);
  work.setPriority(p);

  pos   = new D3dVector();
  dir   = new D3dVector();
  up    = new D3dVector();
  right = new D3dVector();
}

public void run() {
  long startTime, sleepTime;
  while(running) {
    startTime = System.currentTimeMillis();
    Render();

    // adjust camera viewing rotation and position:
    win.camera.getOrientation(win.scene, dir, up);
    win.camera.getPosition(win.scene, pos);
    win.d3drm.vectorCrossProduct(right, up, dir);
    win.camera.setRotation(win.scene, win.rx, win.ry,
                           win.rz, win.rtheta*4.0f);
    float fact = 0.005f * (float)speed;
    pos.x += dir.x * fact;
    pos.z += dir.z * fact;
    pos.y += dir.y * fact;
    win.camera.setPosition(win.scene, pos.x,pos.y,pos.z);
```

```
      // Call the application-specific Update method:
      myGame.UpdateGame();
      // on fast machines, sleep a while...
      sleepTime = 33 - (System.currentTimeMillis() - startTime);
      if (sleepTime > 5) {
        try {
          work.sleep(sleepTime);
        } catch (InterruptedException e) { }
      }
    }
  }


  public void stop() { running = false; }

  public void start() { running = true; work.start(); }

  private Game myGame = null;

  public void setGame(Game a) { myGame = a; }

  public void showStatus(String s) {
    if (myGame != null) myGame.showStatus(s);
  }

  private void Render() {
    win.scene.move(1.0F);
    win.view.clear();
    win.view.render(win.scene);
    win.dev.update();
  }
}
```

The class **GameEngine** calls the Direct3D rendering engine in the method **Render**. In method **Render**, the member variable **win** (an instance of class **GameData**) is used to access the underlying Direct3D objects.

10.3 Design of a 3D game for simulating flight around orbiting planets

The **Game, GameObject, GameData,** and **GameEngine** classes make it fairly easy to create simple games. The game that we will design in this section and implement in Section 10.4 is really more of a virtual reality (VR) experience than a game: you navigate a spaceship around several planets that orbit around a central sun.

The classes **Game** and **GameEngine** automatically handle changing the viewpoint (and rotation and velocity) in a 3D world. For our sample game, we will write two new classes: **PlanetGameObject** (derived from **GameObject**) and **TestGame** (derived from **Game**).

In the game/VR experience, a small white cube, which represents a target to maneuver to, appears in random locations. Using the keyboard arrow keys (for viewing and movement angles) and the number keys (to set the speed of the viewing location), you can try to run over the target without bumping into either of two moving planets. If you collide with a planet, you are repositioned away from the target cube and the two planets.

The following classes seen in Figure 10.3 are used for implementing a test game:

- **TestGame**—derived from **Game**
- **PlanetGameObject**—derived from GameObject

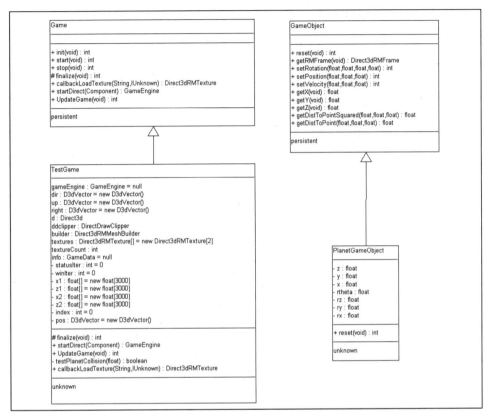

Figure 10.3   *Additional classes used for a simple test game*

10.4   Implementation of a 3D game for simulating flight around orbiting planets

Implementing the sample game is simple; we only have to define two new Java classes: **PlanetGameObject** (Listing 10.5) and **TestGame** (Listing 10.6). The class **PlanetGameObject** adds seven member variables to the base class **GameObject**:

- **x, y, z**—the three spatial coordinates
- **rx, ry, rz**—the three rotational coordinates
- **rtheta**—rotation rate

The method **reset** is overridden to add behavior for restoring the planet object to its initial position and rotation.

Listing 10.5

```
// PlanetGameObject.java
//
// Derived from class GameObject
//

package com.markwatson.d3d;

import com.ms.com.*;
import com.ms.awt.*;
import com.ms.awt.peer.*;
import com.ms.directX.*;

class PlanetGameObject extends GameObject {
  private float x, y, z; // reset position
  private float rx, ry, rz, rtheta; // reset rotation

  public PlanetGameObject(GameData gameData,
                      String model_file,
                      ILoadTextureCallback cb,
                      float x0, float y0, float z0,
                      float rx0, float ry0, float rz0, float rtheta0)
  {
    super(gameData, model_file, cb);
    x = x0; y = y0; z = z0;
    rx = rx0; ry = ry0; rz = rz0; rtheta = rtheta0;
    reset();
  }
  // override the base class reset method:
  public void reset() {
    if (myGameData==null) return;
```

```
    my_frame.setPosition(myGameData.scene, x, y, z);
    my_frame.setRotation(myGameData.scene, rx, ry, rz, rtheta);
  }
}
```

Listing 10.6 shows the implementation of the class **TestGame** that is derived from the base class **Game**. The constructor for class **TestGame** generates 3000 path points for each planet in the test game. The planets move in the *x-z* plane (i.e., the *y*-coordinates for the planets are always zero), so we only allocate storage to hold the *x*- and *z*-coordinates. The arrays **x1** and **z1** hold the path points for the first planet, and the arrays **x2** and **z2** hold the path points for the second planet. The **finalize** method is used to release data that might be allocated outside the Java memory space (i.e., allocated through the COM interface for the Direct3D system); this data is allocated in the **startDirect** method. Most of the Direct3D code in the methods **startDirect** and **finalize** was from the Microsoft "castle" example program. The **startDirect** method performs the following tasks:

- Creates a new instance of the class **Direct3d**.
- Creates a new 3D clipper object.
- Sets a global unique identifier (variable **g**) to a device for either color model **D3DCOLOR_MONO** or **D3DCOLOR_RGB**.
- Creates a new graphics device (stored in **info.dev**).
- Detects the number of bits used for displaying colors and set the storage for texture colors accordingly.
- Creates a new frame to represent the player's viewpoint (stored in **info.scene**).
- Add two instances of class **PlanetGameObject** to the **GameData** object (stored in **info**).

- Add an instance of class **GameObject** (to represent the white target cube) to the **GameData** object (stored in **info**).

The class **Game** has four abstract methods: **startDirect**, **finalize**, **callbackLoadTexture**, and **UpdateGame**. The method **callbackLoadTexture** uses the method **Direct3d.loadTexture** to load color texture information. The **callbackLoadTexture** method is defined in the Java interface **ILoadTextureCallback**. The method **TestGame.UpdateGame** is called automatically by the method **GameEngine.run** from inside the separate work thread. The method **UpdateGame** performs the following tasks for each simulation cycle in the game:

- Get the user's view (or camera) position.
- Update the position of the two planets by moving them to their next path point.
- Periodically (every 17 cycles) check for the distance to the target and update the text display in the test game applet window.
- Periodically (every 11 cycles) check for a collision between the player's viewing position and both planets (using the helper method **testPlanetCollision**).

Listing 10.6

```
// TestGame.java
//

package com.markwatson.d3d;

import java.awt.*;
import java.applet.*;
```

```java
import java.util.Vector;
import com.ms.com.*;
import com.ms.directX.*;
import com.ms.ui.*;
import com.ms.ui.event.*;

public class TestGame extends Game
implements DirectXConstants, ILoadTextureCallback
{
  Direct3d d;
  DirectDrawClipper ddclipper;
  Direct3dRMMeshBuilder builder;
  Direct3dRMTexture[] textures = new Direct3dRMTexture[2];
  int textureCount;
  GameData info = null;

  public TestGame() {
    for (int i=0; i<3000; i++) {
      float theta = ((float)i)*6.28f / 3000.0f;
      x1[i] = (float)(10.0f*Math.sin(theta+0.25));
      z1[i] = (float)(10.0f*Math.cos(theta+0.25));
      x2[i] = (float)(4.0f*Math.sin(2.0f*theta));
      z2[i] = (float)(4.0f*Math.cos(2.0f*theta));
    }
  }

  // Method 'finalize' is abstract in the parent class because
  // different games create different data:
  protected void finalize() {
    for ( int i = 0; i < 2; i++ )
      if ( textures[i] != null )
        ComLib.release(textures[i]);

    //ComLib.release(info.cube_frame_1);
    //ComLib.release(info.cube_frame_2);
    ComLib.release(builder);
    ComLib.release(info.camera);
    ComLib.release(info.scene);
    ComLib.release(info.view);
    ComLib.release(ddclipper);
    ComLib.release(info.dev);
```

(continued)

Listing 10.6 *(continued)*

```
    ComLib.release(d);
    ComLib.release(info.d3drm);
  }


  // Method 'startDirect' is abstract in parent 'Game' class.
  // This method contains all of the game-specific initialization.
  public GameEngine startDirect(Component c) {
    System.err.println("TestGame.startDirect()\n");
    info = new GameData();
    info.d3drm = new Direct3dRM();

    ddclipper = new DirectDrawClipper();
    ddclipper.setComponent(c);

    d = new Direct3d();
    _Guid g = null;
    try {
      g = d.findDeviceForColorModel(D3DCOLOR_MONO, 0);
    } catch (Exception e) {
      g = d.findDeviceForColorModel(D3DCOLOR_RGB, 0);
    }
    info.dev =
      info.d3drm.createDeviceFromClipper(ddclipper, g, 260, 220);

    switch (d.systemBpp()) { // from Microsoft examples:
    case 1:
      info.dev.setShades(4);
      info.d3drm.setDefaultTextureShades(4);
      break;
    case 16:
      info.dev.setShades(32);
      info.d3drm.setDefaultTextureColors(64);
      info.d3drm.setDefaultTextureShades(32);
      info.dev.setDither(0);
      break;
    case 24:
    case 32:
      info.dev.setShades(256);
      info.d3drm.setDefaultTextureColors(64);
```

```
                info.d3drm.setDefaultTextureShades(256);
                info.dev.setDither(0);
                break;
        default:
                info.dev.setShades(1);
                info.dev.setDither(0);
                info.d3drm.setDefaultTextureShades(1);
                break;
        }

        info.dev.setQuality(D3DRMRENDER_UNLITFLAT);
        info.dev.setTextureQuality( D3DRMTEXTURE_NEAREST );

        info.scene = info.d3drm.createFrame(null); // create scene:

        System.out.print("Adding a planet game object...\n");
        // this will be game object at index 0:
        info.addGameObject((GameObject)
                            (new PlanetGameObject(info, "planet1.x",
                                                  (ILoadTextureCallback)this,
                                                  0.0F, 0.0F, 10.0F,
                                                  0.1F, 1.0F, 0.3F, 0.05F)));
        System.out.print("Adding a planet game object...\n");
        // this will be game object at index 1:
        info.addGameObject((GameObject)
                            (new PlanetGameObject(info, "planet2.x",
                                                  (ILoadTextureCallback)this,
                                                  7.0F, 0.0F, 0.0F,
                                                  0.14F, 1.0F, 0.2F, 0.07F)));
        System.out.print("Adding a target (cube) game object...\n");
        // this will be game object at index 2:
        info.addGameObject((GameObject)
                            (new GameObject(info, "target.x",
                                            (ILoadTextureCallback)this)));
        info.gameObjects[2].setPosition(5.0F, 0.0F, 2.0F);
        info.gameObjects[2].setRotation(0.14F, 0.75F, 0.2F, 0.07F);

        info.camera = info.d3drm.createFrame(info.scene);
        info.camera.setPosition(info.scene, 0.0F, 0.0F, -14.0F);
```

(continued)

Listing 10.6 *(continued)*

```
    info.view = info.d3drm.createViewport(info.dev, info.camera, 0, 0,
                                info.dev.getWidth(),
                                info.dev.getHeight());
    info.view.setBack(5000.0F);

    gameEngine = new GameEngine(Thread.NORM_PRIORITY, info);
    return gameEngine;
}

private int statusIter = 0;
private int winIter = 0;

// for planet positions:
private float x1[] = new float[3000];
private float z1[] = new float[3000];
private float x2[] = new float[3000];
private float z2[] = new float[3000];
private int index = 0;

// The Update method is called once per frame by the GameEngine:

public void UpdateGame() {
    info.camera.getPosition(info.scene, pos);

    // update the positions of the two cubes:
    info.gameObjects[0].setPosition(x1[index], 0.0F, z1[index]);
    info.gameObjects[1].setPosition(x2[index], 0.0F, z2[index]);
    index++;
    if (index>=3000)  index=0;

    // check distance to target:
    if (winIter++ > 17) {
      winIter = 0;
      float d0 = info.gameObjects[2].getDistToPoint(pos.x,pos.y,pos.z);
      if (d0 < 1.0f) {
        winIter = -20;
        statusIter = -90;
```

```
          gameEngine.showStatus("retrieved target, now find the next
                             target");
        float x = (float)(10.0f * Math.random() - 5.0f);
        float y = (float)(10.0f * Math.random() - 5.0f);
        float z = (float)( 3.0f * Math.random() - 1.5f);
        info.gameObjects[2].setPosition(x, y, z);
    }
  }

  // test distance to planets:
  if (statusIter++ > 11) {
    statusIter = 0;
    float d0 =
      info.gameObjects[0].getDistToPoint(pos.x,pos.y,pos.z) - 4.2f;
    float d1 =
      info.gameObjects[1].getDistToPoint(pos.x,pos.y,pos.z) - 4.2f;
    if (d0 < d1) {
      if (testPlanetCollision(d0)) {
        gameEngine.showStatus("Collision: blue planet! reset game...");
      } else {
        gameEngine.showStatus("closest planet is blue, distance = " +
                             d0);
      }
    } else {
      if (testPlanetCollision(d1)) {
        gameEngine.showStatus("Collision: green planet! reset game...");
      } else {
        gameEngine.showStatus("closest planet is green, distance = " +
                             d1);
      }
    }
  }
}

private boolean testPlanetCollision(float dist) {
  if (dist > 0.0f)  return false;
  // collision, so reset initial ship/viewing position:
  info.gameObjects[0].setPosition(0.0F, 0.0F, 10.0F);
  info.gameObjects[0].setRotation(0.1F, 1.0F, 0.3F, 0.05F);
  info.gameObjects[1].setPosition(7.0F, 0.0F, 0.0F);
```

(continued)

Listing 10.6 *(continued)*

```
    info.gameObjects[1].setRotation(0.14F, 1.0F, 0.2F, 0.07F);
    info.gameObjects[2].setPosition(5.0F, 0.0F, 2.0F);
    info.gameObjects[2].setRotation(0.14F, 0.75F, 0.2F, 0.07F);
    info.camera.setPosition(info.scene, 0.0F, 0.0F, -14.0F);
    winIter = -90;
    statusIter = -70;
    return true;
}

private D3dVector pos = new D3dVector();

// This callback method must be defined in this subclass, not
// in the abstract parent class:

public Direct3dRMTexture callbackLoadTexture(String name, IUnknown a) {
    return textures[textureCount++] = info.d3drm.loadTexture(name);
}
}
```

In order to compile and run the test game, type the
following commands:

```
cd c:\mjava\d3d
c.bat
r.bat
```

The screen shot in Figure 10.4 shows the application
window. The '1' through '9' keys control the speed of
the viewer (or camera), and the arrow keys rotate the
"camera" point of view.

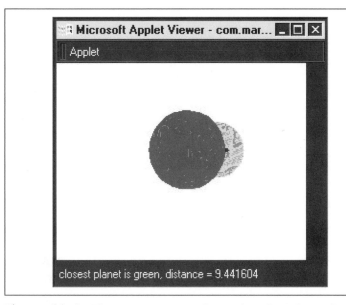

Figure 10.4 *The test game running, using the Microsoft applet viewer. Note that the colors are reversed in this figure to avoid printing the black background behind the two planets. The white target shows as a small black cube to the right of the nearest planet.*

Efficiency note

All Java objects used in the example program are created before we start rendering frames in real time. Once the program starts (and you see the real-time graphics display), hopefully no new data is created in the Java heap (although method calls will allocate and deallocate stack space), so garbage collection should not slow down the example application once it is running.

JScript and DHTML

Most Web browsers now support the European Computer Manufacturing Association (ECMA) standard JavaScript language. JScript is Microsoft's implementation of the ECMA standard, with a few extensions. I will refer to JScript in this chapter, although most of the discussion will also apply to JavaScript. Unfortunately, the use of JavaScript is not completely portable between the Netscape Communicator and Internet Explorer. Incompatibilities are usually the result of different Web page document models for naming different components on a Web page. The examples in this chapter have only been tested using IE 4.0, but most should also work with the Netscape Communicator 4.0. Dynamic HTML (DHTML) allows JavaScript or JScript scripts to be embedded directly inside of Web page documents. This chapter rounds out the material that you need for writing great Web-based (either Internet or private Intranet) distributed applications. After reading this chapter, your toolbox of techniques will include the ability to write

- Java server-side applications
- lightweight client applications built with some combination of DHTML, JScript, and Java

You can download both a JScript tutorial and a complete JScript language reference from *www.microsoft.com/jscript*. This chapter provides a quick tutorial for JScript and a few practical examples of using JScript embedded in DHTML and Java applets.

11.1 Introduction to JScript

JScript is a loosely typed language: variables can hold a value of any data type. There are four built-in data types in JScript:

- Numbers—either integers or floating-point numbers
- Strings—defined inside either single or double quote marks
- Objects—any arbitrary data item
- Boolean—true or false value

A variable has an "undefined data type" if it is created and not assigned a value. A variable can also have a "null" value, which has no meaning.

Since JScript mostly deals with the manipulation of strings, any data values are usually converted to strings. For example:

```
var X = 'I have ';
var Y = " dogs";
var Z = X + 4 + Y;
```

The variable **Z** will have the value "I have 4 dogs". The keyword **var** is used to define a new variable. It is important to note that variables can take on any type of value; for example, the following is legal:

```
var x = "the dog ran down the street";
x = 3.1;  // here, we redefine x as a floating-point number
```

The built-in function **eval** is used to convert strings that contain numeric expressions to numbers. For example:

```
var s = "1 + (10*11)";
var n = eval(s);
```

In this example, **n** will be a number with the value 111. The **substring** method can be used to extract part of a string; for example:

```
var s = "abcdefg";
var z = s.substring(0,4); // z is equal to "abcd"
```

In this example, we note that the variable **s** is considered to be an object, so we use the same syntax as in Java to call a method like **substring**. You can also create arrays in JScript; for example:

```
Var a = new Array(3);
a[0] = 3.14159;
a[1] = "cat";
var a2 = new array(2);
a2[0] = 0;
a2[1] = 111;
a[2] = a2; // this creates a two-dimensional array
var n = a[2][1];  // n will now have the value 111;
```

You should note that any type of object could be stored in any array element. Like Java, arrays are indexed starting at zero. JScript uses the same syntax as Java for **if**, **while**, and **for** statements.

A new line terminates statements in JScript; however, it is a very good idea to always terminate statements

with a semicolon. JScript is block-structured like Java.
JScript can either be stored in a separate file and referenced from an HTML document, or JScript functions
can be directly embedded in HTML using the **<SCRIPT>**
and **</SCRIPT>** tags. Since you already know how to
program in Java, you will find it very easy to write short
JScript functions. The next two sections provide several
short JScript examples; we will discuss the language use
and syntax using examples as needed.

11.2 JScript interaction with Dynamic HTML document objects

Listing 11.1 (file **FontTest.html**) shows a JScript script
that changes the font in a document object using two
JScript functions:

- **my_mouse_over**—sets the text to bold
- **my_mouse_out**—sets the text to italic

Unfortunately, both Microsoft and Netscape have different document object models. Fortunately, both companies have agreed to support the World Wide Web
Consortium's standards in the future. We will only discuss Microsoft's current document model here.

Listing 11.1

```
<HTML>
  <HEAD>
    <TITLE>
      Demo of Dynamic HTML and JScript
    </TITLE>
```

```
</HEAD>
<BODY>
  <P ID="aParagraph"
    onMouseOver="my_mouse_over()"
    onMouseOut="my_mouse_out()">
    This text becomes italic for mouse
    over events.
  <SCRIPT LANGUAGE="JavaScript">
    function my_mouse_over() {
      aParagraph.style.fontStyle='italic'
    }
    function my_mouse_out() {
      aParagraph.style.fontStyle='normal'
    }
  </SCRIPT>
  </P>
</BODY>
</HTML>
```

Figure 11.1 shows two IE 4.0 windows: the one on the right side of the figure shows the effect of the mouse cursor (which is not seen in the figure) moving over the text on the Web page.

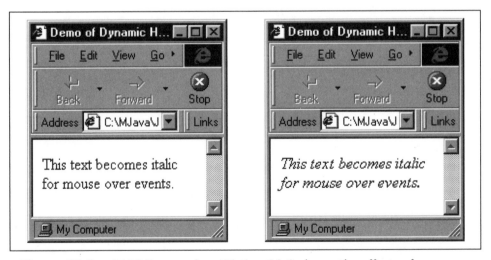

Figure 11.1   *DHTML page from Listing 11.1 shows the effects of mouse over events.*

Listing 11.2 (file **ToggleTest.html**) shows a JScript script that toggles the visibility of document objects by manipulating the value of the **style** variable **display**. Listing 11.2 uses the **DIV** DHTML tag to logically separate blocks of DHTML. The IE 4.0 supports changing styles of content inside **DIV** tags, so we can create cascading menus. In Listing 11.2, the two **DIV** tags have IDs "div1" and "div2". These IDs are referenced in the JScript function **my_mouse_click**. The visibility of the material inside the **DIV** tag with ID "div2" is toggled on and off in the JScript function **my_mouse_click**. The **style** variable **display** of a **DIV** tag can be set to 'none' to hide the contents of a **DIV** tag. The contents of a **DIV** tag can be made visible by setting the **style** variable **display** to the null string (two adjacent single quotes).

Listing 11.2

```
<HTML>
  <HEAD>
    <TITLE>
      Demo of Dynamic HTML and JScript
    </TITLE>
  </HEAD>
  <BODY>
    <B>
      <P>
        This is a test of using the 'document' object.
      </P>
    </B>
    <DIV ID="div1">
      <img src="right.gif" ID="arrow"
        onClick="my_mouse_click()"
      </img>
      This text changes when you click the left arrow
      <DIV ID="div2" STYLE="display:'none';">
        This text becomes visible
      </DIV>
    </DIV>
    <SCRIPT LANGUAGE="JavaScript">
```

Listing 11.2 *(continued)*

```
        function my_mouse_click() {
            if (div2.style.display =='') {
                div2.style.display = 'none';
                arrow.src="right.gif";
            } else {
                arrow.src="down.gif";
                div2.style.display='';
            }
        }
    </SCRIPT>
  </BODY>
</HTML>
```

Figure 11.2 shows the DHTML file in Listing 11.2 with the **DIV** tag with ID equal to "div2" hidden and visible.

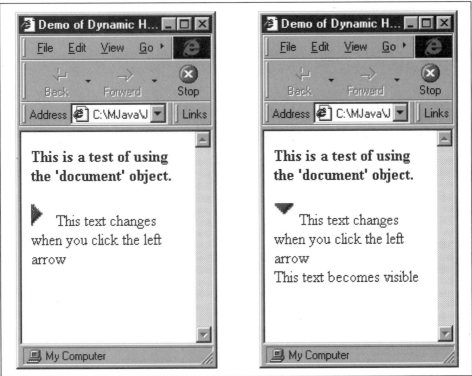

Figure 11.2   *DHTML file from Listing 11.2*

Listing 11.3 shows a JScript script that replaces document contents when the mouse cursor is moved over the text. A pop-up dialog box verifies that the user wants to rewrite the text in the document object.

Listing 11.3

```
<HTML>
  <HEAD>
    <TITLE>
      Demo of Dynamic HTML and JScript
    </TITLE>
  </HEAD>
  <BODY>
    <B>
      <P>
        This is a test of using the 'document' object.
      </P>
    </B>
    <P ID="aParagraph"
      onMouseOver="my_mouse_write()">
      This text changes for a mouse
      over event (move the mouse over this text).
    </P>
    <SCRIPT LANGUAGE="JavaScript">
      function my_mouse_write() {
        var flag =
          window.confirm("Click OK to replace document contents");
        if (flag) {
          document.writeln("This is a test");
        }
      }
    </SCRIPT>
  </BODY>
</HTML>
```

The **document.write** method is used to overwrite the contents of a document.

Figure 11.3 shows the DHTML file in Listing 11.3.

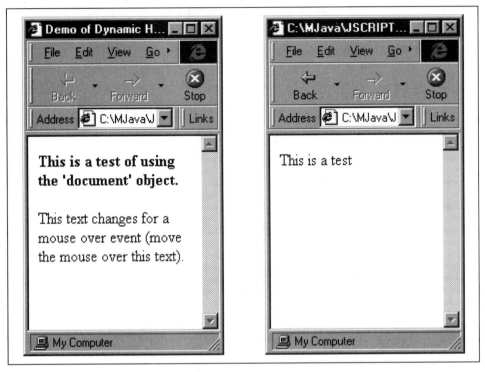

Figure 11.3   *DHTML file in Listing 11.3*

11.3 JScript interaction with Java applets

JScript functions can interact with Java applets embedded in an HTML document. Java applets can also directly call JScript functions. Listing 11.4 shows a Dynamic HTML file (**JavaInterfaceTest.html**) that contains scripts that call methods in a Java applet and are called by methods in a Java applet. The syntax for applet to JScript and JScript to applet communications is very simple. You can use the HTML and JScript example in Listing 11.4 and the simple Java applet in Listing 11.5 as implementation templates.

In Listing 11.4, the **<APPLET> </APPLET>** tags contain the keyword **MAYSCRIPT**. You must add this keyword if you want to call public applet methods from JScript methods and functions. The **<APPLET> </APPLET>** tags also contain the parameter **NAME**; this parameter specifies the name used in JScript functions and methods to access public methods in the Java applet. In Listing 11.4, we call the public method **changeText** of class **TestApplet** by using the following notation:

```
TestApplet.changeText("this is the argument for the Java
method");
```

As seen in Listing 11.4, the **changeText** public Java method is called both in an HTML statement using the **onClick** parameter and inside the JScript function **scriptChangeText**.

Listing 11.4

```
<HTML>
  <HEAD>
    <TITLE>
      Demo of Dynamic HTML and JScript
    </TITLE>
  </HEAD>
  <BODY>
  <APPLET CODE="TestApplet.class"
          CODEBASE="..\class"
          NAME="TestApplet"
          MAYSCRIPT
     WIDTH=300 HEIGHT=120 >
  </APPLET>
  <P ID="aParagraph"
       onClick="document.TestApplet.changeText( &QUOT web mouse click
                    &QUOT )">
  Test Java to JScript interactions. Try clicking this text.
  </P>
```

```
<SCRIPT LANGUAGE="JavaScript">
    function scriptChangeText(arg) {
        window.alert("scriptChangeText(" + arg + ")");
        TestApplet.changeText("text passed through JScript: " + arg);
    }
</SCRIPT>
</BODY>
</HTML>
```

Listing 11.5 shows the Java applet that communicates with the scripts in Listing 11.4. Any public method in an applet can be called from a JScript function or method located on the same Web page as the applet. The class **TestApplet** defined in Listing 11.5 uses two components: a test area and a button. The event handling code for the button is implemented with the inner class **buttonMouseAdapter**. When the button is clicked with the mouse, the applet calls a JScript function named **scriptChangeText**. This JScript function then calls the public method **changeText** in the **TestApplet** class. This is not a very practical example, but it does demonstrate two-way communication between JScript functions and Java methods. The following code from Listing 11.5 is used to find the window that the applet is running in (i.e., the Web page) and how to call JScript functions on that Web page:

```
netscape.javascript.JSObject win =
    netscape.javascript.JSObject.getWindow(applet);
win.call("scriptChangeText", args);
```

This code for accessing JScript (or JavaScript) functions and methods must be executed inside a Java **try** and **catch** block.

Listing 11.5

```
// TestApplet.java
//
// This applet demonstrates communication between
// a JScript function and this applet (in both
// directions).
//

import java.awt.*;
import java.applet.*;

public class TestApplet extends Applet {

  protected String text_to_change = "original text";
  protected Applet applet;

  public void init() {
    applet = this;
    setLayout(null);
    setSize(300,120);
    l = new Label(text_to_change + "            ");
    add(l);
    l.setBounds(5, 20, 260, 25);
    b = new Button("Call JScript");
    b.addMouseListener(new buttonMouseAdapter());
    add(b);
    b.setBounds(5, 60, 60, 25);
  }

  private Label l;
  private Button b;

  protected int count = 0;
```

```
class buttonMouseAdapter extends java.awt.event.MouseAdapter {
  public void mouseClicked(java.awt.event.MouseEvent event) {
    System.out.println("mouse pressed event");
    super.mouseClicked(event);
    text_to_change = "count = " + count++;
    String [] args = {text_to_change};
    try {
        netscape.javascript.JSObject win =
        netscape.javascript.JSObject.getWindow(applet);
      win.call("scriptChangeText", args);
    } catch (Exception e) {
      l.setText("mouseClicked() error: " + e);
    }
  }
}

public void changeText(String text_to_change) {
    l.setText(text_to_change);
  }
}
```

In Listing 11.5, the **TestApplet** class variable **count** is incremented by one each time the applet's button is clicked with the mouse. If the JScript function **scriptChangeText** cannot be found on the same Web page that contains the applet, then the text area of the applet is redrawn with the error message generated when trying to find the JScript function.

Figure 11.4 shows the Web page containing the DHTML file from Listing 11.4 and the Java applet **TestApplet**.

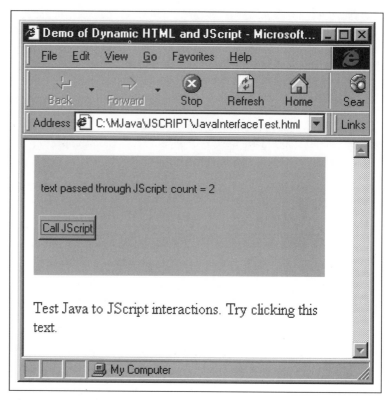

Figure 11.4 *Interacting JScript and Java applet*

J/Direct

The J/Direct interface is provided by Microsoft's Java Virtual Machine and allows fairly direct (and efficient) mechanisms to call the core Windows 32 API from Java programs. The format for using J/Direct is simple, if a little strange, because it relies on using a specially formatted comment statement to declare external interfaces. You must use the Microsoft Java Virtual Machine (JVM) in order to use J/Direct.

In this chapter, we will see how to create native Windows dialog boxes and windows and how to place an icon for running any Java application on the Windows 95/NT 4.0 desktop task bar. We will not attempt to provide exhaustive documentation on the J/Direct API (that is found in the online documentation provided with the Microsoft Java SDK), but we will provide short examples demonstrating most of the techniques commonly used for Java J/Direct programming. If you are writing exclusively for the Windows platform, the use of J/Direct will make your client-side Java applications have the look-and-feel of native Windows 95 and Windows NT applications. Using the AFC class library will also give your Java programs a native Windows look-and-feel.

12.1 Introduction

The Java API for using DLLs is located in the package **com.ms.dll**. This package contains the following classes:

- **Root**—This class allows you to wrap any Java object as a Windows handle. Using this class will prevent a Java object from being garbage collected. Usually, this class is used to prevent instances of the **Callback** class from being garbage collected.

- **Callback**—This class is used to created a DLL callback object. This class must be subclassed with a nonstatic method callback defined that only takes integer arguments.

- **DllLib**—This class contains static public methods for accessing information in DLLs. Hopefully, your applications will not have to use this class directly, except possibly during error handling.

- **ParameterCountMismatchError**—This class will not be directly used in your programs.

- **Win32Exception**—This class extends the **RuntimeException** class and is used for processing errors during calls to DLLs. A runtime error can be retrieved by using the **DllLib.getLast-Win32Error** method.

The **Root** class contains three static public methods:

- **int alloc(Object obj)**—wraps a Java object and returns an integer handle

- **void free(int handle)**—used to free a wrapped Java object when it is no longer required
- **Object get(int handle)**—used to fetch an opaque Java object reference from a handle

In the next section, we will jump right in with short examples of J/Direct programming.

12.2   Using native dialog boxes

Listing 12.1 shows our first effort at accessing native Windows DLLs. The first thing to notice is that we import everything in the package **com.ms.win32** so that we have access to almost all of the standard Windows API. In Listing 12.1, we define a test class **JDMessageBox**. The class constructor has two required arguments: the title of the window used for the message box and a message to appear in the message box. We have already mentioned that a rather strange syntax is used to declare external references to functions in DLLs; here is that syntax (which is embedded in a Java comment):

```
/** @dll.import("USER32") */
private static native int MessageBox(int hwndOwner, String text,
                                     String title, int fuStyle);
```

The program in Listing 12.1 (file **c:\mjava\jdirect \JDMessageBox.java**) must be compiled with the Microsoft **jvc** compiler. The **jvc** compiler recognizes the **@dll.import** statement embedded inside specially formatted comments and makes it possible to directly call a function in a DLL. The Microsoft Java Virtual Machine automatically handles marshalling arguments from a Java format to a Windows-specific data format. Here, we directly call the WIN32 API function **DialogBox** that requires the following arguments (which are marshalled from Java data types to Windows data types by the Java VM):

- Handle to the parent window (this can be the null handle zero for pop-up dialog boxes)
- The string text that should appear inside of the message box
- The title for the window containing the pop-up dialog box
- The window style (which can just default to zero)

Listing 12.1

```
package com.markwatson.ms.jdirect;

import com.ms.win32.*;

class JDMessageBox {

    public JDMessageBox(String title, String message) {
        MessageBox(0, message, title, 0);
    }

    public static void main(String args[])
    {
        new JDMessageBox("test title", "test message");
    }

    /** @dll.import("USER32") */
    private static native int MessageBox(int hwndOwner, String text,
                                         String title, int fuStyle);
}
```

You can run the example in Listing 12.1 by using the command file **c:\mjava\jdirect\r.bat**. Figure 12.1 shows the pop-up dialog box created by the short program in Listing 12.1.

Figure 12.1   *A WIN32 message box created with J/Direct*

This example is simple but serves as a quick introduction to accessing the standard Windows WIN32 API using J/Direct. Section 12.3 shows how to interact with the Windows 95 and Windows NT version 4.0 (or later) desktops. These examples support the basic philosophy of this book to provide Java tools for writing great Windows-specific applications in Java. We will see a complete example in Section 12.4 for adding a Java application, which looks like a native Windows application because we use AFC, to the Windows 95/NT 4.0 desktop task bar.

12.3   Interaction with the Windows 95/98 and NT desktop environment

The example in this section demonstrates how to add an icon for a Java application to the Windows 95/NT 4.0 task bar. A Java class **TaskBarHandler** is developed that encapsulates some of the code in the Microsoft example file

`c:\SDK-Java.30\Samples\Jdirect\TbarIcon\TbarIcon.java`

The class **TaskBarHandler** is an abstract class. In order to use it to add one of your Java applications to the

Windows 95/NT 4.0 desktop task bar, you need to derive your own class from **TaskBarHandler** and define the method

```
public void handleLeftMouseClick()
```

After we develop the class **TaskBarHandler**, we will derive a simple test class **TestTaskBarHandler** as an example for adding a simple Java application to the desktop environment. In the next section, we will develop an Internet newsreader application and add it to the desktop task bar (we will reuse the JavaBean news-reading component that we developed in Chapter 4).

Figures 12.2 and 12.3 show the UML class diagrams for the class **TaskBarHandler**. The class **TaskBarHandler** uses three inner classes (which were defined in the Microsoft **TbarIcon.java** example program) that are shown in Figure 12.3.

Listing 12.2 shows the implementation for the class **TaskBarHandler**. This class is derived from the Microsoft **TaskBar** icon example. The class **TaskBarHandler** has two constructors. The default constructor (no arguments) uses the Windows exclamation mark system icon to represent the program on the desktop task bar. The second constructor takes an integer argument that is the resource ID of any Windows icon. There are comments in this second constructor, which list some other resource IDs that you might want to use.

The inner class **WNDCLASS** (defined at the bottom of Listing 12.2 and taken from a Microsoft example) encapsulates the data for a Windows window class object. If you write Windows applications in C or C++, you will be familiar with the data in **WNDCLASS**; Java programmers can ignore the data defined in **WNDCLASS**. We need to set two **WNDCLASS** data elements:

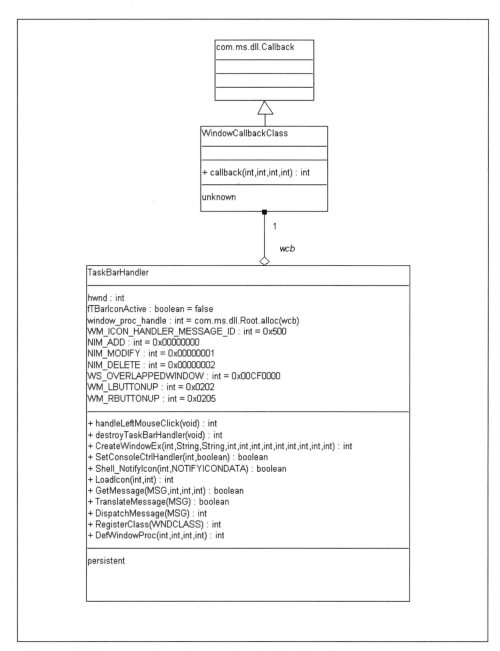

Figure 12.2   *UML class diagram for **TaskBarHandler***

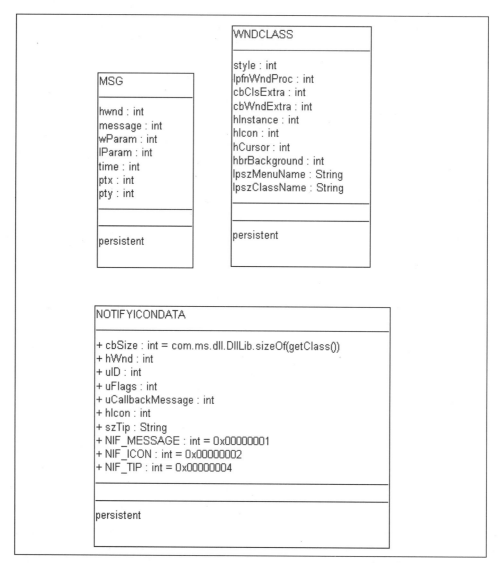

Figure 12.3   *UML class diagram for three inner utility classes defined in*
***TaskBarHandler**. These three classes are provided with Microsoft*
J/Direct example programs to represent Windows-specific data
structures as Java classes.

- **lpfnWndProc**—a reference to an instance of the inner class **WindowCallbackClass** (also defined in Listing 12.3).

- **lpszClassName**—a string containing the class name (this can be arbitrary)

The inner class **WindowCallbackClass** is derived from the class **com.ms.dll.Callback** that was discussed in Section 12.1. This inner class defines one method that will be automatically called whenever any Windows events occur in the **TaskBarHandler**'s icon on the desktop task bar. The method signature is

```
public int callback(int hwnd, int message, int wParam, int
lParam)
```

This method checks the message value to see if it is equal to the constant value **WM_ICON_HANDLER_MESSAGE_ID**, which is set in the instance of class **NOTIFYICONDATA** associated with the **TaskBarHandler** in the class constructor. The class **NOTIFYICONDATA** was defined in the Microsoft J/Direct examples.

The class constructor calls the Windows API function **ShellNotifyIcon** to add the specified icon to the desktop task bar.

The class constructor contains a Windows event loop; it is important to notice that the class constructor does not return until the **TaskBarHandler** instance is destroyed. This works because the callback method **handleLeftMouseClick** is called when the task bar icon is clicked with the left mouse button. Classes that are derived from the **TaskBarHandler** class (e.g., files **TestTaskBarHandler.java** and **TaskBarNews.java** in the directory **c:\mjava**) define a **handleLeftMouseClick** method that can create a new Java application frame and returns control to the Windows event loop in the class constructor. The example in file **TaskBarNews.java** (listed in Section 12.4) has special logic to prevent multiple instances of its application frame. The Windows events are handled by calling three Windows API functions:

- **GetMessage**—checks for an available Windows message in the message queue, waiting until one is available
- **TranslateMessage**—translates Windows virtual key messages to character messages that are placed in the message queue
- **DispatchMessage**—dispatches a message to a Windows procedure (or callback function/method)

Listing 12.2

```
// TaskBarHandler.java
//
// This program installs an icon on the task bar
// that receives mouse messages.  This is an abstract
// base class.  Subclasses must define the method:
//
//     public void handleLeftMouseClick();
//
// Derived from the Microsoft TaskBar icon example.
//

package com.markwatson.ms.jdirect;

/** @dll.import(auto) */
abstract public class TaskBarHandler
{

  public TaskBarHandler() {
    this(32515);  // explanation mark system icon
  }

  public TaskBarHandler(int icon_ID) {
```

```
// Other common icon ID values that you can use:
//
// IDI_APPLICATION =  Default application icon (32512)
// IDI_ASTERISK = Asterisk (32515)
// IDI_EXCLAMATION  = Exclamation point (32515)
// IDI_HAND = Hand-shaped icon (32513)
// IDI_QUESTION = Question mark (32514)
// IDI_WINLOGO = Windows logo (32517)

int icon_handle = LoadIcon(0,  icon_ID);
WNDCLASS wndclass = new WNDCLASS();
wndclass.lpfnWndProc    =
    com.ms.dll.DllLib.addrOf(window_proc_handle);
wndclass.lpszClassName = "MyWindow";

if (0 == RegisterClass(wndclass)) {
  throw new RuntimeException("RegisterClass failed.");
}

m_hwnd = CreateWindowEx(0, wndclass.lpszClassName,
                        "MyWindow",
                        WS_OVERLAPPEDWINDOW,
                        0,0,
                        0,0,
                        0, 0, 0, 0);
if (0 == m_hwnd) {
  throw new RuntimeException("CreateWindow failed.");
}

NOTIFYICONDATA nid = new NOTIFYICONDATA();
nid.hWnd   = m_hwnd;
nid.uID    = 1;
nid.uFlags = nid.NIF_MESSAGE|nid.NIF_ICON|nid.NIF_TIP;
nid.uCallbackMessage = WM_ICON_HANDLER_MESSAGE_ID;
nid.hIcon  = icon_handle;
nid.szTip  = "TaskBarHandler Java Sample. Hit Ctrl-C to quit.";

if (!Shell_NotifyIcon(NIM_ADD, nid)) {
  throw new RuntimeException("Could not add task bar icon.");
}
```

(continued)

Listing 12.2 *(continued)*

```
    m_fTBarIconActive = true;

  MSG msg = new MSG();
  while (GetMessage(msg, 0, 0, 0)) {
    TranslateMessage(msg);
    DispatchMessage(msg);
  }

}

abstract public void handleLeftMouseClick();  // abstract method


static int     m_hwnd;
static boolean m_fTBarIconActive = false;

static void destroyTaskBarHandler()
{
  if (m_fTBarIconActive) {
    m_fTBarIconActive = false;
    NOTIFYICONDATA nid = new NOTIFYICONDATA();
    nid.hWnd = m_hwnd;
    nid.uID = 1;
    nid.uFlags = nid.NIF_ICON;
    Shell_NotifyIcon(NIM_DELETE, nid);
  }
}

WindowCallbackClass wcb = new WindowCallbackClass();

final int window_proc_handle = com.ms.dll.Root.alloc(wcb);

final int WM_ICON_HANDLER_MESSAGE_ID = 0x500;

/** @dll.import("USER32") */
static native int CreateWindowEx(int  dwExStyle
                                 String lpszClassName,
                                 String lpszWindowName,
                                 int    style,
                                 int    x,
```

```
                                    int     y,
                                    int     nWidth,
                                    int     nHeight,
                                    int     hwndParent,
                                    int     hMenu,
                                    int     hInst,
                                    int     pvParam);

/** @dll.import("KERNEL32") */
static native boolean SetConsoleCtrlHandler(int pHandlerRoutine,
                                            boolean fAdd);


/** @dll.import("SHELL32") */
static native boolean Shell_NotifyIcon(int dwMsg,
                                       NOTIFYICONDATA pnid);

static final int NIM_ADD    = 0x00000000;
static final int NIM_MODIFY = 0x00000001;
static final int NIM_DELETE = 0x00000002;


/** @dll.import("USER32") */
static native int LoadIcon(int hinstance, int iconid);


/** @dll.import("USER32") */
static native boolean GetMessage(MSG msg,
                                 int hwnd,
                                 int uMsgFilterMin,
                                 int uMsgFilterMax);
/** @dll.import("USER32") */
static native boolean TranslateMessage(MSG msg);
/** @dll.import("USER32") */
static native int     DispatchMessage(MSG msg);


/** @dll.import("USER32") */
static native int RegisterClass(WNDCLASS wc);
```

(continued)

Listing 12.2 *(continued)*

```java
static final int WS_OVERLAPPEDWINDOW = 0x00CF0000;

static final int WM_LBUTTONUP       = 0x0202;
static final int WM_RBUTTONUP       = 0x0205;

/** @dll.import("USER32") */
static native int DefWindowProc(int hwnd, int msg,
                               int wParam, int lParam);

// Inner class to handle Windows event callback messages:

/** @dll.import(auto) */
class WindowCallbackClass extends com.ms.dll.Callback
{
  public int callback(int hwnd, int message,
                      int wParam, int lParam)
  {
    if (message == WM_ICON_HANDLER_MESSAGE_ID) {
        switch (lParam) {
        case WM_LBUTTONUP:
          System.out.println("Left button up: call subclass handler");
          handleLeftMouseClick();
          break;

        case WM_RBUTTONUP:
          System.out.println("Right button up: destroy task bar icon");
          TaskBarHandler.destroyTaskBarHandler();
          break;
        default:
          break;
        }
        return 0;
    }
    return DefWindowProc(hwnd, message, wParam, lParam);
  }

}
}

// Use the NOTIFYICONDATA class defined in
```

```
// the Microsoft J/Direct example programs:

/** @dll.struct(auto) */
class NOTIFYICONDATA
{
  public int      cbSize = com.ms.dll.DllLib.sizeOf(getClass());
  public int      hWnd;
  public int      uID;
  public int      uFlags;
  public int      uCallbackMessage;
  public int      hIcon;
  /** @dll.structmap([type=TCHAR[64]]) */
  public String   szTip;

  static public final int NIF_MESSAGE = 0x00000001;
  static public final int NIF_ICON    = 0x00000002;
  static public final int NIF_TIP     = 0x00000004;

}

// Use the WNDCLASS and MSG classes defined in
// the Microsoft J/Direct example programs:

/** @dll.struct(auto) */
class WNDCLASS
{
  int      style;
  int      lpfnWndProc;
  int      cbClsExtra;
  int      cbWndExtra;
  int      hInstance;
  int      hIcon;
  int      hCursor;
  int      hbrBackground;
  String   lpszMenuName;
  String   lpszClassName;
}

/** @dll.struct(auto) */
class MSG
```

(continued)

Listing 12.2 *(continued)*

```
{
    int     hwnd;
    int     message;
    int     wParam;
    int     lParam;
    int     time;
    int     ptx;
    int     pty;
}
```

We will close this section by writing a simple test class **TestTaskBarHandler** in order to test the class **TaskBarHandler**. In Section 12.4, we will write a complete Java application using the class **TaskBarHandler**. Figure 12.4 shows the UML class diagram for the class **TestTaskBarHandler**.

Listing 12.3 shows the implementation for the class **TestTaskBarHandler**. This class is derived from the class **TaskBarHandler** and simply defines a **public static void main** method (so that we can run it as a standalone application) and defines the method **handleLeftMouseClick** that was declared abstract in the base class **TaskBarHandler**.

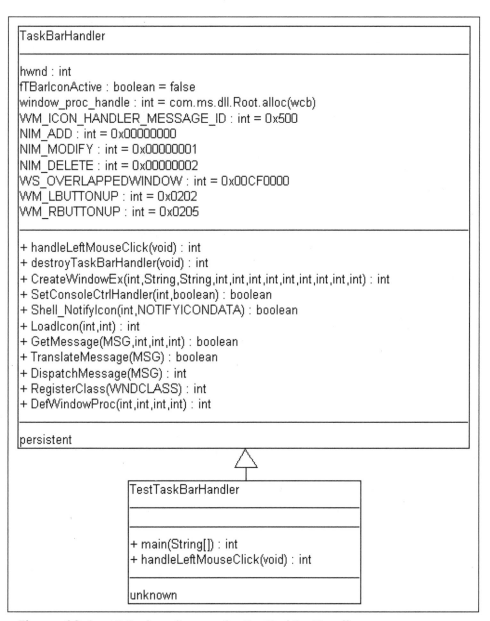

Figure 12.4   *UML class diagram for **TestTaskBarHandler***

Listing 12.3

```
// TestTaskBarHandler.java
//
// This program installs a test icon on the task bar

package com.markwatson.ms.jdirect;

public class TestTaskBarHandler extends TaskBarHandler
{

  static public void main(String [] args) {

    new TestTaskBarHandler();

  }

  public TestTaskBarHandler() {
    super();
  }

  // abstract method in base class
  public void handleLeftMouseClick() {
    System.out.println("TestTaskBarHandler.handleLeftMouseClick");
  }
}
```

The test class in Listing 12.3 shows how easy it is, using the **HandleTaskBar** class, to add an icon to the desktop task bar. You can run the example in Listing 12.3 by using the command file **c:\mjava\jdirect\r_desk_test.bat**.

12.4 Adding a Java newsreader program to the Windows task bar

We have already done most of the work for implementing the example in this section. Our new Java class **TaskBarNews** is derived from the **TaskBarHandler** class and creates an instance of the class **NewsFrame** to create the application frame for reading Internet news. Figure 12.5 shows the class diagram for **TaskBarNews**.

Listing 12.4 shows the implementation of class **TaskBarNews**. The class Boolean variable **active** is used to prevent the creation of multiple newsreader frames. The base class for **TaskBarNews**, **TaskBarHandler**, defines an abstract method **handleLeftMouseClicked** that is called whenever there is a left mouse click on the desktop task bar icon for the newsreader application. The class **TaskBarNews** redefines the method **handleLeftMouseClicked** to create an instance of class **NewsFrame** if there is not already an active instance of class **NewsFrame** on the desktop.

The class **NewsFrame** is also defined in Listing 12.4. This class is very similar to the **NewsFrame** class developed in Chapter 4, with a few minor differences in the Windows close event code in the method **processEvent** and class data:

- The class contains a reference to the **TaskBarNews** object that creates the news frame object.

- The Windows close event logic in **processEvent** coordinates with the **TaskBarNews** object to ensure that only one news frame is visible at any one time.

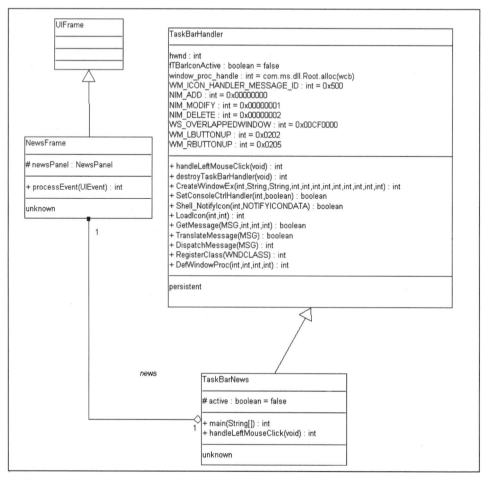

Figure 12.5 *UML class diagram for TaskBarNews*

The class **NewsFrame** does use the class **com.mark-watson.news.NewsPanel** that was developed in Chapter 3 to create both the user interface for the newsreader and to provide the behavior for communication with an Internet news server.

Listing 12.4

```java
// TaskBarNews.java
//
// Example showing how to add a Java application
// to the Windows 95 or Windows NT 4.0 task bar.
//

package com.markwatson.ms.jdirect;

import java.awt.*;
import java.net.URL;
import com.ms.ui.*;
import com.ms.ui.event.*;
import com.ms.fx.*;

import com.markwatson.util.*;
import com.markwatson.news.*;


public class TaskBarNews extends TaskBarHandler {
  protected NewsFrame news;
  protected boolean active = false;

  static public void main(String [] args) {
    new TaskBarNews();
  }

  public TaskBarNews() {
    super();
  }

  // abstract method in base class
  public void handleLeftMouseClick() {
    System.out.println("TaskBarNews.handleLeftMouseClick !!!");
    if (active == false)  {
      active = true;
      new NewsFrame(this);
    }
  }
}
```

(continued)

Listing 12.4 *(continued)*

```java
class NewsFrame extends UIFrame {

  protected NewsPanel newsPanel;
  private TaskBarNews my_parent;

  public NewsFrame(TaskBarNews parent) {
    super("News browser");
    my_parent = parent;
    // enable window events so that we can handle window closing:
    enableEvents(AWTEvent.WINDOW_EVENT_MASK);
    newsPanel = new NewsPanel();
    add(newsPanel);
    setSize(530, 430);
    setVisible(true);
  }
  public void processEvent(UIEvent evt) { // JDK 1.1
    switch (evt.getID())  {
    case Event.WINDOW_DESTROY:
      System.out.println("Save config.news data before quitting.");
      newsPanel.save();
      my_parent.active = false;
      hide();
      dispose();
    default:
      super.processEvent(evt);
    }
  }
}
```

You can run the example in Listing 12.4 by using the command file **c:\mjava\jdirect\r_desk_news.bat**.

The **TaskBarNews** class shown in Listing 12.4 provides a good example of integrating a Java application with the Windows 95/NT 4.0 desktop by adding an icon to the task bar. This example is slightly more complex than the short test program in Listing 12.3 because we need to maintain some state information to prevent multiple application frame windows from showing on the desktop. Here, when the user closes the pop-up application frame window, we see in the method **process-Event** special code to reset the Boolean variable **active** in the **TaskBarNews** class.

12.5 Wrap-up

We have reached the end of the book! I was originally motivated to write this book because of both my belief that Java is one of the most efficient languages for large-scale software development and the desire to use my new favorite language when I write applications specific to the Windows 95 and Windows NT platforms. You may have noticed how I have tried to avoid the political wars concerning Microsoft and Java. For my own programming, I usually write in "pure Java," but since the Windows 95 and Windows NT platforms have become so pervasive, I personally find it reasonable to sometimes give up some portability in order to write specifically for the Windows platform. There are compelling reasons both for writing portable Java code and for tuning Java to a specific platform. Please consider your options, and make an informed decision for each new project. In writing the software examples for this book, I have tried to separate out portable Java classes from Windows-specific Java classes. Even when you do decide to write Java programs specifically for the Windows platform in order to take advantage of desktop integration and the Windows look-and-feel, I urge you to spend the time to design your application so that (hopefully) most of the application code is in separate portable "pure Java" classes, separating out the platform-specific code in separate classes.

JavaDoc Documentation for Example Programs

This appendix contains some of the documentation created by the command file **c:\mjava\make_javadoc.bat** and placed in the files **c:\mjava\html\tree.html** and **c:\mjava\html\AllNames.html**. The material in this appendix has been hand-edited to remove some "uninteresting" entries and to save space. For a complete reference, please check the following HTML documents:

- c:\mjava\html\tree.html
- c:\mjava\html\AllNames.html

Note that underlined text files are on the CD-ROM.

A.1 Class hierarchy

- class java.lang.Object

- class java.awt.Component (implements java.awt.image.ImageObserver, java.awt.MenuContainer, java.io.Serializable)
  - class java.awt.Container
    - class java.awt.Panel
      - class java.applet.Applet
        - class com.ms.ui.AwtUIApplet
          - class com.markwatson.xml.threetier.ViewXML
        - class TestApplet
      - class com.markwatson.ms.activex.BrowserBean (implements com.ms.activeX.ActiveXControlListener, com.ms.ie.WebBrowserEventListener, java.io.Serializable)
      - class com.markwatson.ms.activex.TestBean (implements java.io.Serializable)
- class com.markwatson.util.ConfigFile
- class com.markwatson.xml.threetier.DBInterface
- class com.markwatson.util.Images
- class com.markwatson.ms.jdirect.JDMessageBox
- class com.markwatson.ms.jdirect.MSG
- class com.markwatson.ms.jdirect.NOTIFYICONDATA
- class com.markwatson.util.NewsArticleHeader
- class com.markwatson.news.NewsGroup
- class com.markwatson.util.NewsServer
- class com.markwatson.xml.SampleReader
- class com.markwatson.ms.jdirect.TaskBarHandler

- class com.markwatson.ms.jdirect.<u>Task-BarNews</u>
- class com.markwatson.ms.jdirect.<u>TestTask-BarHandler</u>
- class java.lang.Thread (implements java.lang.Runnable)
  - class com.markwatson.xml.<u>XMLServerConnection</u>
- class com.ms.ui.UIComponent (implements com.ms.ui.IUIComponent, com.ms.ui.IUIAccessible, java.awt.image.ImageObserver, java.lang.Cloneable)
  - class com.ms.ui.UIContainer (implements com.ms.ui.IUIContainer)
    - class com.ms.ui.UIStateContainer
      - class com.ms.ui.UIPanel
        - class com.markwatson.news.-<u>NewsPanel</u>
        - class com.ms.ui.UIApplet
          - class com.markwatson.xml.three-tier.<u>ViewXMLImplementation</u>
        - class com.ms.ui.UIRoot (implements com.ms.ui.IUIRootContainer, com.ms.util.TimerListener)
          - class com.ms.ui.UIWindow
            - class com.ms.ui.UIFrame
              - class com.markwatson.util.-<u>AppTestFrame</u>
              - class com.markwatson.-demo.<u>EventDemo</u>
              - class com.markwatson.-demo.<u>EventDemo2</u>

- ■ class com.markwatson.ms.-
  jdirect.<u>NewsFrame</u>
- ■ class com.markwatson.-
  demo.<u>SplitViewerDemo</u>
- ■ class com.markwatson.-
  demo.<u>TabViewerDemo</u>
- ■ class com.markwatson.-
  demo.<u>TextDemo</u>
- ■ class com.markwatson.-
  demo.<u>TreeDemo</u>
- ■ class com.markwatson.-
  xml.<u>XMLBrowser</u>
- ■ class com.markwatson.-
  demo.<u>test</u>

- ■ class com.ms.ui.UISelector
  (implements com.ms.ui.IUISelector,
  com.ms.util.TimerListener)

  - ■ class com.ms.ui.UITree
    (implements com.ms.ui.IUITree)

    - ■ class com.markwatson.util.-
      <u>EventTree</u>

      - ■ class com.markwatson.-
        demo.<u>SampleTree</u>

  - ■ class com.markwatson.xml.-
    <u>XMLBrowserPanel</u>

- ■ class com.markwatson.ms.jdirect.<u>WNDCLASS</u>
- ■ class com.markwatson.xml.<u>XMLServer</u>

  - ■ class com.markwatson.xml.threetier.-
    <u>DBXMLServer</u>

A.2 Index of all fields and methods

A

active. Variable in class com.markwatson.ms.jdirect.TaskBarNews

ActiveXControlFromIE4. Variable in class com.markwatson.ms.activex.BrowserBean

add(int). Method in class com.markwatson.util.ConfigFile

add(String). Method in class com.markwatson.util.ConfigFile

addDocument(String). Method in class com.markwatson.util.EventTree

addFolder(String). Method in class com.markwatson.util.EventTree

applet. Variable in class TestApplet

AppTestFrame(String). Constructor for class com.markwatson.util.AppTestFrame

author. Variable in class com.markwatson.util.NewsArticleHeader

B

BrowserBean( ). Constructor for class com.markwatson.ms.activex.BrowserBean

BrowserBean(String). Constructor for class com.markwatson.ms.activex.BrowserBean

C

changeText(String). Method in class TestApplet

checkConnection(SQLWarning). Static method in class com.markwatson.xml.threetier.<u>DBInterface</u>

CommandStateChange(int, boolean). Method in class com.markwatson.ms.activex.<u>BrowserBean</u>

configAddButton. Variable in class com.markwatson.news.<u>NewsPanel</u>

configEdit. Variable in class com.markwatson.news.<u>NewsPanel</u>

ConfigFile( ). Constructor for class com.markwatson.util.<u>ConfigFile</u>

ConfigFile(String). Constructor for class com.markwatson.util.<u>ConfigFile</u>

configTree. Variable in class com.markwatson.news.<u>NewsPanel</u>

connectionOK( ). Method in class com.markwatson.util.<u>NewsServer</u>

controlCreated(Object). Method in class com.markwatson.ms.activex.<u>BrowserBean</u>

CreateWindowEx(int, String, String, int, int, int, int, int, int, int, int, int). Static method in class com.markwatson.ms.jdirect.<u>TaskBarHandler</u>

D

data. Variable in class com.markwatson.util.<u>NewsServer</u>

date. Variable in class com.markwatson.util.<u>NewsArticleHeader</u>

DBInterface( ). Constructor for class com.markwatson.xml.threetier.<u>DBInterface</u>

DefWindowProc(int, int, int, int). Static method in class com.markwatson.ms.jdirect.<u>TaskBarHandler</u>

destroyTaskBarHandler( ). Static method in class com.markwatson.ms.jdirect.<u>TaskBarHandler</u>

DispatchMessage(MSG). Static method in class com.markwatson.ms.jdirect.<u>TaskBarHandler</u>

doc. Variable in class com.markwatson.util.<u>EventTree</u>

doClick( ). Method in class com.markwatson.ms.activex.<u>TestBean</u>

DocumentComplete(Object, Variant). Method in class com.markwatson.ms.activex.<u>BrowserBean</u>

doInit( ). Static method in class com.markwatson.xml.threetier.<u>DBInterface</u>

DownloadBegin( ). Method in class com.markwatson.ms.activex.<u>BrowserBean</u>

DownloadComplete( ). Method in class com.markwatson.ms.activex.<u>BrowserBean</u>

E

echoSocket. Variable in class com.markwatson.util.<u>NewsServer</u>

EventDemo( ). Constructor for class com.markwatson.demo.<u>EventDemo</u>

EventDemo2( ). Constructor for class com.markwatson.demo.<u>EventDemo2</u>

EventTree( ). Constructor for class com.markwatson.util.<u>EventTree</u>

EventTree(String). Constructor for class com.markwatson.util.<u>EventTree</u>

F

folder. Variable in class com.markwatson.util.<u>EventTree</u>

G

getColumnNames(ResultSet). Static method in class com.markwatson.xml.threetier.<u>DBInterface</u>

getData( ). Method in class
com.markwatson.util.<u>NewsServer</u>

getHeight( ). Method in class
com.markwatson.ms.activex.<u>BrowserBean</u>

getHeight( ). Method in class
com.markwatson.ms.activex.<u>TestBean</u>

getHostName( ). Method in class
com.markwatson.news.<u>NewsPanel</u>

getImage(int). Method in class
com.markwatson.util.<u>Images</u>

getLine(int). Method in class
com.markwatson.util.<u>ConfigFile</u>

GetMessage(MSG, int, int, int). Static method in class
com.markwatson.ms.jdirect.<u>TaskBarHandler</u>

getMessageRange(String). Method in class com.mark-
watson.util.<u>NewsServer</u>

getNewsArticleHeader(String, int). Method in class
com.markwatson.util.<u>NewsServer</u>

getNewsGroups( ). Method in class
com.markwatson.news.<u>NewsPanel</u>

getNumberLines( ). Method in class
com.markwatson.util.<u>ConfigFile</u>

getSelected( ). Method in class
com.markwatson.util.<u>EventTree</u>

getShowRefreshButton( ). Method in class com.mark-
watson.ms.activex.<u>BrowserBean</u>

getText(String, int). Method in class
com.markwatson.util.<u>NewsServer</u>

getWidth( ). Method in class
com.markwatson.ms.activex.<u>BrowserBean</u>

getWidth( ). Method in class
com.markwatson.ms.activex.<u>TestBean</u>

H

handleLeftMouseClick( ). Method in class com.mark-watson.ms.jdirect.<u>TaskBarHandler</u>

handleLeftMouseClick( ). Method in class com.mark-watson.ms.jdirect.<u>TaskBarNews</u>

handleLeftMouseClick( ). Method in class com.mark-watson.ms.jdirect.<u>TestTaskBarHandler</u>

header. Variable in class com.markwatson.util.<u>NewsServer</u>

host. Variable in class com.markwatson.util.<u>NewsServer</u>

hostName. Variable in class com.markwatson.news.<u>NewsPanel</u>

I

imageNames. Static variable in class com.markwatson.util.<u>EventTree</u>

images. Variable in class com.markwatson.util.<u>Images</u>

Images(String[], int). Constructor for class com.markwatson.util.<u>Images</u>

init( ). Method in class <u>TestApplet</u>

initConfigPanel( ). Method in class com.markwatson.news.<u>NewsPanel</u>

initFirstPanel( ). Method in class com.markwatson.demo.<u>TabViewerDemo</u>

initHelpPanel( ). Method in class com.markwatson.news.<u>NewsPanel</u>

initReadPanel( ). Method in class com.markwatson.news.<u>NewsPanel</u>

initRefreshPanel( ). Method in class com.markwatson.news.<u>NewsPanel</u>

initSecondPanel( ). Method in class com.markwatson.demo.<u>TabViewerDemo</u>

input_strm. Variable in class com.markwatson.xml.XMLServerConnection

K

keyHit(char). Method in class com.markwatson.util.EventTree

keyHit(char). Method in class com.markwatson.demo.SampleTree

L

label. Variable in class com.markwatson.ms.activex.TestBean

leftMouseClicked(String[]). Method in class com.markwatson.util.EventTree

leftMouseClicked(String[]). Method in class com.markwatson.demo.SampleTree

lines. Variable in class com.markwatson.util.ConfigFile

load(String). Method in class com.markwatson.util.ConfigFile

LoadIcon(int, int). Static method in class com.markwatson.ms.jdirect.TaskBarHandler

logOff( ). Method in class com.markwatson.util.NewsServer

logOn( ). Method in class com.markwatson.util.NewsServer

M

main(String[]). Static method in class com.markwatson.ms.activex.BrowserBean

main(String[]). Static method in class com.markwatson.demo.EventDemo

main(String[]). Static method in class com.markwatson.demo.EventDemo2

main(String[]). Static method in class com.markwatson.util.NewsServer

main(String[]). Static method in class com.markwatson.demo.SplitViewerDemo

main(String[]). Static method in class com.markwatson.demo.TabViewerDemo

main(String[]). Static method in class com.markwatson.ms.jdirect.TaskBarNews

main(String[]). Static method in class com.markwatson.demo.test

main(String[]). Static method in class com.markwatson.ms.activex.TestBean

main(String[]). Static method in class com.markwatson.ms.jdirect.TestTaskBarHandler

main(String[]). Static method in class com.markwatson.demo.TextDemo

main(String[]). Static method in class com.markwatson.demo.TreeDemo

main(String[]). Static method in class com.markwatson.xml.XMLBrowser

main(String[]). Static method in class com.markwatson.xml.XMLServer

MAX_FETCH. Static variable in class com.markwatson.news.NewsPanel

my_socket. Variable in class com.markwatson.xml.XMLServerConnection

MyServer. Variable in class com.markwatson.xml.XMLServerConnection

N

NavigateComplete2(Object, Variant). Method in class com.markwatson.ms.activex.BrowserBean

news. Variable in class com.markwatson.ms.jdirect.TaskBarNews

NewsArticleHeader(String). Constructor for class com.markwatson.util.NewsArticleHeader

newsGroups. Variable in class com.markwatson.util.NewsArticleHeader

newsGroups. Variable in class com.markwatson.news.NewsPanel

NewsPanel( ). Constructor for class com.markwatson.news.NewsPanel

NewsPanel(boolean). Constructor for class com.markwatson.news.NewsPanel

NewsServer(String). Constructor for class com.markwatson.util.NewsServer

NewWindow2(Object[], boolean[]). Method in class com.markwatson.ms.activex.BrowserBean

numImages. Variable in class com.markwatson.util.Images

numLines. Variable in class com.markwatson.util.ConfigFile

numNewsGroups. Variable in class com.markwatson.news.NewsPanel

O

OnFullScreen(boolean). Method in class com.markwatson.ms.activex.BrowserBean

OnMenuBar(boolean). Method in class com.markwatson.ms.activex.BrowserBean

OnQuit( ). Method in class com.markwatson.ms.activex.<u>BrowserBean</u>

OnStatusBar(boolean). Method in class com.markwatson.ms.activex.<u>BrowserBean</u>

OnTheaterMode(boolean). Method in class com.markwatson.ms.activex.<u>BrowserBean</u>

OnToolBar(boolean). Method in class com.markwatson.ms.activex.<u>BrowserBean</u>

OnVisible(boolean). Method in class com.markwatson.ms.activex.<u>BrowserBean</u>

output_strm. Variable in class com.markwatson.xml.<u>XMLServerConnection</u>

P

port. Variable in class com.markwatson.xml.<u>XMLServer</u>

process(String). Method in class com.markwatson.xml.<u>XMLServer</u>

processEvent(UIEvent). Method in class com.markwatson.util.<u>AppTestFrame</u>

processEvent(UIEvent). Method in class com.markwatson.demo.<u>SplitViewerDemo</u>

processEvent(UIEvent). Method in class com.markwatson.demo.<u>TabViewerDemo</u>

processEvent(UIEvent). Method in class com.markwatson.demo.<u>test</u>

processEvent(UIEvent). Method in class com.markwatson.demo.<u>TextDemo</u>

processEvent(UIEvent). Method in class com.markwatson.demo.<u>TreeDemo</u>

processEvent(UIEvent). Method in class com.markwatson.xml.<u>XMLBrowser</u>

processMouseEvent(MouseEvent). Method in class com.markwatson.ms.activex.<u>TestBean</u>

processXML(String). Method in class com.markwatson.xml.<u>XMLServer</u>

ProgressChange(int, int). Method in class com.markwatson.ms.activex.<u>BrowserBean</u>

PropertyChange(String). Method in class com.markwatson.ms.activex.<u>BrowserBean</u>

Q

Query(String, String, String, String). Static method in class com.markwatson.xml.threetier.<u>DBInterface</u>

R

readText. Variable in class com.markwatson.news.<u>NewsPanel</u>

readTitleList. Variable in class com.markwatson.news.<u>NewsPanel</u>

readTree. Variable in class com.markwatson.news.<u>NewsPanel</u>

refreshButton. Variable in class com.markwatson.news.<u>NewsPanel</u>

refreshDeleteButton. Variable in class com.markwatson.news.<u>NewsPanel</u>

refreshEdit. Variable in class com.markwatson.news.<u>NewsPanel</u>

refreshTree. Variable in class com.markwatson.news.<u>NewsPanel</u>

RegisterClass(WNDCLASS). Static method in class com.markwatson.ms.jdirect.<u>TaskBarHandler</u>

requestData(String). Method in class com.markwatson.util.<u>NewsServer</u>

resultSetToString(ResultSet). Static method in class com.markwatson.xml.threetier.<u>DBInterface</u>

rightMouseClicked(String[]). Method in class com.markwatson.util.<u>EventTree</u>

rightMouseClicked(String[]). Method in class com.markwatson.demo.<u>SampleTree</u>

run( ). Method in class com.markwatson.xml.<u>XMLServer</u>

run( ). Method in class com.markwatson.xml.<u>XMLServerConnection</u>

S

SampleTree( ). Constructor for class com.markwatson.demo.<u>SampleTree</u>

SampleTree(String). Constructor for class com.markwatson.demo.<u>SampleTree</u>

save( ). Method in class com.markwatson.news.<u>NewsPanel</u>

save(String). Method in class com.markwatson.util.<u>ConfigFile</u>

SetConsoleCtrlHandler(int, boolean). Static method in class com.markwatson.ms.jdirect.<u>TaskBarHandler</u>

setHeight(int). Method in class com.markwatson.ms.activex.<u>BrowserBean</u>

setHeight(int). Method in class com.markwatson.ms.activex.<u>TestBean</u>

setHostName(String). Method in class com.markwatson.news.<u>NewsPanel</u>

setMultiSelect(boolean). Method in class com.markwatson.util.<u>EventTree</u>

setShowRefreshButton(boolean). Method in class com.markwatson.ms.activex.<u>BrowserBean</u>

setURL(String). Method in class com.markwatson.ms.activex.<u>BrowserBean</u>

setWidth(int). Method in class com.markwatson.ms.activex.<u>BrowserBean</u>

setWidth(int). Method in class com.markwatson.ms.activex.<u>TestBean</u>

Shell_NotifyIcon(int, NOTIFYICONDATA). Static method in class com.markwatson.ms.jdirect.<u>TaskBarHandler</u>

showRefreshButton. Variable in class com.markwatson.ms.activex.<u>BrowserBean</u>

splitViewer. Variable in class com.markwatson.demo.<u>SplitViewerDemo</u>

SplitViewerDemo( ). Constructor for class com.mark-watson.demo.<u>SplitViewerDemo</u>

StatusTextChange(String). Method in class com.mark-watson.ms.activex.<u>BrowserBean</u>

subject. Variable in class com.markwatson.util.<u>News-ArticleHeader</u>

T

tabViewer. Variable in class com.markwatson.news.<u>NewsPanel</u>

tabViewer. Variable in class com.markwatson.demo.<u>TabViewerDemo</u>

TabViewerDemo( ). Constructor for class com.markwatson.demo.<u>TabViewerDemo</u>

TaskBarHandler( ). Constructor for class com.markwatson.ms.jdirect.<u>TaskBarHandler</u>

TaskBarHandler(int). Constructor for class com.markwatson.ms.jdirect.<u>TaskBarHandler</u>

TaskBarNews( ). Constructor for class com.markwatson.ms.jdirect.TaskBarNews

test( ). Constructor for class com.markwatson.demo.test

TestApplet( ). Constructor for class TestApplet

TestBean( ). Constructor for class com.markwatson.ms.activex.TestBean

TestTaskBarHandler( ). Constructor for class com.markwatson.ms.jdirect.TestTaskBarHandler

text_to_change. Variable in class TestApplet

TextDemo( ). Constructor for class com.markwatson.demo.TextDemo

TitleChange(String). Method in class com.markwatson.ms.activex.BrowserBean

TranslateMessage(MSG). Static method in class com.markwatson.ms.jdirect.TaskBarHandler

TreeDemo( ). Constructor for class com.markwatson.demo.TreeDemo

U

urlText. Variable in class com.markwatson.ms.activex.BrowserBean

V

ViewXML( ). Constructor for class com.markwatson.xml.threetier.ViewXML

W

window_proc_handle. Variable in class com.markwatson.ms.jdirect.TaskBarHandler

WM_ICON_HANDLER_MESSAGE_ID. Variable in class com.markwatson.ms.jdirect.TaskBarHandler

WM_LBUTTONUP. Static variable in class com.markwatson.ms.jdirect.<u>TaskBarHandler</u>

WM_RBUTTONUP. Static variable in class com.markwatson.ms.jdirect.<u>TaskBarHandler</u>

WS_OVERLAPPEDWINDOW. Static variable in class com.markwatson.ms.jdirect.<u>TaskBarHandler</u>

X

XMLBrowser(String, String). Constructor for class com.markwatson.xml.<u>XMLBrowser</u>

XMLServer( ). Constructor for class com.markwatson.xml.<u>XMLServer</u>

XMLServer(int). Constructor for class com.markwatson.xml.<u>XMLServer</u>

XMLServerConnection(XMLServer, Socket). Constructor for class com.markwatson.xml.<u>XMLServerConnection</u>

Annotated Bibliography

Barret, Edward, ed. 1985. *Text, Context, and HyperText.* Cambridge, MA: MIT Press. An interesting collection of essays dealing with the future of writing, artificial intelligence, and hypertext systems.

Barret, Edward, ed. 1989. *The Society of Text.* Cambridge, MA: MIT Press. An interesting collection of essays dealing with hypertext systems, collaboration using hypertext, and hypertext versus linear texts.

Berk, Emily, and Joseph Devlin, eds. 1991. *Hypertext/ Hypermedia Handbook.* New York: McGraw-Hill. A history of hypermedia and papers dealing with available tools.

Harmon, Paul, and Mark Watson. 1997. *Understanding UML: The Developer's Guide.* San Francisco: Morgan Kaufmann Publishers. An introduction to UML for Java programmers.

Watson, Mark. 1997. *Creating JavaBeans: Components for Distributed Applications.* San Francisco: Morgan Kaufmann Publishers. Presentation of a collection of JavaBeans using sockets, RMI, and CORBA for communication.

Index

– (minus sign) prefacing private methods, 59

+ (plus sign) prefacing public methods, 28

A

ABSTRACT elements (in CDF documents), 194

active variable, 299, 303

ActiveX

  accessing in Java programs, 143–145

  adding controls to IE desktop, 207

  IE, wrapping as JavaBean, 145–152

  in Java programs, 141

  wrappers for nonWindows platforms, 142–143

  writing in Java, 153–159

ACTIVEX subdirectory, 6–7

adapter classes, described, 32

add(int I) method, 123

add(String s) method, 123

addApplication method, 208

AFC (Application Foundation Classes)

  comparison to AWT classes, 20

  components, 24–26

  considerations for Active Desktop customization, 217–218

  containers concept, 20

  event handling, 26–28

  library portability, 18, 37

  packages in, 17–19

  similarity to AWT classes, 17

  split viewer components, 53–57

  tabbed components, 57–62

  text components, 49–53

  tree components, 35–36, 38–49

  See also Internet news browser using AFC; UIComponent class

AFC102 subdirectory, 1

AI (artificial intelligence), advantages of XML for, 178

AllNames.html file documentation, 305

Alt+key combinations. *See* keyboard shortcuts

<APPLET> </APPLET> HTML tags, 276

applications. *See* Java applications

architectural considerations

    file access and security, 218, 219

    See also three-tier application example

artificial intelligence (AI), advantages of XML for, 178

autoexec.bat file, environment variables setup, 4–5

AWT (Abstract Window Toolkit) classes

    comparison to AFC classes, 20

    Component versus Container classes, 20, 21–22

    considerations for Active Desktop customization, 217–218

B

BDK (JavaSoft Bean Development Kit), 139

bibliography, 325

Bin subdirectory, 1, 4

BrowserBean class, 145–148

BrowserBean.java listing, 149–152

browserMouseListener class, 148

Brush graphics object, 70

C

CAB archive files

    applets packaged in, 169–170

    IE support for, 130, 165

    testing applet with HTML file, 170

    using on Web page, 170–171

Café (Java IDE by Symantec), 103

Callback class, 282

callbackLoadTexture method, 258

case and capitalization, of subdirectories, caution on, 6

c.bat command file, 10, 29

    nmake example, 139

CDF (Channel Definition Format)

    customized Web server in Java, 196–206

    described, 174, 192

    example document, 193–196

    Web-based tutorials, 193

    See also XML (Extensible Markup Language)

CD-ROM accompanying this book

    HTML files for CDF examples, 195

    installing code samples from, 5–9

    XML parser from Microsoft, 175, 179

changeText method, 276, 277

CHANNEL elements (in CDF documents), 194

channels, adding to Microsoft Active Desktop, 215

chan1.htm listing, 195

chan2.htm listing, 195

classes

derivation and inheritance, 21–22

hierarchy documentation, 305–308

installation for compile, 3

portable Java versus Windows-specific, 303

separating into packages, 22

See also individual classes by name; AFC (Application Foundation Classes); libraries; packages;UML class diagrams; WFC (Windows Foundation Classes)

classes subdirectory, 4, 9, 10

classes.zip file, caution on installation of J++, 13

CLASSPATH environment variable setup, 4–5

code samples. *See* example programs

COM (Component Object Model) programming

basic concepts, 239–240

javareg program for JavaBeans in windows registry, 153, 155–156

with wrappers, 142–143

com.markwatson.applets.TestApplet.-java listing, 167–168

com.markwatson.apps.NewsFrame.-java listing, 126–128

com.markwatson.beans.NewsBean.-java listing, 132–134

com.markwatson.demo.SampleTree.-java listing, 46–47

com.markwatson.demo.SplitViewer-Demo listing, 55–57

com.markwatson.demo.TabViewer-Demo listing, 60–62

com.markwatson.demo.TreeDemo.-java listing, 48–49

com.markwatson.news.NewsGroup.-java listing, 121–122

com.markwatson.news.NewsPanel listing, 107–120, 300

com.markwatson.util.ConfigFile.java listing, 122–125

com.markwatson.util.DesktopFrame.-java listing, 122–125

com.markwatson.util.EventTree.java listing, 42–44

com.markwatson.util.Images.java listing, 45–46

com.markwatson.xml.threetier.View-XML.java listing, 52, 224–228

com.ms.activeX.ActiveXControlListener (Java interface), 146

com.ms.activeX (Java package), 144

com.ms.com (Java package), 144

com.ms.dll package, 282

com.ms.fx (AFC package), 17

com.ms.ie.WebBrowserEventListener (Java interface), 146

com.ms.ie (wrapped ActiveX control), 145

com.ms.ui (AFC package), 18

com.ms.ui.event (AFC package), 18

com.ms.ui.resource (AFC package), 18

com.ms.util.cab (AFC package), 18

com.ms.xml.Document class, 235

compiling

    with c.bat command file, 10, 29, 103

    classes, installing, 3

    with jvc, 283

components

    adding to Microsoft Active Desktop, 215–217

    AFC, 24–26

    controls as, 19

    stateless and maintaining state, 24

ConfigFile class, 122–123

ConfigFile method, 122

connectionOK method, 93

containers

    AFC concept, 20

    with **null** layout manager, 224

    x-, y-coordinate specification, 52

controls, as "components," 19

copying, code examples from CD-ROM, 5–9

Ctrl+key combinations. *See* keyboard shortcuts

D

database access. *See* three-tier application example

DBInterface class, 221–222, 228–232

DBInterface.java listing, 229–232

DBXMLServer class, 219–220, 222–223, 232–233

DBXMLServer.java listing, 233–235

delegates with WFC, described, 66

delegation event handling, advantages, 26, 32

Delphi (Borland), for ActiveX, 143

DEMO subdirectory, 7

desktop. *See* icons; Internet Explorer (IE) desktop customization

DesktopFrame class, 208–214

DESKTOP subdirectory, 7

DevStudio directory (J++), 13

DHTML (Dynamic HTML)

    document object interaction example with JScript, 270–275

    embedding of scripts, 267

    WFC class support for, 63–64

    See also HTML (HyperText Markup Language); JScript (Microsoft)

dialog boxes, accessing through JScript, 283–285

DirectDraw, 238

DirectInput, 238

DirectSound, 238

Direct3D

    described, 237, 238–239

    orbiting planets game example, 254–265

    See also game library example

Direct3DRM, 238, 239

Direct3dRMDevice, 240

Direct3dRMFrame, 240

Direct3dRMViewport, 240

DirectX, 237, 238, 239

DispatchMessage function, 290

DllLib class, 282

DllLib.getLastWin32Error method, 282

DLLs (dynamic link libraries), accessing with JScript, 282, 283

Docs subdirectory, 2

documentation on all classes, fields, and methods in example programs, 305–322

Document class (in XML documents), 179, 181

DOMs (Document Object Models), standardization, 174

DOS-style window, mouse events revealed in, EventDemo.java, 27–35

doTree method, 179, 181, 184, 221

DTDs (Data Type Documents), 178, 186

d3d subdirectory, 9

E

ECMA (European Computer Manufacturing Association), 267

Element interface (in XML documents), 179

eval function (JScript), 269

event adapters, described, 32

EventDemo.java listing, 30–32

EventDemo2.java listing, 33–35

event handling, AFC, 26–35

EventTree class

advantages, 35

ConfigTree subclass, 107

designing, 35–37

implementing, 38–46

ReadTree subclass, 106–107

RefreshTree subclass, 107

testing, 46–49

example programs

ActiveX control for IE Web browsing, as JavaBean, 145–152

bridge class, 167–168

BrowserBean.java (Web browser), 149–152

CDF Web server, 196–206

com.markwatson.applets.TestApplet.java (bridge class from AwtUIApplet), 167–168

com.markwatson.demo.SampleTree.java (subclass derived from abstract class), 46–47

com.markwatson.demo.SplitViewerDemo (two-part adjustable frame), 55–57

com.markwatson.demo.TabViewerDemo (viewers with tabs), 60–62

com.markwatson.demo.TextDemo (read-only and editable text fields), 50–53

com.markwatson.demo.TreeDemo.java (test for new **SampleTree** class), 48–49 com.markwatson.util.Desktop-Frame.java (desktop-covering Java application platform),122–125

com.markwatson.util.EventTree.-java (event handling with string return), 42–44

com.markwatson.util.Images.java (image file loading utility), 45–46

desktop-covering Java application platform, 122–125

DHTML use in WFC, 67–68

documentation on all classes, fields, and methods, 305–322

EventDemo.java (mouse and keyboard event capture with listener classes), 30–32

EventDemo2.java (mouse and keyboard event capture with adapter classes), 33–35

event handling with string return, 42–44

Form1.java (single instance class implementation), 83–84, 159–163

HTMLtest.java (use of DHTML in WFC), 67–68

icon installation on task bar, 290, 301–302

IE ActiveX control for Web browsing, as JavaBean, 145–152

image file loading utility, 45–46

JAR file reads, 138

JavaBean for listing current news stories from Web news services, 131–139

JavaBean **makefile**, 138–139

Java SDK installation check, 11–12, 13–15

JScript interaction with DHTML document objects, 270–275

JScript interaction with Java applet, 275–280

makefile for creating JavaBeans, 138–139

mouse/keyboard event capture with adapter classes, 33–35

mouse/keyboard event capture with listener classes, 30–32

reading from JAR files, 138

reading from XML documents, 181–183

SampleReader.java (XML document reader), 181–183

single instance class implementation, 83–84, 159–163

socket connection manager, 203–204

subclass derivation from abstract class, 46–47

TaskBarHandler.java (icon installation on task bar), 290

TaskBarNews.java (icon installation on task bar for newsreader), 301–302

TestApplet.java (communication between JScript and applet), 278–279

TestBean.java (packaged JavaBean as ActiveX control), 153–159

test.java (check for installation of Java SDK), 11–12, 13–15

TestTaskBarHandler.java (icon installation on task bar), 298

TicTacToeControl.java (class implementation), 71–83

viewers, split or with tabs, 55–57, 60–62

Web browser, 149–152

Web server, CDF-enhanced, 196–206

XML document browser Java applet, 186–192

XML document reader, URL-based, 181–183

XMLServerConnection.java (socket connection manager), 203–204

XMLServer.java (Web server implementation), 199–202

See also game library example; Internet news browser using AFC; planetary travel game; three-tier application example

F

fields, documentation on example programs, 305–322

file access, security considerations, and application architecture, 218, 219

folders, created by Java SDK setup, 1–3

Font graphics object, 71

FontTest.html listing, 270–271

Form1.java listing, 83–84, 159–163

frames. *See* viewers

Function keys. *See* keyboard shortcuts

G

Game class, 240, 258

GameData class, 241

GameData.java listing, 242–243

GameEngine class, 241, 251

GameEngine.java listing, 251–253

Game.java listing, 244–248

game library example
    GameData.java listing, 242–243
    GameEngine.java listing, 251–253
    Game.java listing, 244–248
    GameObject.java listing, 249–251
    implementation, 241
    requirements, 238–241

GameObject class, 241, 248

GameObject.java listing, 249–251

games. *See* game library example; planetary travel game

getColumnNames method, 222

getData method, 94

getDistToPoint method, 248

getDistToPointSquared method, 248

getIcon method, 132

getLine(int index) method, 123

GetMessage function, 290

getMessageRange method, 94

getNewsArticleHeader method, 94, 95

getNumberLines() method, 123

get/set methods in JavaBeans, 131

getText method, 95, 186

graphics, with WFC, 68–71

Graphics WFC class, 68–70

H

handleEvent method, 26

handleLeftMouseClicked method, 299

handleLeftMouseClick method, 289

host property, 136

HTML (HyperText Markup Language)

    <APPLET> </APPLET> tags, 276

    DOM standardization, 174

    embedding JScript functions, 270

    JFC versus ActiveX, 143

    limitations and improvements, 173–174

    <SCRIPT> </SCRIPT> tags, 270

    See also DHTML (Dynamic HTML)

HTML subdirectory, 7

    AllNames.html file documentation, 305

    tree.html file documentation, 305

HTMLtest.java listing, 67–68

I

icons

    adding for Java application to Windows task bar, 285–298

    adding for newsreader application to Windows task bar, 299–303

    as optional images for menu items, 215

ImageObserver interface, 23

Include subdirectory, 2

index.html file, 2

index of fields and methods used in example programs, 309–322

inheritance

    by classes, 21–22

    for customizing third-party libraries, 36

initConfigPanel method, 106

initHelpPanel method, 106

init method, 244

initReadPanel method, 105–106

initRefreshPanel method, 106

installing

    book examples from CD-ROM, 5–9

    Java SDK, 3–4

    setup of Java SDK, 1–3

int alloc(Object obj) method, 282

interfaces, described, 22

Internet. *See* Web (World Wide Web)

Internet Explorer (IE)

    Active Desktop installation, 216

    ActiveX and WFC, 159–163

    ActiveX in, 141

integration with WFC classes and HTML document model, 67

online documentation for Java SDK, 25

required for this book's examples, 3, 25, 216

server use for receipt of CDF document streams, 196, 197, 205, 206

support for CAB and JAR archive files, 130, 165

WebBrowser ActiveX control, 145

XML parser, 193

Internet Explorer (IE) desktop customization

Active Desktop installation, 216

with ActiveX controls or Java applets, 207

desktop takeover with **DesktopFrame** class, 208–214

Java applets on Microsoft Active Desktop, 215–218

Internet news browser using AFC

adding icon for, to Windows task bar, 299–303

com.markwatson.apps.NewsFrame.-java listing, 126–128

com.markwatson.news.News-Group.java listing, 121–122

com.markwatson.news.NewsPanel listing, 107–120, 300

com.markwatson.util.ConfigFile.-java listing, 122–125

described, 87–88

NewArticleHeader.java listing, 91–92

NewsServer.java listing, 95–100

Panel class design for user interface, 100–104

Panel class implementation, 104–125

portable classes using NNTP: design, 89–90

portable classes using NNTP: implementation, 91–100

portable classes using NNTP: requirements, 88–89

stand-alone Java application design, 125

stand-alone Java application implementation, 126–128

Internet Providers (IPs), troubleshooting connection problems, 198

ITEM elements (in CDF documents), 194

IUIAccessible interface, 23

IUIComponent interface, 23

IUIKeyListener interface, 33

IUIMouseListener interface, 33

IUISelector interface, 38

IUITextListener interface, 50

J

J++ (Microsoft)

DevStudio directory, 13

as Java IDE, 103

J++ (Microsoft) *(continued)*

   using version 1.1 (and later), 13

   using version 6.0, 15–16

j++ subdirectory, 9

jactivex program, 144

JAR archive files

   applets packaged in, 171–172

   example code for reads from, 138

   IE support for, 130, 165

   for JavaBeans, 130, 137–138

   Netscape Communicator support for, 130, 165

   using on Web page, 172

jar.exe program, 172

Java applets

   JavaBeans packaged as, 130

   Java programs as, 29, 165

   JScript interaction example, 275–280

   on Microsoft Active Desktop, 215–218

   packaged in CAB archive file, 169–170

   security considerations of application architecture, 218, 219

   techniques for speeding loading, 165, 169

   See also three-tier application example

Java applications

   with ActiveX, 141–145

   adding icon for, to Windows task bar, 285–298

   as entertainment software, 237

newsreader example, 125–128

platform specificity versus portability, 303

running with r.bat command file, 103

security considerations of architecture, 218, 219

as stand-alone apps, applets, and JavaBeans, 29

See also compiling; example programs; three-tier application example

JavaBeans

   with AFC versus AWT, 130

   BDK (Bean Development Kit) (Web source), 139

   described, 29, 130

   example for listing current news stories from Web news services, 131–139

   properties of, 130–131

   tutorial (Web source), 139

   using **get/set** methods, 131

JAVABEAN subdirectory, 7–8

Java code samples. *See* example programs

Java IDE (Integrated Development Environment), 102–103

javareg program, 153, 155–156

JavaScript (Netscape)

   as HTML extension, 174

   portability problems, 267

   See also JScript (Microsoft)

Java SDK

   ActiveX controls in, 153–159

ActiveX integration into, 144

CLASSPATH and PATH
    environment variables setup,
    4–5

download tips, 1

javareg program, 153, 155–156

JVM (Java Virtual Machine), 3

obtaining, 1

online documentation, 25

patching AFC for OS/2 and Linux,
    18

setup, 1–3

subdirectories for, 1–3, 6–9

testing demo program, 10

testing installation, 3–4, 10–12

updates, 2

Java3D API, 237

Java Virtual Machine (JVM)

installing, 3

See also J/Direct

Jbrowser program, 148

JBuilder (Java IDE by Borland), 103

J/Direct

from JVM (Java Virtual Machine),
    281

on Windows platforms, 281

JDIRECT subdirectory, 8

JDMessageBox class, 283

JScript (Microsoft)

accessing native dialog boxes
    example, 283–285

data types, 268

to ECMA standard, 267

eval function, 269

as extension to HTML, 174

interaction with DHTML
    document objects (example),
    270–275

interaction with Java applets
    (example), 275–280

storage of scripts, 270

string conversions, 268–269

substring method, 269

tutorial source, 268

var keyword, 269

JSCRIPT subdirectory, 8

jvc compiler, 283

jvc.exe, 1

jview.exe, 1

JVM (Java Virtual Machine)

installing, 3

See also J/Direct

K

KeyAdapter class, 32

keyboard event capture, example
    program, 27–34

KeyListener interface, 32

L

libraries

accessing DLLs with JScript, 282,
    283

libraries *(continued)*
  incorporating third-party, 35–36, 37
  portability, 18, 37
  See also game library example
Lib subdirectory, 2
Linux, patching AFC for use with, 18
load(String file_name) method, 123
logOff method, 94
logOn method, 93

M

main method, 222
MAKE_CAB.BAT file, 8
MAKE_JAR.BAT file, 8
Make_javadoc.bat file, 8
MAYSCRIPT keyword, 276
methods
  documentation on those used in example programs, 305–322
  See also individual methods by name
Microsoft Active Desktop, adding Java applets, 215–218
Microsoft Internet Explorer (IE), required, 3
Microsoft Java SDK. *See* Java SDK
Microsoft XML parser, 175, 179
minus sign (-) prefacing private methods, 59
mjava directory
  ACTIVEX subdirectory, 6–7
  classes subdirectory, 4, 9

  copying CD-ROM files to, 6
  DEMO subdirectory, 7
  DESKTOP subdirectory, 7
  d3d subdirectory, 9
  HTML subdirectory, 7
  j++_6.0 subdirectory, 15
  j++ subdirectory, 9
  j++\test, 13–15
  JAVABEAN subdirectory, 7–8
  javadoc documentation, 305–308
  JDIRECT subdirectory, 8
  JSCRIPT subdirectory, 8
  MS subdirectory, 8
  NEWS subdirectory, 8
  3tier subdirectory, 6
  UTIL subdirectory, 8–9
  XML subdirectory, 9
MouseAdapter class, 32
mouse event capture, example program, 27–34
MouseListener interface, 32
MSG class, 288
MS subdirectory, 8
msvmjava.exe, 3

N

Netscape Communicator, support for JAR-packaged applets, 130, 165
NewArticleHeader.java listing, 91–92
NewsArticleHeader class, 88–89, 91
NewsBean class, 131–139

NewsBeanInfo.java listing, 135–136

newsbean.jar listing, 138–139

NewsFrame class, 127–128, 299, 300

NewsGroup class, 121

NewsPanel class, 88, 104, 105, 128

newsreader application

    adding icon for, to Windows task bar, 299–303

    See also Internet news browser using AFC

NewsServer class, 88–89, 92–93

NewsServer.java listing, 95–100

nmake example of c.bat command file, 139

NNTP (Network News Transfer Protocol), 87, 89–90

    advantages of delaying connection to, 93

nonWindows platforms

    disadvantages of WFC for, 63

    Linux, 18, 129

    OS/2, 18, 129

    portability of news browser program, 88

    wrappers for ActiveX and COM components, 142–143

NOTIFYICONDATA class, 288, 289

null layout manager, 224

O

Object get(int handle) method, 283

online documentation for Java SDK, 25

orbiting planets game. *See* planetary travel game

OS/2, patching AFC for use with, 18, 129

P

packages, described, 12, 22

packages of AFC library

    com.ms.fx, 17

    com.ms.ui, 18

    com.ms.ui.event, 18

    com.ms.ui.resource, 18

    com.ms.util.cab, 18

Panel class

    derivations of, 104

    as **NewsPanel** class, 88, 104, 105, 128, 129

ParameterCountMismatchError class, 282

PATH environment variable setup, 4–5

Pen graphics object, 71

planetary travel game

    efficiency note, 265

    implementation, 255–256

    overview, 254

    PlanetGameObject.java listing, 256–257

    TestGame.java listing, 258–264

PlanetGameObject class, 254, 255–256

PlanetGameObject.java listing, 256–257

plus sign (+) prefacing public methods, 28

portability

of AFC libraries, 18, 37

patching AFC versions for, 88, 129

"pure" Java classes versus Windows-specific, 303

private void readFileInJAR(), 138

process event method, 126, 299, 303

process XML method, 197, 222, 232–233

properties

host, 136

of JavaBeans, 130–131

public static void main method, 27

Q

Query method, 222

R

r.bat command file, 103

README.TXT file, 8

register.bat command file, 155–156

RelNotes subdirectory, 2

Render method, 253

requestData method, 93–94

retained mode (in COM programming), 240

Root class, 282

run method, 251

S

SampleReader class (in XML documents), 181

SampleReader.doTree method, 179, 181, 184

SampleReader.java listing, 181–183

Samples subdirectory, 2

save(String save_file) method, 123

<SCRIPT> </SCRIPT> HTML tags, 270

scriptChangeText (JScript function), 276, 277

scripts. *See* JavaScript (Netscape); JScript (Microsoft)

security considerations of application architecture, 218, 219

Serializable interface, 153

server, CDF-enhanced example Java program, 196–206

setBounds method, 224

ShellNotifyIcon function, 289

Shift+key combinations. *See* keyboard shortcuts

source files, directories for, 103

split viewer components, AFC, 53–57

Src subdirectory, 2

stand-alone applications

JavaBeans packaged as, 130

Java programs as, 29

newsreader example, 125–128

startDirect method, 257–258

static int variables, 104

subdirectories

for book examples, 6–9

caution on case and capitalization, 6

created by Java SDK setup, 1–3

See also mjava directory

substring method (JScript), 269

T

tabbed components, AFC, 57–62

task bar (Windows applications). *See* icons

TaskBarHandler class, 285–289

TaskBarHandler.java listing, 290

TaskBarNews class, 299, 302

TaskBarNews.java listing, 301–302

TestApplet class

as component on Active Desktop, 217

described, 166

TestBean.java listing, 153–159

TEST.CAB file, 8

test_cab.html file, 9

TestGame class, 254, 257

TestGame.java listing, 258–264

testing installation of Java SDK, 3–4, 10–12

TEST.JAR file, 8

test_jar.html file, 9

test.java listing, 11–12, 13–15

TestTaskBarHandler class, 286, 296

TestTaskBarHandler.java listing, 298

text components, AFC, 49–53

3D graphics

and Java3D API, 237

See also game library example; planetary travel game

3D transformations (in COM programming), 240

three-tier application example

com.markwatson.xml.threetier.Vie wXML.java listing, 52, 224–228

DBInterface.java listing, 229–232

DBXMLServer.java listing, 233–235

design, 220–223

implementation, 223–.

overview, 218, 219–220

3tier subdirectory, 6

TicTacToeControl.java listing

TITLE elements (in CDF documents), 194

ToggleTest.html listing, 272–273

TranslateMessage function, 290

tree components

AFC, 35–36, 38–49

with **com.ms.ui.UITree** derivations, 35

tree.html file documentation, 305

tree-structured XML documents

displaying, 187

recursive traversal of, 179–186

U

UIApplet class
  described, 20
  example of embedded applet
    implementation class, 165
UICanvas class, described, 20
UIComponent class
  interfaces, 22–23
  public methods, 24
UIDialog class, 20
UIDrawText class, 49
UIEdit class, 49
UIFrame class, 20, 125
UIKeyAdapter class, 33
UILayoutManager class, 20
UIMouseAdapter class, 33
UIPanel class, 20, 125
UIPushButton class, 215
UISelector class, 38
UISplitViewer class, 53
UIStateComponent, 25–26
UIStateContainer class, 38
UITabViewer class, 57, 105
UIWindow class, 20
UML class diagrams
  Component class, 21
  Container class, 21
  DBInterface class, 222
  DBXMLServer class, 223
  DesktopFrame class, 209
  Document and Element class (in
    XML documents), 180

EventDemo class, 28
EventDemo2 class, 33
generic game library classes, 242
MSG class, 288
NewsBean class, 133
NewsFrame class, 127
newsreader Java classes, 120
NOTIFYICONDATA class, 288
portable Java classes for accessing
  Internet news servers, 90
SampleReader class (in XML doc-
  uments), 181
SplitViewerDemo, 55
TabViewerDemo, 59
TaskBarHandler class, 287
TaskBarNews class, 300
TestApplet class, 166
TestTaskBarHandler class, 297
from Togetherj modeling tool, 72
UIComponent and **UIContainer**
  classes, 23
ViewXML class, 221
WNDCLASS class, 288
XMLBrowser class, 187
XMLServer class, 197
UpdateGame method, 258
user interfaces, designing and writ-
  ing, 102–103
UTIL subdirectory, 8–9
U-V coordinates (in COM program-
  ming), 240

V

valid XML documents, 186

var keyword (JScript), 269

Vector class, 105

viewers

splitting in AFC, 53–57

tabbed in AFC, 57–62

ViewXML class, 220, 223

Visual Age for Java (Java IDE by IBM), 103

Visual Basic, for ActiveX, 143

Visual C++, for ActiveX, 143

void free(int handle) method, 283

VR (virtual reality) game. *See* planetary travel game

W

Watson, Mark, Web site, 2

Web (World Wide Web)

popularity of, 173

problems of, 173–174

Web browser (BrowserBean.java example), 149–152

WebBrowser (IE ActiveX control), 145

Web pages

using CAB archive files, 170–171

using JAR files, 172

WFC integration with, 67–68

See also JScript (Microsoft)

Web server, CDF-enhanced example Java program, 196–206

Web sites

Active Desktop for IE 4.0 from Microsoft, 216

author Mark Watson, 2, 88

for BDK (JavaSoft Bean Development Kit), 139

CDF information, 193

DirectX libraries and documentation source, 238

IE's XML parser information, 193

jar.exe source, 172

Java IDEs sources, 103

JavaSoft JDK source, 220

JScript tutorial source, 268

SGML, XSL, and XML tools (ArborText), 194

Sun's Java site and JavaBean tutorial, 139

XML source, 175

WebTop. *See* Internet Explorer (IE) desktop customization

well-formed XML documents, 186

WFC (Windows Foundation Classes)

advantages, 62–63

architecture, 63–64

characteristics of Java applications with, 19

with DHTML, 63, 64

event model, 66–67

example application, 71–85

first release, 15

graphics, 68–71

WFC (Windows Foundation Classes) *(continued)*

with IE ActiveX control, 159–163

integration with Web pages, 67–68

Java packages, 64–65

with WIN32, 63, 64

wfc.app class, 64

wfc.core class, 64

wfc.data class, 64

wfc.html class, 64

wfc.io class, 64

wfc.ui class, 64

wfc.util class, 64

wfc.win32 class, 64

Win32Exception class, 282

WindowCallbackClass class, 289

Windows 95

environment variables setup, 4–5

hiding desktop menu bar/task bar, 212

platform specificity versus portability, 303

portability of this book's material to, 129

task bar icon for Java application, 285–298

task bar icon for newsreader application, 299–303

and use of J/Direct, 281, 283, 285

Windows 98

task bar icon for Java application, 285–298

task bar icon for newsreader application, 299–303

windows

state information in **active** variable, 299, 303

See also viewers

Windows NT

environment variables setup, 4

hiding desktop menu bar/task bar, 212

portability of this book's material to, 129

task bar icon for Java application, 285–298

and use of J/Direct, 281, 285

World Wide Web. *See* Web (World Wide Web)

wrappers

for ActiveX for nonWindows platforms, 142–143

generating, 144

IE ActiveX control as JavaBean, 145–152

X

XMLBrowser class, 187, 188, 191–192

XMLBrowser.java listing, 186–192

XML (Extensible Markup Language)

advantages for development of artificial intelligence (AI), 178

approval and standardization, 174

CDF Web server in Java, 196–206

example program for recursive traversal of tree-structured documents, 179–186

Java Browser for, 186–192

Microsoft's parsers, 175, 179

overview, 176

as tree-structured, 176

use in **DBXMLServer** class, 219

well-formed and valid documents, 186

XSL and SGML tool source Web site, 194

See also CDF (Channel Definition Format)

XMLServer class, 197–199

XMLServerConnection class, 199, 202

XMLServerConnection.java listing, 203–204

XMLServer.java listing, 199–202

XML subdirectory, 9

Xsl (Extensible Stylesheet Language), 194

x-, y-coordinate specification inside containers, 52

About the CD-ROM

Customer note: Please read the following before opening the CD-ROM package.

System requirements: PC with Windows NT, Windows 95, or Windows 98. You will need to install either the Microsoft Java Development Kit version 2 or 3 from *www.microsoft.com/java* to compile and run the programs in this book.

Installation note: When you copy the directory mjava from the CD-ROM, you must use the DOS XCOPY command (and not Windows Explorer). If your CD-ROM drive is D: then please use the following command:

        xcopy d:\mjava c:\mjava /s

You will be asked if the copy operation is for a single file or a directory; respond with "D" to copy the directory. If you use Windows Explorer to copy the directory, then by default all of the files copied will be read-only (which is not what you want!).

No part of this publication or software my be reproduced, stored in a retrieval system, or transmitted in any form or by any means—electronic, mechanical, photocopying, recording, or otherwise—without the prior, written permission of the publisher, except for example programs and Java classes, which may be reused in software if distributed in compiled form only. No source code may be distributed without permission of the publisher.

All programs and supporting materials are presented "as is" without warranty of any kind, either expressed or implied, including but not limited to implied warranties of merchantability and fitness for a particular purpose. Neither Morgan Kaufmann Publishers, Inc. nor anyone else who has been involved in the creation, production, or delivery of this software shall be liable for any direct, incidental, or consequential damages resulting from use of the software or documentation, regardless of the theory of liability.